CATALOGUE

OF THE

PRINCIPAL OFFICERS

OF

VERMONT

AS

CONNECTED WITH ITS POLITICAL HISTORY

FROM

1778 TO 1851

WITH

SOME BIOGRAPHICAL NOTICES, &C.

Leonard Deming

HERITAGE BOOKS
2024

HERITAGE BOOKS
AN IMPRINT OF HERITAGE BOOKS, INC.

Books, CDs, and more—Worldwide

For our listing of thousands of titles see our website at
www.HeritageBooks.com

A Facsimile Reprint
Published 2024 by
HERITAGE BOOKS, INC.
Publishing Division
5810 Ruatan Street
Berwyn Heights, MD 20740

Entered according to Act of Congress, May 29th, 1851, by
Leonard Deming,
In the Clerk's Office of the District Court of
the District of Vermont.

— Publisher's Notice —
In reprints such as this, it is often not possible to remove blemishes from the original. We feel the contents of this book warrant its reissue despite these blemishes and hope you will agree and read it with pleasure.

International Standard Book Number
Paperbound: 978-0-7884-4734-1

INDEX.

	Page.		Page.
Allen, Ethan	5 60	Lamoille County Officers,	97–99
Attorneys, United States	112	" " Representatives,	20-34-46
Aggregate of the Census	112	Lyon, Mathew	26
Addison County Representatives,	17 to 33	Leland, Rev. Aaron	35
" " Officers	75–88	Lost, Children	61
Auditor of Accounts	14	Lowry, Heman	110
Bowker, Joseph	100	Librarian,	14
Bell, Jonathan	110	Members of Congress, Vermont	108
Bennington County Officers	74–88	Marshalls, United States	112
" " Representatives	17–33	Olin, Henry	21
Clerks of the House of Representatives,	9	Orange County Officers,	74–88
" Engrossing "	9	" " Representatives	19-20-47-59
Caledonia County Officers,	89–99	Orleans " Officers	89–99
" " Representatives,	17–33	" " Representatives,	48–59
Chittenden County Officers,	89–99	Paddock, Ephraim Judge	91
" " Representatives,	20-34-46	Preface,	4
Councillors from 1778 to 1835,	12–13	Peck, John	111
Censors, Council of	47–48	Probate, Registers Orleans Co., (in part)	104
Children, Lost	61	Painter, Gamaliel	49
Census of Vermont,	108	Representatives before 1788,	17–20
Constitutional Conventions,	100	" to Congress,	108
Constables of Middlebury,	6	Redding, David	60
Crafts, Samuel C.	22	Robinson, David	109
Chipman, John	110	Rutland County Officers,	74–88
Debentures, Legislative	10	" " Representatives	19-20-47-59
" Constitutional	105	Secretaries to Governor and Council,	10
District Judges and Officers,	112	Secretaries of State,	9
Election Sermons, Preachers of	10	" Senate,	14
Essex County Officers,	90–99	Speakers of the House,	9
" " Representatives	17-18-34-46	Sergeant-at-Arms,	14
Edson, Joseph	111	Sessions, where holden,	10
Franklin County Officers,	89–99	Senators from 1836 to 1850,	14-15-16
" " Representatives,	20-34-46	Safford, Samuel	87-74
First Town Clerks,	6-33-46-59-72	Supreme Judges,	73
First Officers now living,	34	Senators to Congress	73
Fletcher, Samuel	109	Scott, Joseph	110
" Calvin	110	Scott, jr., Joseph	110
" jr., Asaph	111	Scott, Harvey	110
Fuller, Nathan	111	Smith, Israel	111
Governors,	9	Towns, names of altered.	3
Governors, Lieutenant	9	Treasurers,	9
Grand Isle County Officers,	91–99	Vermont,	7
" " Representatives,	34–46	Washington County Officers,	92–99
Hutchinson, Rev. Aaron	75	" " Representives,	60 to 72
" Titus Judge	91	Windham " Officers,	74 to 88
Henry, Hugh	35	" " Representatives,	17-18-60-72
Haight, Stephen	11	Windsor " Officers,	74 to 88
Hall, Prince B.	111	" " Representatives,	17-18-60-72
Judges, Supreme Court	73	Willard, Dubartus	89
Jefferson County Officers,	92	Webb, Greenleaf	111

In the following pages, for Representatives, I have arranged the towns after the first insertion, by figures, alphabetically, by counties, so that a person can easily follow a town through, by observing its number at the beginning, and follow the same to 1850. Before 1788, the Speakers are in small capitals, and after that are in italic. The figures before the county officers, 1 denotes Chief Judge, 2 Side Judges, 3 Clerks, 4 Sheriffs, 5 State's Attorneys, 6 Judges of Probate, 7 Registers of Probate. Where inverted commas and a name are in one column, the person in the previous column served a part of the year.

TO THE PUBLIC.

It is expected in perusing a new book to find some reasons given why such a work is published. In this case an enquiry will be made, why is this work put forth when nothing new can be obtained from it, as the Journals of the Legislatures, Conventions, &c., and even Walton's Registers contain it all? I admit that if a person had those Journals and Registers at his command, he might learn many facts of which he is now ignorant, and will probably remain so, if he depends on that source only for his information. You may go into any Town Clerk's Office in this State, and if you can find a complete set of the Legislative journals, you will succeed better than I have done in any office or Library that I have visited, not even the State Library contain the journals of 1786, but I found one in Rutland. The journals are nearly all scattered "few and far between." The University at Burlington have for many years been collecting a perfect set of those journals, but a short time since, they had not obtained them. As for the Registers nearly every one knows, that notwithstanding all the useful information therein contained, and that which every family ought to purchase yearly and preserve, is, soon after New year's day given to the youngest child to destroy, or deposited in the attic for the mice, to shelter them from the rude blasts of winter. The President of the Antiquarian Society, and some others within my knowledge, have been many years trying to gather up a complete set of Vermont Registers, but as yet have not been successful. As for obtaining the information herein contained, from Journals and Registers without costing a person ten times the price of the book, is folly to think of. But if a person does not wish for the information for himself or family, I have laid him under no obligation to purchase, as I have not a solitary subscriber in the State. A person may go into every town in this State that has been organized sixty years, and in nine out of ten he will be unable to obtain from any source, written or verbal, who have represented the town each year since its organization.

And furthermore, such a bold and fearless body of men as first settled Vermont, and safely carried her through all her various encounters with her numerous enemies, and safely landed her on the shores of this glorious Union with peace and plenty, deserve to have their names written in letters of gold and handed down to the last man of the last generation that shall inhabit the earth.

LEONARD DEMING.

Middlebury, May 30, 1851.

In arranging the following pages, I have endeavored to give the year in which the term of office began. In taking from the journals I found no difficulty of getting it right, nor from the Registers, only, I had to take the year previous. The term of office of the Legislative appointments in nearly all cases commenced on the first of December of the same year, but in Clerks of Courts, and Registers of Probate, it has been more difficult to get right, as some of the Courts and some of the Probate Courts do not sit till after the commencement of the year following, and their appointments being made at those sessions, my correspondents have given me the wrong year. But I have remedied that in many cases, by taking a political view of the Courts that made the appointments, and the time the first Court was holden after the Judges were appointed. I have endeavored to give the facts as they were, but I do not flatter myself to suppose that errors do not exist in the work which I have not yet ascertained. I have already found some which will be mentioned in an errata. I have in some instances had wrong information from correspondents, which they have afterwards discovered, and rectified, but too late to prevent the error occurring.

TOWNS, THE NAMES OF WHICH HAVE BEEN ALTERED.

Alburgh	before 1786	name	Missisco Leg.	Chittenden	in part	1816	"	Philadelphia
Albany	"	1815	"	Lutterloh.	Danville	in part	"	1819	"	Deweysburgh
Bloomfield	"	1830	"	Minehead	Dover	"		1811	"	South Wardsboro
Bradford	"	1788	"	Moretown.	Franklin	"		1817	"	Huntsburgh
Brandon	"	1784	"	Neshobe	Grafton	"		1791	"	Tomlinson
Bristol	"	1789	"	Pocock	Grand Isle	"		1810	"	Middle Hero
Barre	"	1793	"	Wildersburgh	Granville	"		1834	"	Kingston
Brighton	"	1832	"	Random	Hartland	"		1782	"	Hertford
Chester	"	1766	"	Flamstead & N.Fl'd	Huntington	"		1795	"	New Huntington
Chelsea	"	1788	"	Turnersburgh	Isle La Mott	"		1830	"	Vineyard
Craftsbury	"	1790	"	Minden	Kirby	"		1807	"	Hopkinsville
Charleston	"	1825	"	Navy	Londonderry	"		1780	"	Kent
Clarendon	"	1761	"	Socialboro' & Dur'm	Lowell	"		1831	"	Kellyvale
Coventry	in	1842,3	"	Orleans	Morgan	"		1801	"	Caldersburgh

CONTINUED.

Mendon	"	1827	"	Medway&Park's'n	Sutton	" 1812 "	Billymead
Mount Holly	"	1792	"	Jacksons Gore	Troy	" 1803 "	Missisco
Mount Tabor	"	1805	"	Harwick	Vernon	" 1802 "	Hinsdale
Newport	"	1816	"	Duncansborough	Vineyard	" 1802 "	Isle La Mott
Peacham in p'rt		1810	"	Deweysburgh	Waterford	" 1797 "	Littleton
Peru	"	1804	"	Bromley	Whitingham	" 1780 "	Cumberland
Plainfield	"	1797	"	St. Andrews Gore	Waterville	" 1825 "	Coits Gore
Plymouth	"	1797	"	Saltash	Wilmington	" "	Draper
Sheldon	"	1792	"	Hungerford	Westmore	" "	Westford
Sherburne	"	1800	"	Killington	Woodbury from 1838 to 1843 was Monroe		

ERRATA.

Page 9 1st column, 3d line from bottom for 45 read 48.
" 18 5th " 3d name " top " Silas Goodrich read John Gray.
" " " " 4th " " " " Oliver Smith " Silas Goodrich.
" " " " 9th " " " " John Gray " Oliver Smith.
" " " " 12th " " " " Israel Smith " Joseph Clark.
" " " " 14th " " " " Burgess " Ebenezer Burgess.
" " " " below Daniel Jewett insert Samuel Taylor.
" " " " above Elias Weld " John Davison. Strike out Ryegate.
" 20 " " between Noah White & Bildad Andrus, insert, Pelatiah Bliss.
" " " " strike out Thomas P. Loid, he was from Alburgh.
" 27 2d " Richard Skinner should be in Italic.
" 33 last " 4th line from top, for Calvin Eastman read Henry M'Laughlin.
" 34 11th line from bottom, for Jairus Hall 1810, read, John Roberts 1817.
" 38 bottom long line, for 1786, read, 1781.
" 53 " " " after the word "that," read, declared Vermont independent.
" 58 4th and 5th columns, Ebenezer N. Briggs should be in Italic.
" 64 1st " Aaron Leland " " "
" 73 3d " for 1843, for Daniel Kellogg, read, Wm. Hebard, K. declined.
" " " for the bottom 3 but one, read 4
" 75 7th line from bottom, for Elisha, read, Aaron.
" " 6 " " " " The first Minister of, read, Of.
" " 2d column for Jonathan Robinson, read, Josiah Fay.
" 76 1st " against 7 insert, Josiah Fay
" " 2d " " " " Jonathan Robinson till 1794.
" 77 last " and first on page 78 insert, Wm, A. Griswold, to 1798.
" 78 4th column " Jonathan Hunt.
" " 5th " " Andrew Seldon to 1807.
" 80 3d " " Jonathan E Robinson to 1813.
" 81 4th " " Charles Wright and Marshall Carter.
" " and 82 for 1815 and 16 " Orsamus C. Merrill.
" 82 and 3 " 1817 to 1820 and 22 " Uel M. Robinson.
" 83 " 1821, 23 and 24 " Hiland Hall.
" " " 1825 " Stephen Robinson.
" 84, 85, 86, 87, to 1844 " William Haswell.
" 87 for 1845 " Samuel H. Blackmer.
" 88 " 1846--7 " William Haswell.
" " from 1848 " A. B. Gardner.
" 108 1st blank under 1830 should be filled with 33.
" " the " against Goshen Gore North, same column, should be 200.
" " " " Harris Gore, " " " 19.
and the footings added to correspond.
" " the last column against Sheffield should be 797, the footing is right.
" 109 the blank against Easthaven for 1830 should be 33 and same added to footing.
" 111 last column, 11th line from top for 1787 read 1788.

GENERAL ETHAN ALLEN,

Was born in Roxbury, Conn., in 1739, and died at Colchester, Vt., Feb. 15, 1789. The following is related of him as having taken place while a prisoner in irons on his passage to England. While closely confined to his cabin, he discovered that a pin or wire that fastened one of his handcuffs was broken. Extricating the pieces with his teeth, he was enabled to loosen the bolt and set one hand at liberty, by the aid of which, and his teeth, he soon had both at liberty, and he was not long in liberating his feet. But fearing a discovery might lead to worse treatment, he replaced his irons, bolts

TOWN CLERKS.

and pins before the arrival of his keeper. It soon became a fine recreation for the General to take off and put on his irons at pleasure.

One day the Captain wishing to afford the crew some merriment, ordered that Allen be brought on deck. Hoping to frighten him, the Captain said : "There is a probability that the ship will founder—if so, what *will* become of us, especially you, Mr. Allen, a rebel against the King ? "Why," said Allen, "that would be very much like our dinner hour." "Why so ?" said the Captain not reflecting that Allen was not allowed to come on deck only when he the captain went down into his cabin to dine. "Well, you see, answered Allen, "I'd be on my way *up* just as you would be going *below*." This answer did not please the Captain, and he began a regular tirade of abuse against the American people. "In a short time," said the Captain, "all the rebels will be in the same situation as yourself." This was too much for Allen, and raising his hands to his teeth, soon snapped the bolts and pins, took off his irons and threw them overboard—seized the panic struck Captain by the collar, and threw him headlong upon the deck, then turning to the affrighted crew, he exclaimed in a voice of thunder . "If I am insulted again during the voyage, I'll sink the ship and swim ashore." This exploit had such an effect on the Captain and crew, that no further insult was offered to the General during the passage.

The following persons were elected Town Clerks in the years set to them, and have continued in the office to 1851.

Cabot, Thomas Osgood and jr.	1802	Dorset, Heman Morse	1835 Elmore, Martin Elmore 36
Danville, Archelaus Sias	1819	Woodstock, Nahum Haskell	1835 Topsham, Lemuel Tabor 34
Bakersfield, Silas B. Hazeltine	1821	Sturksboro, William Worth 2d	1835 Halifax, Darius Bullock 32
		St. Albans, William Bridges	1836 Newfane, Nathan Stone 32
Middlesex, Horace Holden	1822	Wilmington, Stephen P. Flagg	1836 Stockbridge, Rufus Lyon 30
Walden, Daniel Wooster	1822	Stowe, Joseph H. Bennett	1837 Sandgate, George Peck 27
Salem, Samuel Blake	1822	Jericho, John Lyman, jr.	1837 Ryegate, James Whitelaw 27
Ira, John Mason	1823	Wheelock, John W. Brown	1837 Lemington, Mills De Forrest 26
		Hartland, E. M. Stocker	1838 St. Albans, Jonathan Hoit 26
Fairfield, Joseph Soule	1824	Cornwall, Marcus O. Potter	1838
Rupert, Henry Sheldon (one out)	1824	Albany, Luther Delano	1838 ADDITIONAL FIRST TOWN CLERKS.
Shaftsbury, Hiram Barton	1825	Newfane, Otis Warren	1839 Bakersfield, Stephen Maynard 1795
		Guilford, John Lynde	1839 Fletcher, Elisha Woodworth 1790
Lunenburgh, Stephen Howe, jr.	1825	Somersett, Ephraim Rice	1839 Highgate, Jonathan Butterfield
Pittsford, Samuel H. Kellogg,	1826	Royalton, Calvin Skinner 2d	1839 St. Albans, Jonathan Hoit 1788
Rochester, John Trask	1827	Sudbury, James K. Hyde	1839 Monkton, Samuel Barnum 1786
Brandon, Barzillia Davenport	1827	Bridport, Ervin E. Grovenor	1839 Rutland, Joseph Hawley
		Shelburne, Lyman Hall	1839 Weybridge, ——— Jackson
Rutland, Ambrose L. Brown	1827	Northfield, Volney H. Averill	1839
Shoreham, Levi O. Birchard	1827	Newport, Seymour Lane	1839 FIRST SUPREME COURT CLERKS
Barnet, John Shaw	1827	Plymouth, Thomas Moore	1839 IN ADDISON COUNTY.
Burke, Asahel Burrington	1827	Whitingham, Hosea F. Ballou	1840 N Brush, before 1793
		Hartford, Geo. E. Wales	1840 Samuel Painter, from 93 to June 97
St. Johnsbury, Jerry Dickerman	1827	Shrewsbury, Lowell W. Gurnsey	1840 Loyal Case, Aug. 2d. 97 to Jan. 98
Isle La Mott, Ira Hill	1828	Pantou, George Spencer	1840 Darius Mathews, after that to 1819
Essex, Amasa Bryant	1829	Weybridge, Isaac Drake	1840
		Cavendish, Otis Robbins	1841
Craftsbury, Joseph Scott, jr.	1829	Middlebury, James M'Donald	1841 CONSTABLES OF MIDDLEBURY.
Ludlow, Artemas Spafford	1831	Newbury, David Johnson	1841 Martin Foote, appointed in 1787
Castleton, Olver R. Harris	1831	Barre, Alvan Carter	1841 Joseph M'Donald " 1796
Concord, Harvey G. Fry	1831	Groton, Isaac N. Hall	1841 and Erastus Hawley " 1798
Stockbridge, Merrick Gay	1832	Brownington, Chester Gilbert	1841 are now living ; the two first in this town, and the other in Cambridge.
		Morgan, Charles Cummins	1841 Out of fourteen that held the office
Moretown, Lester Kinsley	1832	Johnson, Stoughton S. Pike	1841 of Constable since 1807, all but two
Grafton, Benjamin H. Bridgman	1833	There are others who have here-	or three are living.
Fairhaven, Benjamin T. Gilbert	1833	tofore served longer as Town Clerks,	Of the nine Town Clerks that
		West Fairlee, Elisha Thayer 50 y's	have been elected since 1786, two
Orwell, Roswell Bottum, jr.	1833	Berlin, Abel Knapp 49	only remain. Samuel Swift, appointed in 1819, and James McDonald in 1841.
Hancock, Zerah Barnes	1833	Fairlee, Samuel Smith 45	
Randolph, Benjamin T. Blodgett	1833	Wells, Ansel Goodspeed, 43	
Halifax, Rufus K. Henry	1834	Brattleboro, Step'n Greenleaf 42	By this it may be inferred that
		North Hero, Nathan Hutchins 39	exercise tends to longevity.
Sharon, Samuel Shuttleworth	1834	Craftsbury, Samuel C. Crafts 37	
Pomfret, Otis Chamberlin	1834	Hinesburgh, Erastus Bostwick 36	

By a letter which came a little too late, I make the following additions to Windham County.

Noah Sabin, Judge of Probate from 1781 till 1801, and Noah Sabin from and after 1801, should be, Noah Sabin, jr. Stephen R. Bradley was Register from 1781 to March, 1791, Noah Sabin, jr., to Dec, 1801, Phinehas White, to Dec , 1809, Elijah Knight, Judge and Register, to 1813, Horace Baxter, R. to 1814, Asa Keyes, to 1815, Horace Baxter, to 1816, Stephen Tyler, to 1819, Daniel Kellogg, to March, 1820, Charles Phelps, to May, 1820. Horace Baxter, to 1821, Munnis Kinney, to 1822, Charles Phelps and Ebenezer Hunington, to 1823, A. Keyes, to 1824, H. Baxter, to 1825, Alexander S. Campbell, to 1827, Epaphroditus Ransom, to 1828, A. S. Campbell, to 1831, A. Keyes, to 1833, E. Ransom, to Oct. 2, 1833, James Crawford, to Dec., 1834, David L. Putnam, to 1836, James Crawford, to 1838, Charles Phelps, to 1841, James H. Phelps, to 1846, Abishai Stoddard, to 1849, Nathaniel Tracy Sheafe, to April, 1851, Benjamin W. Dean, to ———. In the above dates, Dec. 1st is meant, when not otherwise mentioned.

VERMONT.

The tract of country now known by the name of Vermont, was, previous to the American Revolution, known by the name of "*The New Hampshire Grants*," and was divided into four counties, by the Government of the then Colony of New York, viz: Cumberland and Gloucester on the east, and Bennington and Charlotte on the west of the range of Green Mountains. But by a careful perusal of facts of those times it does most plainly appear that the inhabitants of the Grants were not very obedient subjects to those New Yorkers who volunteered to rule over them. Soon after the Declaration of Independence at Philadelphia, in July, 1776, the *Green Mountain Boys*, concluded they were not under the rule of any earthly nation or government except their own. They therefore called a Convention of Delegates from the several towns, which Convention met at Dorset, July 24, 1776, but no records show what steps were then taken, only it was adjourned to Sept. 25th, same year, when it again met at the same place, as appears from the following record:

NEW HAMPSHIRE GRANTS.

DORSET, September 25th, 1776.

At a General Convention of the several Delegates from the towns on the west side of the Green Mountains, the 24th of July last, consisting of fifty one members, representing 35 towns, and holden this day by adjournment, by the delegates on the east and west side of the Green Mountains, the following members being present at the opening of the meeting:

Capt. JOSEPH BOWKER, in the Chair.   Jonas Fay, *Clerk.*

Towns.	Delegates.	Towns.	Delegates.
Pownal,	Capt. Samuel Wright, Dr Obadiah Dunham.	Poultney,	Mr. Nehemiah Stow, Mr. William Ward.
Bennington,	Mr. Simeon Hathaway, Dr. Jonas Fay, Capt. John Burnham, Nathan Clark, Esq. Maj. Samuel Safford, Col. Moses Robinson.	Castleton, Bridport, Addison, Stamford, Williston, Colchester,	Capt. Jos. Woodward, Mr. Samuel Benton. Mr. David Vallance. Mr. Thomas Morgan. Col. Thomas Chittenden. Lieut. Ira Allen.
Shaftsbury,	Maj. Jeremiah Clark, John Burnham, Sen.	Middlebury, Neshobe now	Mr. Gamaliel Painter. Capt. Timothy Barker,
Sunderland,	Lieut. Joseph Bradley, Col. Timothy Brownson.	Brandon,	Mr. Thomas Tuttle.
Manchester,	Col. William Marsh, Lieut. Martin Powell, Lieut. Gideon Ormsby.	Rutland, Wallingford,	Capt. Joseph Bowker, Col. James Mead. Mr. Abraham Ives.
Dorset,	Mr. John Manly, Mr. Abraham Underhill.	Tinmouth,	Capt. Ebenezer Allen, Maj. Thomas Rice.
Rupert,	Mr. Reuben Harmon, Mr. Amos Curtis.	Danby, Panton,	Capt. Micah Veal, Mr. William Gage. Mr. John Gale.
Pawlett,	Capt. William Fitch, Maj. Roger Rose.	Bromley or Peru,	Capt. William Utley. Col. Seth Warner and Capt. Heman Allen,
Wells,	Zacheus Mallery, Ogden Mallery.		present.

Members from the east side of the Green Mountains:

Marlboro,	Capt. F. Whittemore.	Rockingham,	Dr. Reuben Jones.
Guilford,	Col. Benjamin Carpenter, Maj. John Shephardson.	Dummerston,	Mr. Joseph Hildrick, Lieut. Leonard Spaulding,
Windsor,	Mr. Eben Hoisington.	Westminster,	Mr. Joshua Webb, Nathan Robinson, Esq.
Kent, now Londonderry,	Mr. Edward Aiken, Col. James Rogers.	Halifax,	Col. Benjamin Carpenter.

Wilmington and *Cumberland* were represented by letters from some of the principal inhabitants.

Among the proceedings of this Convention at that time were the following: To take suitable measures as soon as may be, to declare the New Hampshire Grants a free and separate district, which vote passed without a dissenting voice. A committee of seven reported the wrongs and grievances suffered from New York, and the impolicy of any further connection with them, directly or indirectly. *Resolved*, Therefore, that this Convention being fully convinced, that it is absolutely necessary that every individual in the United States of America should exert themselves to the utmost of their abilities in the defence of the liberties thereof; therefore, that this Convention, may the better satisfy the public of their punctual attachment to the said common cause at present as well as heretofore, we do make and subscribe the following covenant, viz.:

We, the subscribers, inhabitants of that district of land commonly called and known of New Hampshire Grants, being legally delegated and authorized to transact the public and political affairs of the aforesaid district for ourselves and constituents, do solemnly covenant and engage, that for the time being, we will strictly and religiously adhere to the several resolves of this, or any future convention constituted on said district by the free voice of the friends to American liberties, which shall not be repugnant to the resolves of the honorable the Continental Congress, relative to the cause of America.

VERMONT.

The Convention met again at Westminster, January 15, 1777. The committee appointed to bring in a draught of a Declaration of Independence reported:

Right 1. That whenever protection is withheld, no allegiance is due, or can of right be demanded. The committee then after repeating the wrongs from New York, offered the following declaration: "This Convention, whose members are duly chosen by the free voice of their constituents in the several towns, on the New Hampshire Grants, in public meeting assembled, in our own names, and in behalf of our constituents, do hereby proclaim and publicly declare, that the district of territory, comprehending and usually known by the name and description of the New Hampshire Grants, of right ought to be, and is hereby declared forever hereafter to be considered, as a free and independent jurisdiction, or State; by the name, and forever hereafter to be called, known, and distinguished by the name of New Connecticut, *alias* Vermont, &c."

This Convention after informing the Continental Congress of their doings, adjourned to meet at Windsor, on the first Wednesday in June.

The above declaration brought down upon us the wrath of New York, but notwithstanding that, those brave Green Mountain Boys, whom any nation or people on earth might well be proud of, followed up their declaration by the adoption of a Constitution the same year, and a Legislative session in March following. In February, 1779, the Legislature passed an act in the face and eyes of the New York law dividing the State into two counties, Bennington on the west and Cumberland on the east of the Green Mountains, and divided each county into two shires each, Westminster and Newbury on the east, and Bennington and Rutland on the west. That division of counties remained till the extra session of the Legislature in Feb. 1781, when the County of Rutland was incorporated, from Bennington, and Windsor and Orange counties were incorporated from Cumberland, and the name of Cumberland altered to Windham.

Zadock Thompson, in his history of Vermont, says, that Chittenden County was incorporated October 22d, 1782, and Addison County Feb. 27, 1787. This is a mistake as to both Counties, as will be seen by the following extract of a letter from Mr. Thompson to a friend, who had addressed him on the subject: "While in Montpelier a few days since, I was induced, by your suggestions, to examine the manuscript acts in the office of the Secretary of State, and I there found that Addison County was incorporated October 18th, 1785, and that Chittenden County was incorporated October 22nd, 1787." This explanation explains a mystery which was hard to solve, which was, "how came Addison County Court to set in Colchester at their Nov. Term, 1786, and one of Chittenden County citizens for the first Sheriff, in 1785, and one of her citizens for side Judge 1785, and another in 1786," for such are the facts, and as appeared it was all done over one year before Addison County was incorporated. When the County of Addison was incorporated it included within its boundaries the present county, (except Granville and Orwell,) the whole of Chittenden, Franklin, Grand Isle, and Lamoille, nine towns from Orleans, and eight from Washington Counties, and that was the size of the County till Oct. 19. 1787, when Kingston, now Granville, was annexed to it from Orange County, and three days after by the incorporation of Chittenden County. Addison County was reduced to its present dimensions, except Starksboro' has been added from Chittenden, and Orwell from Rutland, and a part of Philadelphia in Rutland has been added to Goshen, and a part of Goshen has been set to Rochester, and the town of Warren in 1829 was annexed to Washington County. Avery's Gore has been annexed to Lincoln, altering no County lines. The first County Court in Addison County, was holden at Addison, on the first Tuesday in March, 1786, and continued to be holden there, (with the exception of the November term of that year which was held at Colchester,) till the first of April, 1792, and since that all the sessions have been holden at Middlebury.

The Counties of Caledonia and Franklin were incorporated Nov. 8th, 1796, the former from Orange and the latter from Chittenden Counties. The Legislature on the 2d day of March, 1797, passed an act defining the boundaries of eleven counties, including the whole State, but left the Counties of Essex and Orleans to be connected with Caledonia and Franklin for all purposes till a future Legislature should elect their County officers, which was done at the October Session, 1797 as to Orleans County, and for Essex County, the County officers were appointed at the Oct. session 1800. Thus the State remained with eleven Counties till the organization of Grand Isle County, which took place in November, 1805. After the sessions of the Legislature were established at Montpelier, and that became a thriving town, the Legislature saw fit in 1811, to organize a new County of which Montpelier was near the centre, by the name of Jefferson, containing 15 towns from the adjoining Counties of Orange, Caledonia and Chittenden. In 1814, when the Federal party were predominent in every branch of the government, the name of the County was changed to "Washington," and has retained that name since. In 1836, the County contained 19 towns by the addition of Elmore from Orleans, Woodbury from Caledonia, Roxbury from Orange, and Warren from Addison. In 1336, the County of Lamoille was incorporated by taking Stowe and Elmore from Washington, Mansfield, which has since been annexed to Stowe from Chittenden; Eden, Hydepark, Morristown and Wolcott from Orleans, and the other five towns from Franklin, and the State has remained in that situation since till 1848, when the towns of Windsor, and Montpelier were divided into two towns each, West Windsor and East Montpelier, making 240 organized towns in the State.

OFFICERS OF VERMONT LEGISLATURES.

Years.	Governors.	Lt. Gov's.	Treasurers	Sec. of State.	Speakers.	Clerks.	En'g. clerk.
March 12							
1778	Thomas * p	Joseph	Ira Allen.	T. Chandler	Nathan Clark.	Benjamin Baldwin	
O 78	Chittenden, p	Marsh p	"	p	Joseph Fay.	Thomas Chandler.	Bezaleel Woodard
79	" " p	Benjamin p	"	p	"	"	Roswell Hopkins.
80	" "	Carpenter. p	"	p	"	"	"
81	" " p	Elisha Payne	"	p	Micah	Thomas Porter.	"
82	" " p	Paul	"	p	Townshend.	Increase Moseley.	"
83	" " p	Spooner. p	"	p	"	Isaac Tichenor.	"
84	" " p	" p	"	p	"	Nathaniel Niles.	"
85	" " p	" p	"		"	Stephen R. Brad-	"
86	" " p	" p	Samuel		"	Gideon Olin. ley.	"
87	" " p	Joseph p	Mattocks. p		"	"	"
88 p	" (Robinson	Marsh. p	"	p	Roswell	"	Stephen Jacobs.
89	Moses p	" p	"	p	Hopkins.	"	"
90	Thomas p	Peter Olcott.	"	p	"	"	Lewis R. Morris.
91	Chittenden. p	" p	"	p	"	"	William Eaton.
92	" p	" p	"	p	"	"	"
93	" " p	" p	"	p	"	Daniel Buck.	Richard Whitney.
94	" " p	Jonathan	"	p	"	"	" Thomas
95	" " p	Hunt. p	"	p	"	Lewis R. Morris.	" Tolman
96	" " p	Paul	"	p	"	"	"
97	Isaac	Brigham. p	"	p	"	Abel Spencer.	"
98	Tichenor. p	" p	"	p	"	Daniel Farrand.	Samuel C. Crafts.
99	" p	" p	"	p	"	Amos Marsh.	"
1800	" p	" p	"	p	Benjamin	"	Nathan Osgood.
1	" p	" p	"	p	Swan. p	"	James Elliott.
2	" p	" p	"	p	"	Abel Spencer. ton	"
3	" p	" p	"	p	David	Theophi's Harring	Anthony Haswell.
4	" p	" p	"	p	Wing, jr.	Aaron Leland.	Martin Post.
5	" p	" p	"	p	"	"	"
6 p	" (Smith.	" p	"	p	Thomas	"	"
7	Israel p	" p	"	p	Leavcrett.	"	Orsam's o.
8 I.	Tichenor. p	" p	"	p	"	Dudley Chase.	Merrill
9	Jonas p	" p	"	p	"	"	William D. Smith.
10	Galusha. p	" p	"	p	"	"	"
11	" p	" p	"	p	"	"	"
12	" p	" p	"	p	"	"	"
13	Martin	William	"	p	Josiah	Daniel Chipman.	" Azro
14	Chittenden.	Chamberlin.	"	p	Dunham.	"	" Loomis
15	Jonas p	Paul p	"	p	William	William A. Gris-	"
16	Galusha. p	Brigham. p	"	p	Slade, jr.	" wold.	Timothy
17	" p	" p	"	p	"	Richard Skinner	" Merrill
18	" p	" p	"	p	"	Wm. A. Griswold.	"
19	" p	" p	"	p	"	Daniel A. A. Buck	"
20	Richard p	William	"	p	"	"	"
21	Skinner. p	Cahoon. p	"	p	"	"	Timothy Merrill.
22	" p	Aaron p	"	p	"	"	" S. S Conant
23	Cornelius p	Leland. p	"	p	Norman	George E. Wales.	" Oramel n.
24	P. Van Ness p	" p	"	p	Williams.	" Isaac Fletcher.	" Smith
25	" p	" p	"	p	"	Daniel A. A. Buck.	"
26	Ezra Butler. p	" p	"	p	"	"	"
27	" p	Henry Olin. p	"	p	"	Robert B. Bates.	"
28	Samuel p	" p	"	p	"	"	"
29	C. Crafts. p	p" [Richards	"	p	"	Daniel A. A. Buck.	"
30	" p	Mark	"	p	"	Robert B. Bates.	" Daniel P.
31	William A.	Lebbeus p	"	p	Timothy	John Smith.	Charles Davis. Thompson
32	Palmer.	Edgerton.	"	p	Merrill.	"	Robert Pierpoint. "
33	" p	" p	Augustine p		"	Ebenezer N. Briggs	Edward D. Barber. O.H. Smith
34	" p	" (Jenison.	Clarke.		"	"	Oramel H. Smith. Daniel P.
35	no choice	Silas H. p	"	p	"	Ebenezer N. Briggs	Edward D. Barber. Thompson
36	Silas H. p	David M. p	" (Wardner		Chauncey	Carlos Coolidge.	Ahiman L. Miner. Ferrand F.
37	Jenison p	Camp. p	Allen		L. Knapp.	Solomon Foot.	" Merrill
38	" p	" p	Henry F. p		"	"	Ferrand F. Merrill Oel Bilings
39	" p	" p	Janes.. p		"	Carlos Coolidge.	" "
40	" p	" p	" p		"	"	" "
41	Charles p	Waitstill R.	John		Alvah Sabin	"	" Ambrose
42	Paine. p	Ranney. p	Spaulding. p		James Mc.	Andrew Tracy.	" L. Brown
43	John Mattocks. p	Horace Eaton	"	p	M. Shafter.	"	" "
44	William p	" p	"	p	"	"	" Eno'h Davis
45	Slade. p	" p	" (Jewett.		"	Eben. N. Briggs.	" Norman
46	Horace Eaton. p	Leonard	Elisha P.		"	"	" Durant
47	" p	Sargeant.	George		"	Solomon Foot.	" "
48	Carlos p	Robert	Howes.		"	William C. Kitt-	" "
49	Coolidge. p	Pierpoint.	"		Ferrand F.	redge.	Chalon F. Davey "
50	Charles K. p	Julius p	"	p	Merrill.	Thomas E. Powers.	" None
	Williams.	Converse.					

* Those with a p, added, were elected by the People.

SESSIONS, DEBENTURES AND PREACHERS.

Where holden.	Began.		Ended.	Days.	Debentures.	Preachers Election day.	Sec. Gov. & C.
Windsor	Mar. 12	1778	Mar. 26	15		Rev. Peter Powers	Joseph Fay
Bennington	June 4	1778	June 18	15			"
Windsor	Oct. 8	"	Oct. 24	17		' Eden Burroughs	"
Bennington	Feb. 11	1779	Feb. 26	16			"
Windsor	June 2	"	June 4	3			"
Manchester	Oct. 14	"	Oct. 27	14		' Benajah Root	"
Westminster	Mar. 8	1780	Mar. 16	9			"
Bennington	Oct. 12	"	Nov. 8	28	1,506 38		"
Windsor	Feb. 7	1781	Feb. 23	17	1,178 44		"
"	Apr. 4	"	Apr. 16	13	1,377 48		"
Bennington	June 13	"	June 28	16	1,860 83		"
Charlestown N. H.	Oct. 11	"	Oct. 27	17		' ———— Olcott	
Bennington	Jan. 31	1782	Feb. 28	29			"
Windsor	June 13	"	June 21	9			"
Manchester	Oct. 10	"	Oct. 24	15		' Gershom C. Lyman	
Windsor	Feb. 13	1783	Feb. 27	15			"
Westminster	Oct. 9	"	Oct. 24	16		' Joseph Bullen	
Bennington	Feb. 19	1784	Mar. 9	20			
Rutland	Oct. 14	"	Oct. 29	16		' Job Swift	Joseph Fay
Norwich	June 2	1785	June 18	17			Thomas
Windsor	Oct. 13	"	Oct. 27	15		' Asa Burton	Tolman
Windsor	Oct. 12	86	Oct. 31	20		' Peletiah Chapin	Joseph Fay
Bennington	Feb. 15	87	Mar. 10	24			"
Newbury	Oct. 11	"	Oct. 27	17		' Lyman Potter	"
Manchester	Oct. 9	88	Oct. 25	17		' Elijah Sill	"
Westminster	Oct. 8	89	Oct. 29	22		' Dan Foster	"
Castleton	Oct. 14	90	Oct. 28	15		' Mathias Cazier	"
Bennington	Jan. 10	91	Jan. 27	18			"
Windsor	Oct. 13	"	Nov. 3	22		' Saml Shuttleworth	"
Rutland	Oct. 11	92	Nov. 8	29		' Caleb Blood	"
Windsor	Oct. 10	93	Nov. 4	26		' Benjamin Bell	"
Rutland	Oct. 9	94	Oct. 30	22		' Samuel Williams	Truman
Windsor	Oct. 8	95	Oct. 27	20	5,180 42	' Asa Burton	Squier
Rutland	Oct. 13	96	Nov. 8	27	6,334 15	' Dan Kent	"
"	Feb. 4	97	Mar. 10	35			"
Windsor	Oct. 12	"	Nov. 10	30		' Samuel Whiting	"
Vergennes	Oct. 11	98	Nov. 8	29		' Danl C. Saunders	Richard
Windsor	Oct. 10	99	Nov. 5	27		' William Forsythe	Whitney
Middlebury	Oct. 9	1800	Nov. 7	30	9,105 98	' Benjamin Wooster	"
Newbury	Oct. 8	1	Nov. 6	30	10,967 64	' Nathaniel Lambert	"
Burlington	Oct. 14	2	Nov. 12	30	11,483 41	' Jeremiah Atwater	"
Westminster	Oct. 13	3	Nov. 14	33	12,449 58	' Sylvester Sage	William
Windsor	Jan. 26	4	Feb. 6	12	4,489 92		Page jr.
Rutland	Oct. 11	"	Nov. 9	30	11,007 52	' Heman Ball	"
Danville	Oct. 10	5	Nov. 8	30	12,057 26	' John Fitch	"
Middlebury	Oct. 9	6	Nov. 11	34	12,727 68	' Thomas A. Merrill	"
Woodstock	Oct. 8	7	Nov. 11	35	12,841 63	' Thomas Gross	Rollin C.
Montpelier	Oct. 13	8	Nov. 11	30	11,952 47	' Tilton Eastman	Mallary
"	Oct. 12	9	Nov. 8	28	10,973 04	' Sylvanus Haynes	Wm. Page
"	Oct. 11	10	Nov. 5	26	10,227 21	' Chester Wright	Rollin C.
"	Oct. 10	11	Oct. 31	22	9,217 81	' Thomas Skeel	Mallary
"	Oct. 8	12	Nov. 9	33	13,057 42	' Isaac Beal	"
"	Oct. 14	13	Nov. 17	35	13,838 42	' Daniel Marsh	Samuel
"	Oct. 13	14	Nov. 11	30	12,177 06	' Elijah Lyman	Swift

SESSIONS. CONTINUED. 11

Where holden.	Began.	Ended.	Days.	Debentures.	Preachers.	Sec. to Gov. & Council.
"	Oct. 12	15 Nov. 13	33	13,129 69	' Henry Davis	Rollin C.
"	Oct. 10	16 Nov. 6	28	11,457 95	' Samuel Austin	Mallary
"	Oct. 9	17 Nov. 7	30	11,480 75	' Phinehas Peck	"
"	Oct. 8	18 Nov. 12	36	13,258 01	' Clark Kendrick	"
"	Oct. 14	19 Nov. 17	35	13,110 71	' James Converse	"
"	Oct. 12	20 Nov. 16	36	13,921 78	' George Leonard	Robert
"	Oct. 11	21 Nov. 16	37	13,536 68	' Joshua Bates	Temple
"	Oct. 10	22 Nov. 13	35	13,372 86	' John Linsley	"
"	Oct. 9	23 Nov. 7	30	12,057 81	' Joseph W. Sawyer	Daniel
"	Oct. 14	24 Nov. 19	37	14,116 26	' Amariah Chandler	Kellogg
"	Oct. 13	25 Nov. 18	37	14,631 58	' Robert Bartlett	"
"	Oct. 12	26 Nov. 16	36	14,622 96	' Wilber Fisk	"
"	Oct. 11	27 Nov. 15	36	14,830 05	' Thomas Goodwillie	"
"	Oct. 9	28 Oct. 31	23	10,616 19	' Jona'n Woodman	George B.
"	Oct. 8	29 Oct. 30	23	10,472 70	' Charles Walker	Shaw
"	Oct. 14	30 Nov. 11	33	12,443 20	' George G. Ingersol	" [Barber
"	Oct. 13	31 Nov. 10	29	12,291 87	' Leland Howard	Edward D.
"	Oct. 11	32 Nov. 9	30	12,780 85	' William S. Perkins	George B.
"	Oct. 10	33 Nov. 8	30	13,286 22	' Tobias Spicer	Manser
"	Oct. 9	34 Nov. 7	30	12,737 87	' Warren Skinner	"
"	Oct. 8	35 Nov. 7	31	14,895 31		
"	Oct. 13	36 Nov. 17	37	18,392 03		
"	Oct. 12	37 Nov. 1	22	12,613 02		
"	Oct. 11	38 Nov. 6	27	14,468 50		
"	Oct. 10	39 Nov. 19	41	21,003 84		
"	Oct. 8	40 Oct. 30	23	13,016 69		
"	Oct. 14	41 Nov. 12	30	16,283 25		
"	Oct. 13	42 Nov. 14	33	17,270 65		
"	Oct. 12	43 Nov. 2	22	12,236 40		
"	Oct. 10	44 Oct. 31	23	11,536 70		
"	Oct. 9	45 Nov. 6	29	13,858 50		
"	Oct. 8	46 Nov. 3	27	13,305 24		
"	Oct. 14	47 Nov. 16	34	16,063 60		
"	Oct. 12	48 Nov. 14	34	17,011 00		
"	Oct. 11	49 Nov. 14	35	17,877 55		
"	Oct. 10	1850 Nov. 14	36	23,552 84		

This year ended the old Connecticut practice of calling in the Clergymen going to Election, and dining at the expense of the State, and have a sermon from one of them. Some of the most radical members came to the conclusion that the money and time thus spent might be put to a better use. They therefore resolved to have no more Election Sermons with accompanying expenses after 1834 unless it should be otherwise ordered in future This has not yet been done; but whether any very material benefit has been effected by the change is a doubt in the minds of many. If a Farmer hired a man to mow in his meadow six days, & he should go earley to the meadow and swing his sythe a few times on the sixth day. then quit and go home, there is a doubt whether that farmer would feel disposed to pay full price for that last day. But if the man had taken his pay for the six days, and quit on the fourth day morning, it might be some less doubtful how that farmer would act, but would he be apt to hire him again?

HON. STEPHEN HAIGHT,

Of Monkton, commenced in legislation while young, he first represented the town in 1812, and was elected each year to 1822, eleven years, and three years afterwards. He was four years judge of the County Court, and four years Sheriff, ending the last office in 1832. In the fore part of his public life he belonged to the old Federal School in politics, and figured very adroitly in effecting the election of Martin Chittenden, Governor in 1813. The federal members of the legislature and many others of the party met at Montpelier the fore part of election week, and there found, on comparing notes, that unless some of the freemens votes were rejected, there would be a federal majority of four in the House, and a republican majority of ten in the Council. It was then found that rejecting the votes from Colchester on account of a part of them being given by the U. S. troops, and altering the votes of a few other towns, it would elect three more federal members in the Council, and bring the Joint Assembly to a tie, 112 each. The canvassing committee with a large federal majority carried out the measures concocted in Caucus, and brought the legislature to a tie. Thus legislation stood nearly still for a week, but tampering with a republican member to carry a load to Boston, at a great profit did not stand so still, a few federal leaders kept that moving, but not to much purpose, as he staid in the house and voted for Jonas Galusha throughout, making a tie, 112 each. After a number of ballots the votes were reported 112 for Martin Chittenden, and 111 only for Jonas Galusha. It has caused many conjectures as to who was guilty, or negligent, as to that vote

COUNCILLORS FROM 1778 TO 1835.

March 12.

1778	Jonas Fay, Ben-	Timothy Brownson	Jeremiah Clark	Ira Allen, Colches	Benj. Carpenter,	Peter Olcott,	
Oct. 78	" nington	" Sunderland	" [Bennington	" [ter	" [Guilford	" [Norwich.	
'79 & 80	"	"	"	"	John Fassett, jr.	Thomas Chandler,	
'81	"	"	Bezleel Woodward	"	" [Arlington	Peter Olcott,	
'82	"	"	Thos Porter [N.H	"	"	"	
'83	"	"	" [Tinmouth	"	"	"	
'84	"	"	"	"	Thomas Moredock.	"	
'85	Samuel Mattocks,	Nathaniel Niles	"	"	"	"	
'86	" Tinmouth	" Fairlee	"	"	"	"	
'87 8&9	Isaac Tichenor	John Fassett	"	Timothy Brownson	"	"	
'90	" Bennington	"	, "	"	Jonathan Arnold,	"	
'91	"	"	"	"	"	Ebenezer Marvin,	
'92	Paul Brigham,	"	"	"	"	"	
'93	" Norwich	"	"	Ebenezer Marvin	Jonas Galusha,	Gideon Olin,	
'94	"	"	"	"	" Shaftsbury.	"	
'95	"	Elijah Robinson	Sam'l Williams	" [Tinmouth	"	"	
'96	"	" Weathers'd	" [Rutland	"	"	"	
'97	Stephen Jacobs	"	"	"	"	"	
'98	" Windsor	"	"	"	"	Timothy Todd,	
'99	"	"	Abel Spencer	"	Elisha Allis,	" [Arlington.	
1800	"	"	"	"	" [Brookfield.	"	
'1	"	"	Noah Chittenden	"	"	Beriah Loomis,	
'2	Eliakim Spooner	Stephen Williams	" [Jericho	James Witherill	"	"	
'3 & 4	" Westm'ns'tr.	Nathaniel Niles	"	" [Fairhaven	Asaph Fletcher,	"	
'5 & 6	"	"	"	"	" Cavendish.	"	
'7	" [Thetford	"	"	Samuel Shaw, Cast	"	"	
'8	Jed. T. Buckingham	Daniel Dana	"	John Ellsworth	Chauncey Langdon	Asa Lyon, G. Isle.	
'9	Beriah Loomis	Gilbert Denison	"	Samuel C. Crafts	Apollos Austin,	Haines French,	
'10	Thetford	" Guilford	"	"	& Pliny Smith, of	" [Maidstone.	
'11	"	"	"	"	" Orwell.	John Cameron,	
'12	"	William C. Bradley	Wm. C. Harrington	"	"	" [Ryegate.	
'13	"	Mark Richards	" [Burlington	Daniel Dana	Gamaliel Painter,	Solomon Miller,	
'14	Moses Robinson	William Hall jr.	John Ellsworth	"	"	" [Williston.	
'15	Josiah Wright	Mark Richards	William. Cahoon	Timothy Stanley	Joel Doolittle,	Truman Chitenden	
'16	"	Theoph's Crawford	" [Lyndon	" [Greensboro'	"	" (do.	
'17	David Fay, Bennin	" Putney	"	"	"	"	
'18	" ton	"	"	"	Abel Tomlinson,	"	
'19	"	"	"	"	"	"	
'20	"	Charles Phelps	Joseph Warner	"	Henry Olin,	"	
'21	Joel Pratt, Manches-	" Townsend	" [Sudbury	"	"	"	
'22	"	"	Uriel C. Hatch	"	Eben W. Judd,	"	
'23	"	John Roberts	Chauncey Langdon	"	Samuel H. Holley.	"	
'24	Orsamus C. Merrill	" Whitingham	"	"	" [Bristol	"	
'25	" Bennington	"	"	Samuel C. Crafts	"	"	
'26	"	"	"	"	"	"	
'27	"	John C. Thompson	"	"	"	" [Windsor.	
'28	Myron Clark	" [Burlington	"	Ira H. Allen	Ezra Hoyt,	Abner Forbes,	
'29	" Manchester	"	"	" [Irasburgh	" [Newhaven	Job Lyman,	
'30	" "	"	Henry F. Janes	"	" [Middlebury	William G. Hunter	
'31	John S. Pettibone	John Phelps	" [Waterbury	Jasper Robinson	Samuel S. Phelps,	Sam'l. C. Loveland	
'32	Isaac Sherman	" [Guilford	"	" [Browning'n	Silas H. Jenison,	" [Reading.	
'33	"	Austin Birchard	"	"	"	"	
'34	"	" [Newfane	"	"	"	Allen Wardner,	
'35	John S. Pettibone	David Crawford	Milton Brown	E. H. Starkweather	Harvey Bell,	" Windsor.	
	Manchester	[Putney	[Worcester	[Irasburgh	[Middlebury.		

lacking. From an examination of the Journal it might be readily inferred that Judge Kinne, a republican member from Plainfield, was at fault, but although he was very feeble, and scarsely able to leave his lodgings, he did attend on the election of Governor and voted till all was done, and the fault must lie at anothers door. There were four test votes taken during the maneuvering to get the two branches together, and one after, and at each the federal vote was 108, and the highest on the other side was 103, and that only once. There was a member of the house that year from a small town in the southerly part of Bennington County, and for the first time, and last but one, that was counted with the republicans; but by an examination of the five test votes as stated, he voted twice on the federal side, twice on the republican, and on the other he did not vote, and if he carried out his principles as he began, I shold look no further to find where that missing vote did not come from.

Whenever Mr. De Forest, a federalist, or the Speaker, did not vote, the name of the gentleman from Bennington County would help up the number to 108 on all the test votes. And it is possible that Mr. De Forest being unwell, retired before the last vote was taken, being satisfied that his old helper would help him again.

In the latter part of Judge Haight's term of legislation he became quite radical, and was influential in procuring the passage of a bill for reducing the fees of many officers, including the County Court Judges, of which he was one. When the Clerk of the court had counted out the amount due each Judge at the end of a session, which was much reduced under his own bill. The Judge looked on the money as if in a quandary about

COUNCILLORS CONTINUED.

John Throop,	Paul Spooner,	Thomas Moredock,	Benjamin Emmons.	Joseph Bowker,	Jacob Bailey.	
Moses Robinson,	" [Hartland	" [Norwich	Elisha Payne, N. H	" [Rutland.	Samuel Fletcher	
" [Bennington	"	John Throop,	Benjamin Emmons	"	" [Townshend	
"	"	" [Pomfret	" [Woodstock	"	"	
"	Samuel Safford,	"	"	John Fassett,	"	
"	" [Bennington	"	"	" [Bennington	"	
Eben'r. Walbridge	"	John Streng,	Jonathan Hunt.	Jacob Bailey,	"	
" [Bennington	"	" Addison.	" [Vernon.	" [Newbury.	"	
"	"	"	"	"	Luke Knowlton	
"	"	"	"	"	" [Newfane.	
Wm. Chamberlin,	"	"	Cornelius Lynde,	"	"	
"	"	"	" [Williamston	"	"	
"	"	"	"	Noah Smith.	"	
"	"	"	Solomon Miller,	Benjamin Burt.	"	
"	"	"	"	Jonas Galusha.	John White.	
Elias Keyes,	"	Eben'r Wheelock,	Sam'l Shepherdson	"	"	
"	Josiah Wright.	" [Whiting.	" [Guilford	"	"	
"	" [Pownal.	"	"	"	"	
"	Samuel Fletcher,	Daniel Chipman, &	Reuben Hatch,	Solomon Miller.	Zerah Willoughby	
"	Josiah Wright,	Horatio Seymour,	William Hunter,	Ezra Butler.	Frederick Bliss.	
"	"	" [Middlebury	" [windsor.	"	"	
"	"	"	"	Samuel Fletcher.	"	
Elias Stevens,	James D. Butler,	Zerah Willoughby.	John w. Chandler,	Josiah Hubbard.	Nicholas Baylies.	
Elias Keyes,	Pliny Smith,	Frederick Bliss,	James Tarbox,	William Hunter,	Ezra Butler	
"	"	" Georgia	Daniel Penslee,	Thomas Hammond	"	
Aaron Leland,	"	"	" [washington.	" [Pittsford.	"	
" [Chester.	Joseph Berry,	Seth Wetmore,	John H. Cotton,	"	"	
"	" [Guildhall.	" St. Albans	" [Bradford.	John H. Andrus.	"	
Jabez Proctor,	"	"	Josiah Dana,	" [Danby.	"	
" [Cavendish.	"	"	" [Chelsea.	Israel P. Dana.	"	
"	Robert Pierpoint,	"	"	" [Danville	"	
"	" [Rutland	"	Lyman Fitch,	"	John Peck.	
Benj'n. F. Deming.	"	"	" [Thetford.	David Hopkinson.	Geo' Worthington	
" [Danville.	"	"	Jedediah H. Harris	Samuel Clark,	" [Montpelier.	
"	"	James Davis,	" [Strafford.	" Brattleboro'	"	
"	Zimri Howe,	Joseph H. Brainard	Daniel Cobb,	N. Leavenworth.	Richardson Graves	
"	" [Castleton.	" [St. Albans	" [Strafford.	Wm. A. Griswold	" [St. Albans.	
George C. Cahoon	"	"	"	"	H. R. Beardsley,	
" [Lyndon	"	George Green,	Martin Flint,	George P. Marsh,	Richardson Graves	
Walter Harvey,	Tho. D. Hammond	" [Swanton.	Randolph	Burlington.	[Guildhall.	
[Barnet	Orwell					

taking it. Judge Olin observed, "O! take it by all means, Judge, and nurse it up as it is one of your own children.,'

In 1821 he got a law passed for enlarging the jurisdiction of justices of the peace to $100, and restricting appeals for a less amount claimed than $10 This law very materially affected the attornies, as it much reduced their business in the higher courts; and they tried to prevent the passage of the bill, and to get it repealed afterward. In 1824 a violent effort was made to repeal the 5th. section, which prevented appeals from a justice under $10. Judge Haight arose and began, "Mr. Speaker, we have heard much said against this little 5th. section of the act of 1821, and I challenge any gentleman upon this floor, if he knows of any injustice being done under the operation of that section, let the house have the facts, we can then act understandingly", Mr. Fletcher of Lyndon informed the house of a case within his knowledge. Mr. A had given a note to Mr. B for a good likely cow at a stated time, which was not paid, and a suit brought, and the justice concluded that a good likely cow was worth $17, and gave a verdict accordingly, which was paid. Soon after Mr. A found a justice who thought that $15 was as much as a good likely cow was worth, and he gave out a writ against Mr. B, and gave judgment that Mr. A recover back $2 and cost, and not appealable as the law now stands. Some other cases were mentioned, and one by Esq. Bell of Walden, in his peculiar mode of delivery, about an old saw, in which it appeared that some injustice had been done. Judge Haight wished to know whether those corrupt justices

VERMONT SENATE, FROM 1836 TO 1850.

1836	1837	1838	1839	1840
BENNINGTON CO.				
Orsamus C. Merrill	Nathan Burton	"	William Hoyt	Noadiah Swift
Winslow C. Watson	Heman Swift	John S. Robinson	"	Ahiman L. Miner
WINDHAM CO.				
Phinehas White,	"	David Chandler	"	David Crawford
Wait'll R. Ranney	"	"	Calvin Townsley	"
William Henry.	John Phelps	Laban Jones	"	Emery Wheelock
RUTLAND CO.				
T. D. Hammond,	"	Obadiah Noble	"	Isaac Norton
Zimri Howe,	"	Wm. C. Kittredge	"	Orson Clark
Robert Pierpoint,	"	"	"	Anderson G. Dana
WINDSOR CO.				
Francis E. Phelps.	"	Daniel Bowen	"	Abel Gilson
Samuel W. Porter.	"	Ptolemy Edson	"	Barnabas Dean
William Steele.	"	"	Andrew Tracy	Walter Palmer
Julius Converse	"	"	"	Thomas P. Russell
ADDISON CO.				
Eben. N. Briggs	"	"	Joseph Simonds	Dorastus Wooster
Jesse Grandey	Ville Lawrence	"	"	Elias Bottom
Harvey Bell	"	Samuel Swift	"	Isaac Chipman
ORANGE CO.				
A. B. W. Tenney	Lebbeus Edgerton	A. B. W. Tenney	Lebbeus Edgerton	Timothy Morse
Thomas Keyes	Jonathan Jenness	Simeon Short	Daniel Cobb	Simeon Short
William Hebard	Daniel Cobb	William Hebard	Jonathan Jenness	Nathaniel Wheatly
CHITTENDEN CO.				
John Van Sicklin jr	"	Truman Chitenden	Lyman Burgess	Thad's R. Fletcher
Harry Miller	"	Joseph Clark	Joseph Marsh	"
WASHINGTON CO.				
Arunah Waterman	"	Joseph A. Curtis	"	Orion W. Butler
Newell Kinsman	"	Israel Goodwin	"	Nathaniel Eaton
FRANKLIN CO.				
Nathan Smilie	"	"	Joseph Waterman	"
Joshua w. Sheldon	Timothy Foster	Alden Sears	Timothy Foster	"
Homer E. Hubbell	Horace Eaton	Homer E. Hubbell	Horace Eaton	"
CALEDONIA CO				
William A. Palmer	"	Robert Harvey	"	Walter Harvey
John Beckwith	Joseph H. Ingalls	Andrew M'Millan	"	Elias Bemis jr,
ORLEANS CO.				
Augustus Young	"	"	S. S. Hemenway	Jacob Bates
ESSEX CO.				
William Gates	Wm. Heywood jr.	"	George E. Holmes	Stephen Howe
GRAND ISLE CO.				
Melvin Barnes	Joel Allen	"	Samuel Adams	"
SECRETARY to Gov				
George B Manser	"	"	"	"
SEC'T to SENATE				
Norman Williams	"	"	"	D. W. C. Clarke
ASSISTANT SEC'Y,				
Edmond Weston	William Weston	"	"	Ed. A. Stansbury
SERGEANT at ARMS				
Milton Brown	Abel Carter	C Ware, R. Riker	Edward H Prentiss	Erastus S. Camp
LIBRARIAN.				
Heman Carpenter	"	Jackson A. Vail	"	"
AUD. OF ACOUNTS				
David Pierce	"	"	"	"

were now in office, and found they were not. That is the best way, said the judge, if you find justices that are corrupt, and do injustice, turn them out of office, and let the law remain as it is. This brought up Isaac N. Cushman, of Hartland, who said "Mr. Speaker, the argument of the gentleman from Monkton reminds me of a French King who kept a Jester, and this jester had offended one of the Lords of the Court, and the Lord threatened to kill him-

SENATE CONTINUED.

	1841	1842	1843	1844	1845
BENNINGTON CO.					
	Noadiah Swift	Josiah Wright	Leonard Sargeant	Asahel Hurd	"
	Henry Sheldon	"	Benj'n w. Morgan	"	Black'r E Brownell
WINDHAM CO.					
	David Crawford	Calvin Townsley	William Harris	"	Ebenezer Howe jr.
	John Barrett	"	Sam'l F. Thompson	"	John Campbell
	Emery Wheelock	Sandford Plumb	"	Reuben Winn	"
RUTLAND CO.					
	Isaac Norton	Eben. N. Briggs	"	"	George T. Hodges
	Orson Clark	Elisha Allen	"	Frederick Button	"
	Anderson G. Dana	Alanson Allen	"	Joseph H. Chitendn	"
WINDSOR CO.					
	Abel Gilson	Hampden Cutts	"	James Barrett	"
	Barnabas Dean	John Porter	"	Thomas S. Barrett	"
	Walter Palmer	Salmon F. Dutton	"	Benjamin Billings	"
	Thomas P. Russell	Abner Field	"	Justin Morgan	
ADDISON CO,					
	Dorastus Wooster				
	Elias Bottom	Peter Starr	"	Davis Rich	"
	Isaac Chipman	Harvey Munsill	"	E. D. Woodbridge	"
ORANGE CO.					
	Calvin Blodgett	"	Elijah Farr	"	Horace Fifield
	Royal Hatch	"	Loren Griswold	"	Reuben Page
	Tappan Stevers	"	Ebenezer Bass	"	Levi B. Vilas
CHITTENDEN CO.					
	T. R. Fletcher	David A. Smalley	David Read	"	Harry Bradley
	David French	"	Luther Stone	"	Daniel H. Onion
WASHINGTON CO.					
	Paul Dillingham jr	"	Jacob Scott	"	Oramel H. Smith
	Nathaniel Eaton	Wooster Sprague	"	Rode'k Richardson	"
FRANKLIN CO.					
	Alvah Sabin	William Green	Alvah Sabin	"	"
	Moses Fisk	Homer E. Hubbell	George Green	"	Hiram Bellows
	Horace Eaton	"	Jon. H. Hubbard	"	William Clapp
CALEDONIA CO.					
	Daniel w. Aiken	"	George C. Cahoon	"	Welcome Bemis
	Thomas Bartlett jr.	"	John Phillips	"	William Sias
ORLN CO.					
	S. S. Hemmenway	David M. Camp	"	"	Enoch B. Simonds
ESSEX C.					
	Moody Rich	Warner Bingham	"	George Marshall	"
GRAND ISLE CO.					
	William L. Sowle	"	Wallis Mott	H. H. Reynolds	Lewis Ladd
LAMOILLE CO.					
		Orion W. Butler	"	David P. Noyes	"
SECRETARY GOV,					
	Harry Hale	"	"	George H. Beaman	"
SEC. TO SENATE					
	D. W. C. Clarke	"	"	"	"
ASSISTANT SEC,					
	Ed. A. Stansbury	"	Enoch Davis	"	Frederick Billings
SERG'T at ARMS					
	Wm. T. Burnham	"	"	"	"
LIBRARIAN					
	A. W. Kenney	"		Gusta's H. Loomis	"
AUDITOR					
	David Pierce	"	"	"	Silas H. Hodges

The jester informed the King what the Lord had threatened. Said the King, "if he kills you I will have him hung in fifteen minutes *afterwards*." I do wish your Majesty would hang him fifteen minutes *before*, it would make no materiel differ- ence with him, but a very essential difference with me. Just so with the argument of the gentleman from Monkton, he would hang those corrupt justices who have done injustice under this law, but I am for repealing that law under

SENATE CONTINUED.

	1846	1847	1848	1849	1850
BENNINGTON CO.					
	Heman Morse	"	George R. Draper	John L. Wilmarth	Joel Ranney
	B. E. Brownell	"	Francis Kidder	"	Ira K. Bachelder
WINDHAM CO.					
	Ebenezer Howe jr.	Larkin G. Mead	"	"	Asa Wentworth
	John Kimball	"	"	Frederick Holbrook	"
	Austin Birchard	Peter w Dean	"	John Tufts	"
RUTLAND CO.					
	George T Hodges	"	Ezra June	"	James K. Hyde
	John Fox	"	"	"	Elisha Lapham
	J. H. Chittenden	Henry Stanley	"	John Crowley	
WINDSOR CO.					
	Artemas Cushman	"	Oliver P. Chandler	"	"
	Harvey Burton	"	Joseph W. Colburn	"	"
	Robert B. Cram	"	Solon Danforth	"	Daniel L Lyman
	Dearborn H. Hilton	"	Calvin French	"	Warren Currier
ADDISON CO.					
	Davis Rich	Ira Stewart	"	Joel Rice	"
	William Nash	"	Zuriel Walker	"	Edward Seymour
ORANGE CO.					
	Horace Fifield	Henry Keyes	"	J. W. D. Parker	"
	Reuben Page	William Sweatt	"	Simeon M. Bigelow	"
	Levi B. Vilas	Jefferson P. Kidder	"	Stephen Thomas	"
CHITTENDEN CO.					
	Harry Bradley	Jamin Hamilton	"	Lemuel B. Platt	"
	Daniel H Onion	Alexan'r Ferguson	"	William Weston	"
WASHINGTON CO.					
	Oramel H. Smith	Nath'l Bancroft	"	Asaph Town	"
	Moses Robinson	"	Wliam Carpenter	"	Leonard Keith
FRANKLIN CO.					
	George w. Foster	"	Jona. H. Hubbard	Homer E. Royce	"
	Hiram Bellows	Rufus Hamilton	"	Jacob Wead	"
	William Clapp	Lucius R. Beeman	"	John S. Foster	"
CALEDONIA CO.					
	Welcome Bemis	Sam'l B. Mattocks	"	Eph'm Chamberlin	David Goss jr.
	James D Bell	Sewall Bradley	Isaac N. Hall	John M'Lean	"
ORLEANS CO.					
	Enoch B. Simonds	Elisha White	Timo. P. Redfield	Elisha White	Henry M. Bates
ESSEX CO.					
	David Hibbard jr.	"	Oramel Crawford	"	John Dewey
GRAND ISLE Co		"			
	Giles Harrington		Solomon J. Davis	Frederick Hazen	David Marvin
LAMOILLE CO.					
	Burrell S. Miner	"	William W. White	Nathan Robinson	"
SEC. to the Gov.					
	Frederick Billings	"	Geo. F. Houghton	"	Rufus F. Andrews
SEC. to SENATE					
	D. W. C. Clarke	"	"	"	"
ASSISTANT SEC.					
	Thomas E. Powers	"	"	"	Samuel M. Conant
SERG. at ARMS.					
	Wm. T Burnham	Luther Cross	"	"	"
Librarian					
	Gustavus H Loomis	"	C. N. Carpenter	George Nichols	"
AUDITOR					
	Silas H Hodges	"	"	"	F. B. Woodbridge

which they do the injustice."

The Judge was subsequently admitted as an attorney at the Bar, and removed to Burlington, where he vigorously advocated the election and measures of Andrew Jackson to the Presidency. He afterwards removed to Washington City, where he acted as an agent in the Pension business. He was a number of times appointed Sergeant at Arms, in the Senate, which office he held at his death, January 12, 1841, aged 58.

REPRESENTATIVES BEFORE 1788.

	March 12, 1778	Oct. 1778	1779	1780	1781
BENNINGTON Co.					
1 Arlington	Thomas Chittend'n	John Fassett, jr.	" Jacob Galusha	Eli Pettibone	Lemuel Buck
		Ethan Allen	Mathew Lyon	"	"
2 Bennington	†NATHAN CLARK	Eben'r. Walbridge	Nathan Clark	Samuel Robinson	Samuel Safford
	John Fassett	"	Nathan Robinson	Eben'r Walbridge	Isaac Tichenor
3 Dorset	Cephas Kent	Abrah'm Underhill		Abraham Underhill	"
			John Strong	"	"
6 Manchester	Steph'n Washburn	Martin Powell	"	"	"
	Gideon Ormsby	"	"	"	Lewis Beebe
8 Pownal	Thomas Jewett	Joseph Williams	Abiather Angel	Joseph Briggs	ned'h Aylesworth
		Eli Noble	Benj'n. Gardner	Elisha Barber	Benjamin Gardner
10 Rupert	Moses Robinson				Wareham Gibbs
		"		Reuben Harmon	Stephen Pearl
11 Sandgate		Reuben Thomas	Bethel Hurd	Abner Hurd	Reuben Thomas
13 Shaftsbury	John Burnham	John Millington	John Burnham	William Ward	Peter Wright
	Gideon Olin	"	David Galusha	Gideon Olin	
14 Stamford					Jonathan Munger
15 Sunderland		Joseph Bradley	David Comstock	Samuel Bartlett	Joseph Bradley
WINDHAM Co.					
1 Athens				Abel Mattoon	
2 Brattleboro'				Samuel Wells	Samuel Knight
					John Sargeant
5 Dummerston	Leonard Spaulding	Jonathan Knight	"	"	Leonard Spaulding
6 Grafton			John Duncan	Miles Oatman	Thomas Kinne
7 Guilford	Benja. Carpenter	Comfort Starr	David Stowell	David Thurber	William Bullock
	John Shepherdson	Levi Goodnoe	John Noyes	Levi Goodnoe	John Shepherdson
8 Halifax	Edward Harris	"	"	"	"
	Hubbel Wells	"	"	Hazael Shepherd	Benjamin Henry
9 Jamaica					William H. Church
10 Londonderry	Edward Aiken	"		"	"
11 Marlboro'	Samuel King			"	"
12 Newfane			Jona'n Underwood		Zadock Granger
			Ebenezer Myrick	William Ward	Ebenezer Myrick
13 Putney		Abner Miles	"	Daniel Martin	Daniel Taylor
					Lucus Wilson
14 Rockingham	Joshua Webb	"	Amos Hale	"	Daniel Jewett
	Reuben Jones	"	"	"	Colburn Preston
17 Townshend	Samuel Fletcher	"	"	Silas Hayward	Joshua Wood
18 Vernon			"	Arad Hunt	John Bridgman
20 Westminster	Nathan'l Robinson	"	"		Benjamin Burt
				Steph'n R. Bradley	
21 Whitingham	Silas Hamilton	"	"	Moses Bratton	Silas Hamilton
22 Wilmington	Elijah Alverd		"	"	James Flagg
			William Williams		Jesse Cook
WINDSOR Co.					
1 Andover					John Simonds
3 Barnard	Edmond Hodges	"	Asa Whitcomb	John Foster	Benjamin Cox
4 Bethel				Joel Marsh	
6 Cavendish	John Coffein		John Russell		John Coffein
7 Chester	Thomas Chandler	THO. CHANDLER	THO. CHANDLER	THO. CHANDLER	Reuben Jones
					Thomas Chandler
8 Hartford		Stephen Tilden	Amos Robinson	Elkanah Sprague	"
					Joseph Marsh
9 Hartland	William Gallup	"	Elias Weld	Daniel Spooner	Elias Weld
11 Norwich		Abel Curtis		Thomas Moredock	Abel Curtis
		Joseph Hatch		Elisha Burton	Peter Olcott
13 Pomfret	John W. Dana	John Throop		John W. Dana	"
14 Reading			Andrew Spear	Thomas Hapgood	
16 Royalton		Joseph Parkhurst		Calvin Parkhurst	Comfort Seaver
17 Sharon		Benja'n Spaulding		Ebene'r Parkhurst	Joel Marsh
18 Springfield	John Barrett	Samuel Scott			Abner Bisbee
					John Barrett
20 Weathersfield	Israel Burlingame	William Upham	"	Israel Burlingame	Walters Chilson
23 Windsor	Ebenezer Curtis	"	"	"	"
	Thomas Cooper	"	Benjamin Wait	Joel Eli	Stephen Jacob
24 Woodstock	John Strong	"	Stephen Powers	Warren Cottle	
		Phinehas Williams	Nathan Howland	John King	Jesse Safford
ADDISON Co.					
4 Cornwall		Nathan Foot	"		
CALEDONIA Co.					
1 Barnet	Alexander Harvey	"			Alexander Harvey
11 Peacham					"
ESSEX County.				11 James Bailey	
8 Guildhall				8 Ward Bailey	Timothy Nash
10 Lunenburgh					10 Reuben Howe
11 Maidstone					11 Abraham Gild

'Supposed to be the first white person born in Vermont.   [Speakers in small Caps.

REPRESENTATIVES BEFORE 1788, CONTINUED.

BENNINGTON CO.

	1782	1783	1784	1785	1786	1787
1	Jonathan Fassett		Thomas Tolman			
1	Mathew Lyon	Lemuel Buck	"		Nathan Canfield	
2	Samuel Safford	Henry Walbridge	"			
2	Isaac Tichenor	ISAAC TICHENOR	Isaac Tichenor	Jonath'n Robinson	Elijah Dewey	"
3	Benja'n Baldwin	John Shumway	Benj'n Baldwin			
2	John Strong	Timothy Brown	Abra'm Underhill	John Shumway	Silas Goodrich	John Shumway
6	Gideon Ormsby	"		"		
6	Thomas Bull	Timothy Bliss	Martin Powell		Oliver Smith	Gideon Ormsby
8	Benja'n Gardner	Thomas Jewett	John Niles	"		
8			Benjamin Gardner		Benjamin Gardner	Thomas Jewett
10	Moses Robinson					
10	Amos Curtis	Richard Bailey	David Sheldon	Israel Smith	David Sheldon	
11		Edward Hurd	"		Joseph Bristol	Richard Hurd
13	Peter Wright	"	Parker Cole		GIDEON OLIN	
	Bigelow Lawrence	Gideon Olin	"	"		GIDEON OLIN
14	Asa Hickock			Perez Deane	John Gray	
15	Joseph Bradley	Samuel Bartlett	Joseph Bradley	"	Gideon Brownson	

WINDHAM CO.

	1782	1783	1784	1785	1786	1787
1						
2	Ben'n Butterfield	"	Samuel Bailey	"	James Shafter	"
2		Samuel Knight	"	"	Israel Smith	"
5	Alexan'r Kathan	"				
5		Jonathan Knight	LeonardSpaulding	Hosea Miller	Leonard Spaulding	"
6					—— Burgess	William Stickney
7		Benja'n Carpenter	Lovewell Bullock			
7	William Smalley	Thomas Cutler	William Bullock	William Bigelow	Peter Briggs	"
8	Edward Harris	"				
8		Joseph Tucker	Hubbel Wells	"	"	"
9				"		
10	Edward Aiken		"	"	Phinehas Freeman	"
11		Benjamin Olds	"	"		
11	J. Underwood	"	"		Wm. Ward Feb 87	"
12	Daniel Taylor	"		"	" Oct. '86	
12		William Ward	Luke Knowlton			
13	Lucus Wilson	"	"		Daniel Jewett	
13	Noah Sabin	Joshua Webb	James Hale			Noah Sabin
14		John Roundy	Oliver Lovell	Jehiel Webb		Jehiel Webb
14	Elias Olcott	Joseph Tyler				
17		Jonathan Hunt	"	Joshua Wood	"	"
18	Arad Hunt		John Bridgman	Arad Hunt	John Bridgman	Arad Hunt
19	WARDSBORO'				Aaron Hudson	
20	John Norton	John Tuthil				
20		Elijah Ranney	S. Roe Bradley	S. R. BRADLEY	Benjamin Burt	John Sessions
21	Silas Hamilton	Isaac Lyman	"	"	James Roberts	Isaac Lyman
22	Josiah Lock	"	Chipman Swift	"	Jesse Cook	"

WINDSOR CO.

	1782	1783	1784	1785	1786	1787
1	John Simonds	Samuel Brown	John Simonds jr.			
3	Benja'n Stebbens	Benjamin Cox	Aaron Barlow	"	Beriah Green	Benjamin Cox
4		Rice Wheeler	Michael Flynn	Joel Marsh	Nathaniel Throop	"
5	BRIDGWATER.		John Hawkins	"		John Hawkins
6			Jonathan Atherton			
7			William Gilkey	John Coffein		
7	Thomas Carroll	Daniel Heald	"	"	"	
8	Joseph Marsh		Joshua Hazen	"	"	Thomas Chandler
8	Joshua Hazen	Stephen Tilden	"	"		Joshua Hazen
9	Roger Enos		Roger Enos			
9	Elias Weld	William Gallup	"		Elias Weld	"
11	Abel Curtis		Elisha Burton			
11	Tho. Moredock	Paul Brigham	Elijah Gates	Jacob Burton	Paul Brigham	Elisha Burton
13		Abidah Smith	William Perry	"	Abidah Smith	John Throop
14	Andrew Spear	Joseph Sawyer	John Weld			John Weld
16	Cal'n Parkhurst	Elias Stevens	Silas Wiliams	Elias Stevens	Calvin Parkhurst	Elias Stevens
17	Daniel Gilbert	"	Anthony Morse	Daniel Gilbert	James Carpenter	"
18			Nathaniel Weston	"	Abner Bisbee	Jotham White
18		Simeon Stevens	Daniel Gibb			
20	Elijah Robinson	"	Walters Chilson	Hilkiah Grout	Joseph Hubbard	Elijah Robinson
23	Ebenezer Curtis	"	Bryant Brown	Benjamin Wait	Bryant Brown	
23	Benjamin Wait		Charles Leavens			
24	Jabez Cottle	Phinehas Thomas	Jabez Cottle			
24	John Strong	Jesse Safford	"	"	Benjamin Emmons	"

CALEDONIA CO.

	1782	1783	1784	1785	1786	1787
1						
11					Alexander Harvey	"
12	RYEGATE.			Wm. Chamberlin		Wm. Chamberlin

ESSEX CO.

	1782	1783	1784	1785	1786	1787
8				John Rich	"	"
10			Samuel Howe	"	Eliozer Rosbrook	"

REPRESENTATIVES BEFORE 1788.

	March, 12, 1778	Oct. 1778	1779	1780	1781
RUTLAND CO.	Thomas Tuttle	Josiah Powers	Timothy Barker		
2 Brandon	Zado'k Remington	Jesse Belknap	"	Brewster Higley	"
3 Castleton			Ezekiel Clark	Joseph Smith	"
5 Clarendon	Abner Lewis	"	Nebediah Angel	Elihu Smith	Lewis Walker
5	Thomas Rowley	"	"	"	Ebenezer Wilson
6 Danby			William Gage	"	Daniel Sherman
6			Isaac Clark	George Sherman	"
9 Ira			William Fitch	"	Simeon Edgerton
14 Pawlet	Zadock Everest	Gideon Adams	Ebenezer Drury	"	"
16 Pittsford	Jonathan Fassett	"	"	"	" Abisha Moseley
17 Poultney	William Ward	"	William Roberts	Roswell Post	John Smith
18 Rutland	Joseph Bowker	Roswell Post	John Smith	Benjamn Whipple	"
18	John Smith	Zebulon Mead			Benedict Webber
20 Shrewsbury			Solomon Bingham	"	Samuel Mattocks
22 Tinmouth	Charles Brewster		Charles Brewster	Thomas Porter	THOMAS PORTER
22			Abraham Ives	Abraham Jackson	"
23 Wallingford	Abraham Jackson	"		Barnabas Moss	Daniel Culver
24 Wells	Daniel Culver	Ithamer Hibbert			
ORANGE CO.				Steph'n M'Connell	John Barron
1 Bradford	Benjamin Baldwin	"			Joe Thurber
1				John Taplin	"
5 Corinth		Joshua Nutting		Samuel Smith	Icabod Ormsby
6 Fairlee		Icabod Ormsby		Jacob Kent	"
7 Newbury	Jacob Kent	"			John G. Bailey
7	John G. Bailey			John Powell	Elijah Beaman
10 Strafford		Frederick Smith	"	Tim. Bartholomew	" Israel Smith
11 Thetford	Tim' Bartholomew	"	Silas Webb		

From NEW HAMP-
SHIRE. *

				1780	1781
1 Charlestown				1 William Page	"
2 Canaan		2 Thomas Baldwin		1 Sam'l Witherbee	"
3 Claremont				3 Mathias Stone	"
4 Haverhill		4 James Bailey		3 Oliver Ashley	Benjamin Sumner
5 Chesterfield				5 Samuel King	"
6 Enfield		6 Bela Turner		5 Silas Thompson	"
7 Dresden		Bezaleel Woodard		"	"
8 Hanover		8 David Woodard		"	7 Eb'z'r Brewster
8		8 Jonath' Freeman		"	8 Jonathan Wright
9 Lebanon		9 Joshua Wheatley		8 John House	8 Jonath. Freeman
9		Nehe'h. Estabrook		9 Elisha Payne	"
10 Keene				9 Elihu Hyde	"
10					10 Isaac Wyman
11 Cardigan		11 Elisha Payne		11 Sawyer Bullock	10 Ezra Stiles
12 Walpole				12 John Graves	12 "
12					12 Jonathan Hall
13 Westmoreland					13 Jonathan Cole
13					Archelaus Temple
14 Lyme				14 Jonathan Child	14 "
15 Oxford		15 Israel Morey		15 Eben. Fairfield	14 Ebenezer Green
16 Acworth				16 John Duncan	16 Peleg Sprague
17 Cornish				17 William Ripley	17 "
18 Bath					Elisha Cleaveland
19 Gunthwaite		19 John Young		"	19 "
20 Landaff		Nathaniel Rogers		20 Absolem Peters	"
21 Gilsum				Ebenezer Dewey	"
22 Plainfield				22 Jona'n Stevens	22 Francis Smith
23 Piermont		Abner Chandler		22 Josiah Russell	23 Thomas Russell
24 Hinsdale					24 Daniel Jones
25 Richmond				25 Silas Gaskill	
25				25 Daniel Cass	
26 Alstead				Nath'l S. Prentiss	
27 Croydon				27 Moses Whipple	
28 Grafton				28 Russel Mason	
29 Marlow				29 Samuel Canfield	
30 Lempster				30 Elijah Frink	
31 Lyman				31 Nathan Hodges	
32 Newport				32 Benjamin Giles	
33 New Grantham				33 Abel Stevens	
34 Orford				Davenport Phelps	
35 Saville				35 Moses True	
36 Surry				Walston Brockway	

*By an examination of SLADE'S VERMONT STATE PAPERS, you will find the particulars of a Union formed by a part of New Hampshire, and a part of New York, with Vermont, for the extension of the latter; and representatives were admitted from those states to act in the legislature a number of times, till their October session 1781, holden at Charlestown, N. H., the connection was brought to an end. On this and the next page you will find the names of the representatives from those two states, one of which was chosen Clerk in 1778, and another Lieut. Governor in 1781.

REPRESENTATIVES BEFORE 1788.

RUTLAND CO. 1782	1783	1784	1785	1786	1787
1 Benson				1 Asahel Smith	
2				2 Iohn Mott	Nathan Daniels
3		Isaac Clark	Brewster Higley		
3 Reuben Moulton	Eli Cogswell	Noah Lee	"	3 Isaac Clark	"
5 Elihu Smith [LY	Joseph Smith	Daniel Marsh		"	"
5 INCREASE MOSE-	Thaddeus Curtis	Abel Cooper			
6 Thomas Rowley		Darius Lobdell			
6 Roger Williams	Peter Lewis	Edward Vail			
7 Fairhaven	Mathew Lyon		"	"	5 Peter Lewis
8 Hubbardton				8 David Hickock	Nathan Rumsey
9 Lemuel Roberts	Joseph Wood	Lemuel Roberts	Cephas Carpenter	"	"
11 Middletown		. "	Joseph Spaulding		
14 Sime'n Edgert'n	Joel Harman	William Fitch		Lemnel Chipman	Joseph Spaulding
16 Eben. Drury	Jonathan Fassett	Eleazer Harwood		Ionathan Fassett	"
17 Titus Watson		James Brookings			16 Gideon Cooley
17 William Ward	"	"	"	"	Thomas Ashley
18 Roswell Post	Samuel Williams	"	"		Samuel Williams
18 Benj. Whipple	"	"		18 Iohn Stevens	
20 Icab'd Robinson	Benedict Webber	Nathan Finney	"	Icabod Robinson	"
22 Sam. Mattocks	. "				
22 Thomas Potter	Ebenezer Marvin	Nathani'l Chipman		Ebenezer Marvin	"
23 Ebenez Murray	Abraham Ives	Nathaniel Ives	Abraham Jackson	Ioseph Randall	Stephen Clark
24 Abel Merriman	. "	Daniel Culver	Abel Merriman	"	Samuel Lathrop
ORANGE Co.					
1		John Barron			
1	Benjamin Baldwin	"	Noah White		Bildad Andrus
5 Nehe'h Lovewell	"				5 Reuben Foster
6		NATHANI'L NILES	Nathaniel Niles	6 Israel Morey	Samuel Smith
7		Ebenezer White			
7		Jacob Bailey	John G. Bailey	Thomas Johnson	"
10	Heber Gilbert				
10 Elijah Beaman	Enoch Bean	Timothy Blake	Heber Gilbert	Samuel Bliss	Alexand'r Pennock
11 Moody Freeman	Israel Smith				
11 Beriah Loomis	"	"	"	Tim. Bartholomew	Beriah Loomis
14 Vershire			Joel Walker		
9 Randolph		9 Asa Edgerton	James Blodgett	9 James Steele	Asa Edgerton
ADDISON CO.					
1 Addison		1 John Strong	"	"	Zadock Everest
4 Cornwall				4 Hiland Hall	Samuel Benton
15 Panton			15 Zadock Everest	15 Peter Ferris	"
23 Whiting		23 Samuel Beach			
2 Cambridge			2 Daniel Kinsley	2 Thomas P. Loid	John Fassett
4 Colchester			4 Tho. Butterfield	4 Ira Allen	"
Members from	June session, 1781	Oct. session, 1781	6 Ferrisburgh	5 Abel Thompson	"
NEW YORK.			9 Leicester	John Smith	9 Thomas Sawyer
1 Black Creek	John Shepherd		11 * Middlebury	Gamaliel Painter	"
2 Cambridge	Phine's Whiteside	"	12 Monkton		Ebenezer Barnum
2	Joseph Caldwell	"	13 Newhaven	Phinehas Brown	Bezaleel Rudd
3 Hoosick	John Abbott	Stutson Benson	14 Orwell	Ebenezer Wilson	"
3		Jonathan Walton	ORANGE Co.		
4 Greenfield	Gideon Warren		3 Brookfield	Jonathan Pierce	Timothy Cowle
5 Granville	Asaph Cook		13 Tunbridge		13 Seth Austin
6 Little Hoosick	Abraham Burdick	"	17 Williamstown		17 Elijah Paine
6	David Randall	"	2 Burlington	Samuel Lane	Frederick Saxton
7 North Granville		Benjamin Baker	5 Essex	Dubartus Willard	Timothy Bliss
8 South Granville		Joseph Craw	8 Jericho	Jedediah Lane	James Farnsworth
9 Skeensboro'	Aaron Fuller	Silas Child	11 Shelburne		11 Caleb Smith
10 Schaghticoke	Thomas Benedict	David Smith	15 Williston	Jonathan Spafford	
10		Bezaleel Phelps	4 Fairfax		4 Thomas Russell
11 Saratoga	Thomas Smith		9 Highgate	9 Tho. Butterfield	
11	John Rogers		12 Ryegate	James Whitelaw	"

*The town of Salisbury claim Judge Painter as their Representative in 1787, in consequence of a new running of town lines, taking his house unexpectedly, two or three rods south of the south line of Middlebury, and the journals of that year support their claim ; but I have not yet learned that they claim him in 1786, although living in the same house both years. Nor have I been informed of their laying any claim to Thomas Sawyer who represented Leicester in 1787, 8 and 9, although he resided on the disputed territory between the two towns, and on that part which is now Salisbury village.

The foregoing pages contain all the Representatives previous to the year 1788, that are to be found. The journals of March, 1778, and of October, 1786, do not contain a catalogue of the members, but I think I have both nearly accurate.

The remainder will be arranged by counties alphabetically, and will come as even as any mode without dividing counties. By the figures before the towns, the reader will be enabled to follow any town through the work to 1850.

REPRESENTATIVES, ADDISON, BENNINGTON, CALEDONIA 21

ADDISON CO.	1788	1789	1790	1791
1 Addison	Zadock Everest	"	David Whitney	Samuel Strong
2 Bridport	Philip Stone		Philip Stone	Marshall Smith
3 Bristol				
4 Cornwall	Samuel Benton	"	Thomas Tolman	Samuel Benton
5 Ferrisburgh	Abel Thompson	"	"	"
9 Leicester	Thomas Sawyer	"	John Smith	Benja'n Whitman
11 Middlebury	Gamaliel Painter	"	"	"
12 Monkton	Samuel Barnum	"	"	Joseph Willo'ghby
13 Newhaven	Alexander Brush	Phinehas Brown	Flijah Foot	"
14 Orwell	William Smith		Ebenezer Wilson	"
15 Panton	Gideon Spencer	Peter Ferris	Benjamin Holcomb	"
17 Salisbury	Stephen Hard	"	Eleazer Claghorn	Stephen Hard
18 Shoreham	Josiah Pond		Josiah Pond	James Moore
20 Vergennes		Samuel Chipman	Jabez Fitch	Enoch Woodbridge
22 Weybridge		Abel Wright	"	Samuel Clark
23 Whiting	Samuel Beach	Ezra Allen	Ebenezr Wheelock	
BENNINGTON Co.				
1 Arlington	Nathan Canfield		Timothy Todd	"
2 Bennington	Elijah Dewey	Jonathan Robinson	"	"
3 Dorset	William Dunton	John Shumway	William Dunton	John Shumway
6 Manchester	Thomas Barney	Gideon Ormsby	"	Job Giddings
8 Pownal	Thomas Jewett	"	"	"
10 Rupert	Israel Smith	"	"	Moses Sheldon
11 Sandgate	Richard Hurd		Richard Hurd	"
13 Shaftesbury	*Gideon Olin*	Gideon Olin	Gideon Olin	Gideon Olin
14 Stamford	Benjamin Tupper	Perez Deane	Andrew Selden	"
15 Sunderland	Gideon Brownson		"	"
CALEDONIA Co.				
1 Barnet	Alexander Harvey	James Cross	Alexander Harvey	"
3 Cabot				
4 Danville	Abraham Morrill	Jesse Leavenworth	David Whither	Jesse Leavenworth
11 Peacham	Wm. Chamberlin	"	"	"
12 Ryegate			John Gray	"
14 St. Johnsbury				Joel Roberts

HON. HENRY OLIN

Came into Leicester at an early day, and from his large dimensions and rather awkward habits, the people were not at first much prepossessed in his favor. But being of a strong mind and full of wit and anecdote, prejudices began to wear away, and he was chosen a Representative in 1799 and continued to be chosen for twenty-two out of twenty-six years. He was two years a member of the Council, and three years Lieutenant Governor, and one short session was a member of Congress to supply the place of the Hon. Charles Rich, deceased. He was one of the Assistant Judges of the County Court for eight years, and Chief Judge fifteen years in succession from 1801 to 1824.

When he first began legislation it was a new business to him, and the sound of his own voice would sometimes embarrass him in that body of talented men. An anecdote is related of him as follows: He arose from his seat and began "Mr. Speaker. I rise for information," and halted. Upon which another member arose and said: "Mr. Speaker I very much rejoice that the gentleman should arise with such a commendable object, for no man needs it more."

*Speakers in Italics.

He had among his townsmen an old gentleman that had taken a dislike to the Judge, but being politically agreed, he would support the Judge for office. On one occasion he came into meeting while the ballotting was going on,—pushed himself through the crowd to the box and spoke out in a loud voice, "here Mr. Constable is a vote for Judge Olin, but I hope God will forgive me." During his services on the bench he had given some offence to one of the young attornies, that has since disappointed many of his enemies. A person informed the Judge that this attorney was going to the Legislature to prevent him from being re-appointed. Well, said the Judge, I will tell the company a story. When I first came into Leicester, I built a log hut and began cutting down the forest east of it which enabled me to see the sun and moon as they rose, earlier than usual. I had a little dog, and he seeing the moon lower down than he had before, and shining through the trees concluded some mischief was on foot, and began to bark at the moon, and kept at it, and paused. Well, says one, "what next?" Why, I could not discover that it had any effect whatever on the moon, that kept on its course the same as if the dog had been silent, but I discovered the little dog was

REPRESENTATIVES, AD., BEN., CAL., CONTINUED.

ADDISON CO. 1792	1793.	1794.	1795.	1796.
1 David Whitney	"	Josiah Clark	Zadock Everest	Josiah Clark
2 Marshall Smith	"	"	"	"
3 Jona. Eastman	Henry M'Laughlin	"	Jona. Eastman	Gurdon Munsill
4 William Slade	Joel Linsley	"	"	"
5 Abel Thompson	"	"	"	"
9 Benj. Whitman	John Smith	"	Benj. Whitman	"
11 Gaml. Painter	"	Joshua Hyde	"	Gamaliel Painter
12 John Ferguson	Joseph Willoughby	"	John Fergason	"
13 Miles Bradley	William Eno	Miles Bradley	Elijah Foot	"
14 Jabez Warren	Ebenezer Wilson	Amos Spafford	Jabez Warren	Ebenezer Wilson
15 Peter Ferris	"	Edmond Grandey	"	"
17 Stephen Hard	"	"	"	Eleazer Claghorn
18 James Moore	Ephraim Doolittle	James Moore	Josiah Pond	"
20 E. Woodbridge	"	"	Gideon Spencer	Amos Marsh
22 Samuel Clark	Samuel Jewett	"	"	"
23 Ebe'r Wheelock	"	Joel Foster	Eben'r Wheelock	"
BENNINGTON CO.				
1 Nathan Canfield	Timothy Todd	"	"	Jonathan Baker
2 Jona. Robinson	"	"	"	Elijah Dewey
3 John Shumway	Jona. Armstrong	Stephen Martindale	John Shumway	Jona. Armstrong
6 Job Giddings	"	Martin Powell	Gideon Ormsby	George Sexton
8 Josiah Wright	"	"	"	Solomon Wright
9 *Readsboro'*	Samuel Thayer	"	Elijah Bayley	
10 David Sheldon	Moses Sheldon	"	David Sheldon	Grove Moore
11 Richard Hurd	Samuel Bristol	Simeon Hazletine	Reuben Thomas	"
13 Gideon Olin	Gideon Olin	Peter Wright	"	"
14 Andrew Selden	"	"	"	Benj. Tupper
15 Samuel Bartlett	Gilbert Bradley	Lemuel Bradley	Samuel Bartlett	Gilbert Bradley
16 *Winhall*				Asa Beebe
CALEDONIA CO.				
1 A. Harvey	"	"	Enos Stevens	"
3 James Morse	"	Joseph Morse	Samuel Warner	"
4 J. Leavenworth	Benjamin Sias	"	"	"
7 *Hardwick*				
9 *Lyndon*	Josiah Arnold	Daniel Cahoon	"	"
11 W. Chamberlin	"	"	"	"
12 Josiah Page	"	"	John Gray	Josiah Page
14 Joel Roberts	Josias L. Arnold	"	"	Joel Roberts
16 *Walden*			Nathaniel Perkins	"
17 *Waterford*			Jonathan Grow	John Grow
18 *Wheelock*		John Beane	"	"

some hoarse for a few days, and I never knew him to bark at the moon again.

When the Judge took his seat in Congress in Dec., 1824, the weather was unpleasant and very different from what he was accustomed to see, and having but a short time to stay, his brother members were not very anxious for an acquaintance; and he was lonely. One of the members in conversation with him, wished to know how he liked Washington as compared with Vermont. The Judge said he liked some things in Washington very well, but he preferred Vermont in many respects, and one in particular, which is, here you have white butter and yellow girls, and in Vermont we have yellow butter and white girls.

The Judge removed to Salisbury in the spring of 1837, where he died the same year, aged about 70 years.

HON. SAMUEL C. CRAFTS

Is a son of Col. Ebenezer Crafts, who began the first settlement of Craftsbury in 1788, though he did not remove his family there till February, 1791, but was there himself and experienced many of the hardships incident to a life in the wilderness, having to draw the female part of his family, with others who came with him, from Cabot, 18 miles, on hand sleds with snow shoes, and snow four feet deep. The town was organized in March, 1792, and Samuel C. Crafts was the first Town Clerk, which office he held, by annual elections, till March, 1829, in which Joseph Scott (then Jun., was elected and has held it till Feb., 1851.) Samuel C. Crafts was born at Woodstock, in the county of Windham, State of Connecticut, on the 6th day of October, A. D. 1768. He graduated at Harvard University, Massachusetts, in July, 1790; and in the winter

REPRESENTATIVES, AD., BEN., CAL., CONTINUED.

ADDISON CO. 1797	1798.	1799.	1800.	1801
1 David Whitney	"	Levi Hanks	"	Gideon Segar
2 Philip Stone	Marshall Smith	"	"	Phinehas Kitchel
3 H M'Laughlin	Timothy Allen	Robert Holley	"	"
4 Joel Linsley	William Slade	Joel Linsley	William Slade	Joel Linsley
5 Abel Thompson	"	Theo Middlebrooks	Amos Thompson	T. Middlebrooks
8 *Hancock*			Esaias Butts	"
9 Benj. Whitman	John Smith	Henry Olin	"	"
10 *Lincoln*				Jedediah Durfey
11 Samuel Miller	Daniel Chipman	"	"	Gamaliel Painter
12 Jos. Willoughby	Josiah Willoughby	Samuel Barnum	Daniel Smith	Samuel Barnum
13 Ezra Hoyt	"	William Eno	"	Elisha Fuller
14 Jabez Warren	Pliny Smith	"	"	"
15 Edm'nd Grandy	Silas Pond	"	"	"
17 E. Claghorn	Stephen Hard	Salathiel Bump	"	"
18 Josiah Pond	Thomas Rich	Josiah Pond	Charles Rich	"
19 *Starksboro*	John Ferguson	"	John Ferguson	"
20 Amos Marsh	"	Amos Marsh	Amos Marsh	Amos Marsh
22 S. Jewett	Simon Dickinson	Samuel Jewett	"	Silas Wright
23 Joel Foster	"	"	"	Aaron Beach
BENNINGTON CO.				
1 Jonathan Baker	Aaron C. Collins	Tyrus Hurd	Nathan Canfield	Jonathan Baker
2 Jona. Robinson	"	"	Jona. Robinson	"
3 John Shumway	"	"	Jona. Armstrong	Steph'n Martindale
5 *Landgrove*			David Carpenter	Daniel Tuthil
6 George Sexton	Gideon Ormsby	"	Jacob Odel	Gideon Ormsby
8 Josiah Wright	"	"	Josiah Wright	"
9			Elijah Bailey	"
10 Grove Moore	David Sheldon	"	"	"
11 Richard Hurd	"	"	Reuben Thomas	John Watkins
13 Peter Wright	"	Gideon Olin	Jonas Galusha	Jacob Galusha
14 Bethuel Finney	"	"	"	Simeon Stevens
15 Samuel Bartlett	Lemuel Bradley	"	Gilbert Bradley	"
16 Russel Day	John Brooks	Russel Day	Asa Beebe Jr	Asa Beebe
17 *Woodford*			Elkanah Danforth	"
CALEDONIA CO.				
1 Walter Brock	"	"	"	James M'Leran
3 Samuel Warner	Horace Beardsley	"	"	Joseph Fisher
4 Benj. Sias	Jesse Leavenworth	Benjamin Sias	David Dunbar	"
7 Paul Spooner	"	"	Levi Goodrich	"
9 Daniel Cahoon	"	"	"	"
11 J. W. Chandler	Reuben Blanchard	"	David Elkins	Jonathan Elkins
12 John Cameron	"	Wm. Neilson Jr.	"	John Cameron
14 Joel Roberts	Joseph Lord	Joel Roberts	"	Joseph Lord
16	Nicholas Gilman	Nathaniel Perkins	"	Nath'l Farrington
17 John Grow	"	Asa Grow	"	"
18 Abra'am Morrill	"	John Beane	Abraham Morrill	"

following came with his parents to Vermont. He was soon after chosen a delegate to a Convention which formed the Constitution at Windsor, July 4, 1793, and was the youngest member of that convention, and is believed to be the only one of that convention now living. He was also a member of the House of Representatives in 1796, 1800,-1, 3, and 5, and Clerk of the Assembly in 1798, and 9. He was a member of the Council in 1809, 1810, 1811, 1812, and would have been in 1813, had not the canvassing committee of that year viewed it be their duty to reject the votes returned from the town of Colchester.

He was appointed first Assistant Judge of Orleans County Court, on its first organization in 1800, and continued in that office till 1810, at which time he was appointed Chief Judge, and held that office till December 1st, 1816, in which year he was elected a member of Congress to commence March 4, 1817, and was three times subsequently elected and continued to March 3d, 1825; when he was again elected Councillor, which office he held for the two succeeding years. In October, 1825 he was appointed first Judge of the County Court which he held till December, 1828. In 1828 and 1829, he was chosen Governor of the State by the people, and in 1830 was Governor, but chosen by the Legislature. In the winter of 1842 he re-

REPRESENTATIVES, AD., BEN., CAL., CONTINUED.

ADDISON CO. 1802	1803.	1804.	1805.	1806.
1 Gideon Segar	"		"	"
2 Phine'as Kitchel	"	Asa Hemenway	"	William Myrick
3 Robert Holley	"	"	"	Ezekiel Dunton
4 Joel Linsley	David Foot	"	Benjamin Sanford	"
5 T. Middlebrook	"	"	John Frasier	The'l Middlebrooks
6				
7				
8 Esaias Butts			Esaias Butts	"
9 Henry Olin	"	"	Abijah Perry	Henry Olin
10 Ebenezer Durfey	"	"	Howland Delong	Ebenezer Durfey
11 Daniel Chipman	Gamaliel Painter	Daniel Chipman	Gamaliel Painter	Daniel Chipman
12 Daniel Smith	"	"	"	"
13 E. Fuller	"	"	"	"
14 P. Smith	"	"	"	"
15 Silas Pond	"	Saml. Shepherd	Silas Pond	"
16				
17 Salathiel Bump	Reuben Saxton	Salathiel Bump	Reuben Saxton	Salathiel Bump
18 Charles Rich	John S. Larabee	Charles Rich	"	"
19 John Ferguson	"	"	Samuel Hill	John Ferguson
20 E'h Woodbridge	Amos Marsh	Samuel Strong	"	Thomas Byrd
21				
22 Silas Wright	"	"	Samuel Jewett	"
23 Eb'nr Wheelock	David Brown	"	Aaron Beach	David Brown
BENNINGTON CO.				
1 Jonathan Baker	"	"	"	Tyrus Hurd
2 Moses Robinson	Nathan Robinson	Martin Norton	William Henry	Wm. Henry Jr
3 Ste'n Martindale	John Shumway	"	Samuel Collins	"
5 David Carpenter	" Daniel Tuthil	Asa Utley	Daniel Tuthil	"
6 Gideon Ormsby	Robert Anderson	Nath'l Collins	"	And'w Richardson
7	Reuben Bigelow	"	"	"
8 Josiah Wright	Solomon Wright	"	Benj. Gardner	"
9 John Whitney	Elijah Bailey	"	"	"
10 David Sheldon	"	Josiah Rising	"	"
11 Reuben Thomas	Richard Hurd	"	"	"
13 Jacob Galusha	"	"	"	"
14 Bethuel Finney	"	James Millard	S. Wilmarth Jr	Shubael Wilmarth
15 Edmond Graves	"	Gilbert Bradley	Edmond Graves	"
16 Asa Beebe	Jacob Hale	"	Asa Beebe	Jacob Hale
17 Elka'h Danforth	"	"	"	"
CALEDONIA CO.				
1 Alex. Harvey	"	John Bachop	David Goodwillie	Wm. Strowbridge
2 *Burke*			Thomas Bartlett	"
3 Joseph Fisher	"	John W. Dana Jr	Joseph Fisher	Pearly Scott
4 David Dunbar	Saml. Chamberlain	Joseph Moffet	Christop'r Sargeant	Joseph Moffet
5 *Deweysburgh*			Stephen Crossman	Ford Placestead
6 *Groton*	Jona. M'Cumber	Jesse Heath	"	"
7 Levi Goodrich	"	Samuel French	"	"
9 William Cahoon	Isaiah Fisk	"	William Cahoon	Abraham Smith
11 Reub Blanchard	"	Jonathan Elkins	Wm. Chamberlain	Jona. Elkins Jr.
12 John Cameron	"	"	"	James Neilson Jr
13 *Sheffield*				Stephen Drown
14 Nathaniel Edson	"	"	Pres West	Nath'l Edson
15 *Sutton*			Caleb Fisk	"
16 N. Farrington	"	Nath'l Perkins	"	"
17 Jos. Armington	"	"	"	Silas Davison
18 Abram Morrill	"	"	John Beane	Abraham Morrill

ceived from the Governor the appointment of Senator in Congress, in room of the Hon. Samuel Prentiss, who had resigned on being appointed a District Judge in the room of Judge Paine deceased. In the fall of that year he was elected by the Legislature to fill the vacancy in the Senate till March 3d, 1843. He was President of the Constitutional Convention of 1829. In all the duties he has performed, "doing right" has been his principal object, and none has been able to say that he ever swerved from that. He still lives in Craftsbury, enjoying remarkable health and strength for one of his age.

REPRESENTATIVES, AD., BEN., CAL., CONTINUED.

ADDISON CO. 1807	1808.	1809.	1810.	1811.
1 Gideon Segar	David Whitney	"	"	"
2 Wm. Myrick	"	"	"	"
3 Amos Eastman	Ezekiel Dunton	Amos Eastman	Noble Munson	Robert Holley
4 David Foot	Joel Linsley	"	Titis Fenn	Darius Mathews
5 Obadiah Walker	"	"	"	T. Middlebrooks
7 Joel Rice	Joseph Patrick	"	"	"
8 Esaias Butts	"	Zenas Robbins	"	Esaias Butts
9 Henry Olin	"	"	"	"
10 E. Durfey	"	David Corbin	Ebenezer Durfey	Joseph Delong
11 Daniel Chipman	"	Gamaliel Painter	"	Samuel Mattocks
12 Frederick Smith	Daniel Smith	"	Jos. Willoughby Jr	Daniel Smith
13 Elisha Fuller	Ezra Hoyt	Jonathan Hoyt jr.	"	Mathew Phelps Jr
14 Pliny Smith	"	"	Joab Smith	"
15 Saml Shepherd	"	"	"	"
17 Salathiel Bump	Reuben Saxton	"	"	Salathiel Bump
18 Charles Rich	"	"	"	"
19 Samuel Hill	John Ferguson	"	Elisha Ferguson	Samuel Hill
20 John H. Sherrill	David Edmond	"	Amos W. Barnum	E. D. Woodbridge
22 Samuel Jewett	"	* "	Asaph Hayward	John Brittol
23 Stukely Stone	"	Elijah Kirkum Jr	Stukely Stone	"
BENNINGTON CO.				
1 Jonathan Baker	Sylvester Deming	"	"	"
2 Wm Henry Jr	"	"	William Henry	"
3 John Shumway	Samuel Collins	"	"	"
5 Daniel Tuthil	"	"	Peabody Utley	Daniel Tuthil
6 Christ'r Roberts	Joel Pratt 2d	"	"	"
7	Peter Dudley	"	"	"
8 Benj. Gardner	"	"	"	Samuel Wright
9 Elijah Bailey	"	"	"	"
10 Josiah Rising	"	Asaph Sheldon	Josiah Rising	David Sheldon
11 Richard Hurd	Sherman Prindle	"	George Peck	"
13 Jacob Galusha	"	"	"	Charles Dyer
14 S. Wilmarth	"	"	Otis Phillips	"
15 Edmond Graves	"	"	"	"
16 Asa Beebe Jr	"	"	"	"
17 E. Danforth	"	William Park	D. Lyman	Moses Robinson jr
CALEDONIA CO.				
1 Enos Stevens	John Duncan	"	"	"
2 Thomas Bartlett	Roman Fyler	"	Daniel Newell	Abner Coe
3 J. W. Dana Jr	—— Damon	Joseph Fisher	John W. Dana Jr.	Joseph Fisher
4 W. A. Griswold	"	"	"	Wm. A. Palmer
5		Zenas Crossman	"	Set to Danville & Peach'm
6 Jesse Heath	"	Jeremiah Hidden	"	Jesse Heath
7 Mark Norris		Amos Farley	"	Alpha Warner
8 *Kirby*		Theophilas Grout	Leon'd Harrington	"
9 Abraham Smith	William Cahoon	"		William Cahoon
10 *Newark*				Eleazer Packer
11 John Mattocks	Wm. Chamberlin	Jonathan Elkins	"	Jesse Merrill
12 John Cameron	"	"		Hugh Laughlin
13 Jos. H. Ingalls	Reuben Miles	Stephen Drown	Joseph H. Ingalls	"
14 Pres West	Ariel Aldrich	"	"	Calvin Jewett
15 Caleb Fisk	Jethro Sanborn	Thomas Colby	Caleb Fisk	"
16 David Gilman	Nath'l Farrington	"	Joseph Perkins	Nath'l Farrington
17 Jos. Armington	Sylv's Hemenway	"	"	"
Samuel Fellows jr.	Abraham Morrill	Edward Fifield	"	Abner Morrill

*The town of Weybridge, politically, has been about even. This year, Samuel Jewett was returned a member by one majority. He took his seat in the House, which was politically against him, and it was contested, and the Committee on Elections reported that he was not duly elected. The House accepted the report by a vote of 98 to 77, and the seat left vacant. The old gentleman remarked, "I am on the gain, I had but one majority to come here, and I have got twenty-one majority to go home."

ADDISON CO. 1812.	1813.	1814.	1815	1816.
1 David Whitney	"	"	"	Gideon Segar
2 Phine's Kitchell	Benjamin Skiff	John B. Catlin	"	Samuel Buck
3 Luther Barnard	Ezekiel Dunton	Henry Soper	Luther Newcomb	Noble Munson
4 D. Mathews	"	"	"	"
5 Obadiah Walker	The'l Middlebrooks	"	"	Benjamin Field
6 *Goshen*			Phinehas Blood	"
7 Joseph Patrick	"	"	"	"
8 Esaias Butts	John Hartshorn	"	Esaias Butts	"
9 Henry Olin	"	"	"	Isaac Morse
10 Ebenezer Durfey	Joseph Delong	E. Durfey	Joseph Delong	Jeremiah Hatch
11 Daniel Chipman	*Daniel Chipman*	*Daniel Chipman*	Peter Starr	Samuel Swift
12 Step'n Haight jr	"	"		"
13 Ezra Hoyt	"	"	Levi Warner	"
14 Joab Smith	"	Jas. Q. M'Farland	"	"
15 S. Shepherd	"	Henry Chamberlin	Abner G. Holcomb	Samuel Shepherd
17 Reuben Saxton	"	"	Jonathan Gibson	"
18 Charles Rich	Elisha Bascom	Joseph Smith	Charles Rich	Joseph Smith 2d
19 Elisha Ferguson	"	"	Ezekiel Pease	E. Ferguson
20 A. W. Barnum	David Edmond	"	"	E. D. Woodbridge
22 G. Cleaveland	Samuel Jewett	"	"	"
23 David Brown	"	"	"	"
BENNINGTON CO.				
1 Joshua Judson	Sylvester Deming	Nathan Canfield	"	"
2 Elijah Dewey	"	Noadiah Swift	Stephen Robinson	Aaron Robinson
3 Benj. Deming	"	"	John Underhill	"
5 Peabody Utley	Daniel Tuthil	David Willey		
6 C. Chamberlin	Joel Pratt	Elijah Littlefield	Richard Skinner	E. Littlefield
7 Peter Dudley		Peter Dudley		P. Dudley
8 Samuel Wright	"	Thos Brownal 2d	Solomon Wright	"
9 Elijah Bailey	Joshua Dupy	"	Elijah Bailey	Henry Davison
10 A. Harmon jr	"	Josiah Rising	Amos Harmon jr.	Silas Harwood
11 George Peck	Joseph Tuttle	Thomas Tuttle	Joseph Tutile	Isaac Sherman
13 Charles Dyer	"	Gardner Barton	"	Elihu Cross
14 Otis Philips	"		Timothy Cook	Otis Phillips
15 Edmond Graves	"	Ethan Bradley	Edmond Graves	
16 Asa Beebe	Asa Beebe jr	Russell Day	Asa Beebe	"
17 M. Robinson	Moses Robinson	Oliver Perry	Jona. Danforth	Luther Park
CALEDONIA CO.				
1 Adam Duncan	"	Alex. Gilchrist	"	"
2 Isaac Denison	Abner Coe	Sylvester Hall	Roman Fyler	"
3 Joseph Fisher	John Damon	Joseph Fisher	David Haynes	"
4 Wm. A. Palmer	Wm. A. Griswold	"	*Wm. A. Griswold*	Wm. A. Griswold
6 Jesse Heath	Peter M'Lacklin	"	"	"
7 Alpha Warner	Amos Tuttle	"	"	"
8 Theo. Grout	"	Leon'rd Harrington	"	Theophilus Grout
9 William Cahoon	Isaiah Fisk	"	"	"
10 Eleazer Packer	James Ball	Eleazer Packer	"	"
11 Jesse Merrill	Jonathan Elkins	Nicholas C. Buswell	John Mattocks	"
12 Hugh Laughlin	James Henderson	John Neilson	James Henderson	Hugh Laughlin
13 Stephen Drown	Reuben Miles	Joseph H. Ingalls	"	"
14 Calvin Jewett	"	"	"	Ariel Aldrich
15 Thomas Colby	Ezra Child	"	Benj. Campbell	Caleb Fisk
16 T. Farrington	Wm. Montgomery	"	James Bell	Thos. Farrington
17 S. Hemenway	Sylv's Hemingway	"	"	"
18 Abra'm Morrill	Samuel Fellows jr	Elijah Sargeant	Abner Morrill	Saml Fellows jr

MATHEW LYON,

Who first represented Arlington in 1779, &c., and afterwards Fairhaven many times, endeavored to obtain the passage of an act giving him the exclusive right of Slitting Iron in Vermont. He had counted a member from a town very near Bennington, a political friend, as one of the supporters of his bill, but after hearing argument on both sides, the project looked like asking too much, and when his name was called to vote on the question, he asked to be excused; reasons were

REPRESENTATIVES, AD., BEN., CAL., CONTINUED.

ADDISON CO. 1817	1818.	1819.	1820.	1821.
1 Robert Chambers	Aaron Merrill	"	Robert Chambers	"
2 Samuel Buck	John B. Catlin	"	Benjamin Miner jr	"
3 Henry Soper	Luther Newcomb	Henry Soper	"	Noble Munson
4 Darius Mathews	Aaron Delong	"	Tho's P. Mathews	Benjamin Sanford
5 Benjamin Field	"	Thomas Marsh	Robert B. Hazard	"
6				
7	Thomas King	"	Benjamin Pinney	Joel Rice
8 Esaias Butts	"	Icabod Eastman	Esaias Butts	Omri Dodge
9 Henry Olin	"	"	William Gile	"
10 Jeremiah Hatch	Ebenezer Durfey	"	"	"
11 Samuel Swift	Daniel Chipman	Jonathan Hagar	"	Daniel Chipman
Stephen Haight jr.		"	"	"
13 Ezra Hoyt	Silas Doud	"	Othniel Jewett	Ezra Hoyt
14 Joab Smith	Jam's Q M'Farland	Apollos Austin	John Jackson	"
15 Silas Pond	Samuel Shepherd	Silas Tappan	"	"
17 Reuben Saxton	Salathiel Bump	"	"	"
18 Elisha Bascom	"	Joseph Smith, 2d.	Elisha Bascom	John S. Larrabee
19 Elisha Ferguson	"	Eber Blodgett	David Kellogg	Elisha Ferguson
20 David Edmond	E'h D. Woodbridge	William White	"	David Edmond
22 Samuel Jewett	Samuel Childs	Samuel Jewett	Asaph Drake	"
23 Eb'nr Wheelock	"	"	"	James O. Walker
BENNINGTON CO.				
1 Daniel Church	"	Sylvester Deming	Cyrus Canfield	"
2 Aaron Robinson	Jonathan Robinson		Moses Robinson	
3 John Underhill	"	"	"	"
			Gideon Davis	
6 Joel Pratt	Richard Skinner	Elijah Littlefield	Calvin Sheldon	Joseph Burr
	Peter Dudley			
8 Solomon Wright		Benjamin Gardner	Stoddard Merchant	Solomon Wright
9 Rich'd Carpenter	John Walker	"	Jeremiah Amidon	Jonath'n Houghton
10 Silas Harwood	Nathan Burton	"	Seth Moore	"
11 George Peck	Isaac Sherman	"	Abraham Hurd	John H. Sanderson
13 Elihu Cross	Jonathan Draper	"	Norman Hinsdell	"
14 Otis Phillips	Levi Gilmore	"	John M'Elwain	"
15 Edmond Graves	Timothy Brownson	William Landon	"	"
16	Russel Day	Reuben Brooks	"	
17 Luther Park	Jonathan Danforth	William Park	Joseph C. Hollister	David Weeks jr.
CALEDONIA CO.				
1 Henry Oakes	"	Wm. Gilkerson	"	"
2 Isaac Denison	Roman Fyler	Abner Coe	Isaac Denison	"
3 David Haynes	John W. Dana	"	"	Enoch Hoyt
4 Wm. A. Griswold	William A. Palmer	Wm. A. Griswold	Joseph Morrill	"
6 James Renfrew	"	Peter M' Lacklin	"	David Vance
7 Joel Whipple	Joshua Cutler	Levi Goodrich	"	Solomon Aiken
8	Theophilas Grout	"	"	Ebenezer Damon
9 Isaiah Fisk	"	Isaac Fletcher	"	Isaiah Fisk
10 Eleazer Packer	James Ball	Philemon Hartwell	"	
11 Nehemi' Bradlee	Jesse Merrill	"	Nehemiah Bradlee	"
12 Hugh Laughlin	Alexan. Henderson	"	John Cameron	John Neilson
13 Jos'h H. Ingalls	"	Stephen Drown	Benjamin Conner	Joseph H. Ingalls
14 Ariel Aldrich	"	Pres West	Abner Miles	Ephraim Paddock
15 James Way	"	Caleb Fisk	Jacob C. Morrill	"
Wm. Montgomery	James Bell	"	"	"
17 Jos'h Armington	Nathan Pike	"	Jacob Benton	
18 S. Fellows jr.	Abner Morrill	"	Israel Porter	

called for, he said, "Mr. Speaker, I cannot in conscience vote upon this question, my conscience will not let me vote upon it, and I must be excused." Thereupon arose a Scotch member from Caledonia County, and began, Mr. Spaker, I think the jointleman must have a werry coorious kind of a konshunts that 'wont let him say ees nor noo.

28   REPRESENTATIVES, AD., BEN., CAL., CONTINUED.

ADDISON CO. 1822.	1823.	1824.	1825.	1826.
1 Rob't Chambers	"	David Whitney	Henry Brevoort	"
2 Benj. Miner jr	Phinehas Kitchel	"	Benj. Miner jr	Calvin Solace
3 Henry Soper	Luther Newcomb	"	Daniel E. Parmelee	Henry Soper
4 Asahel Bingham	Benj. Sanford	"	Horace Janes	"
5 Josiah Taft	"	Stodard Martin	"	Daniel Marsh
6				
7 Joel Rice	"	"	Joseph Patrick jr	Benj. Pinney
8 Charles Church	"	Zerah Barnes	Omri Dodge	Charles Church
9 Henry Olin	"	"	Pearley Enos	"
10 Nathan Page	Robert Johnson	"	John Bush	Robert Johnson
11 Jonathan Hagar	Robert B Bates	Joel Doolittle	R. B. Bates	"
12 S. Haight jr	John Smith	Stephen Haight	John Smith	Johnson Finney
13 Elias Bottum	Othniel Jewett	Ezra Hoyt	William Nash	"
14 John Jackson	"	"	"	Ira Smith 2d
15 Silas Tappan	"	Jonathan Spencer	Silas Tappan	Enoch Kent
17 Salathiel Bump	Harvey Deming	"	"	Aaron Barrows
18 Elisha Bascom	John S. Larrabee	"	Elisha Bascom	S. H. Jenison
19 Elisha Ferguson	"	Myron Bushnell	"	Elijah Ferguson
20 Edward Sutton	"	E. D. Woodbridge	Amos W. Barnum	"
21 *Waltham*		C. Denison jr	"	
22 Asaph Drake	Samuel Childs	Milo Stow	"	Wight. Chapman
23 Jas. O. Walker	"	Josiah Simonds	Esquire Brown	James O. Walker
BENNINGTON CO.				
1	Abel Aylsworth	A. Aylsworth jr	Asahel Hurd?	Samuel S. Baker
2 O. C. Merrill	Moses Robinson		Noadiah Swift	C. H. Hammond
3 John Underhill	Reub. H. Blackmer	"	Johnson Marsh,	Reub. H. Blackmer
5				David Willey
6 J, S. Pettibone	Josiah Burton	Joseph Burr	John S. Pettibone	Major Hawley
7				
8 L· Staunton	Solomon Wright	Lodowick Staunton	Stod't Merchant	Abel W. Porter
Richard Carpenter	Jedediah Amidon	Jona. Houghton	James Carpenter	Henry Holbrook
10 Seth Moore	Myron Clark	Elisha Hopkins	Abram C. Sheldon	"
11 J. H. Sanderson	"	"	Samuel Thomas	"
13 Asa Mattison	"	Nathan H. Bottum	G. Barton jr	N. H. Bottum
14 John W. Elwain	Levi Gillmore	James Millerd	"	Otis Phillips
15 William Landon	"	Gideon Brownson	James A Graves	Joseph Bradley
16 Reuben Brooks	Asa Thatcher jr	Reuben Brooks	Benj. Thatcher	"
17 J· C. Hollister	David Weeks jr	Perry Jewett	"	Hymen Tuttle
CALEDONIA CO				
1 Wm. Gilkerson	"	Walter Harvey	"	Henry Stevens
2 G. W. Denison	"	Sylvester Hall	Geo. W. Denison	Ira Walter
3 Jer. Babcock	"	"	"	"
4 Joseph Morrill	George W Drew	Augustine Clarke	Wm. A. Palmer	"
5				
6 David Vance	Peter. M'Lacklin	David Vance	Peter M'Lacklin	David Vance
7 Solomon Aiken	Timothy P. Fuller	"	"	Samuel Warner
8 Timothy Locke	Ebenezer Damon	"	"	"
9 Isaac Fletcher	Isaiah Fisk	*I. Fletcher* 4 *days*	William Cahoon	"
10 Phile'n Hartwell	"	"	Miles Coe	"
11 N. Bradlee	John Mattocks	"	Jonathan Elkins	Josiah Shedd
12 John Cameron	Robert Whitelaw	"	"	John Cameron
13 Stephen Drown	"	Joseph H. Ingalls	Stephen Drown	Joseph H. Ingalls
14 Calvin Jewett	Ephraim Paddock	"	"	"
15 Ira Goodrich	"	Andrew Brown	"	"
16 James Bell	"	"	"	"
17 S. Hemingway	Jonah Carpenter	S. Hemingway	Silas Davison	"
18 Abner Morrill	Israel Porter	Abner Morrill	"	Josiah Lane

REPRESENTATIVES, AD., BEN., CAL., CONTINUED.

ADDISON CO. 1827.	1828.	1829.	1830	1831.
1 Aaron Merrill	"	"	Marshall S. Doty	"
2 Calvin Solace	Zenus Myrick	"	Abner Wilcox	"
3 John Howden	"	Harvey Munsill	Rufus H. Barnard	Harvey Munsill
4 Horace Janes	"	Chauncey Cook	"	William Hamilton
5 Daniel Marsh	David Hazzard	Heman Barnum	David Hazzard	Heman Barnum
6		Abiathar Knpp	Nathan Capen	"
7 Benj. Pinney	Joel Rice	Benj. Pinney	Isaac Parker	"
8 Charles Church	"	Nathan Claflin	"	John Hackett
9 Pearley Enos	William Gile	"	John Bullock	"
10 O. W. Burnham	Hezekiah Hatch	"	Isaac Houstin	"
11 *Robert B. Bates*	*Robert B. Bates*	Samuel Swift	*Robert B. Bates*	
12 John Smith	Johnson Finney	Daniel Collins	John Smith	Stephen Haight
13 David P. Nash		Elias Bottum	Daniel Twitchell	"
14 Ira Smith 2d	T. D. Hammond	"	Samuel Young	"
15 Enoch Kent	William H. Smith	"	Jesse Grandey	
17 Aaron Barrows	"	Jonathan Gibson	Elnathan Darling	Ebenezer N. Briggs
18 S. H. Jenison	"	"	"	J. S. Hunsden
19 E.F. sick at home	Myron Bushnell	Asel Wentworth	Myron Bushnell	"
20 Noah Hawley	"	Philip C. Tucker	"	Belden Seymour
21 B. Tomlinson	Solomon Hobbs	George Fields	"	Richard Burroughs
22 W. Chapman	Joseph Hayward	"	Benjamin Wales	"
Moulton Needham	"	"	John Branch	"
BENNINGTON CO.				
1 Samuel Baker	Anson Canfield	"	Martin C. Deming	"
2 Hiland Hall	Noadiah Swift	John Norton	Saml. H. Blackmer	Jedediah Dewey
3 John Cochran	S. Martindale	John Cochran	Azel Morse	"
5	David Willey	Simeon Leland	Gideon Davis jr	David Willey
6 J. S. Pettibone	"	"	Leonard Sargeant	"
7	Reuben Bigelow			
8 S. Merchant	John Wright	"	"	Samuel Wright
9 Caleb Bailey	"	Henry Holbrook	James Carpenter	Elijah Bailey
10 James Weed	Seth Moore	David Sheldon jr	"	Silas Harwood
11 Joseph Tuttle	"	"	"	"
13 N. H. Bottum	Hiram Barton	Asa Matteson	Jesse Blackmer	"
14 D. N. Stroud	"	Joel Houghton	"	Thomas Bratton
15 Joseph Bradley	William Landon	"	Noah Landon	N. B. Landon
16	Nath'l Mellen jr	"	Nathaniel Mellen	"
17 Hymen Tuttle	Joseph C. Hollister	William Park jr	Joseph C. Hollister	Joseph Knapp
CALEDONIA CO.				
1 Henry Stevens	Hugh Somers 2d	Walter Harvey	William Gilkerson	"
2 Ira Walter	Ebenezer Darling	Joel Trull	"	Elam White
Jeremiah Babcock	"	Anthony Perry	"	Nathan Wheeler
4 *Wm. A. Griswold*	Augustine Clark	William A. Palmer	Augustine Clark	George W. Drew
6 Septimus Lathrop	David Vance	"	Peter M'Lacklin	David Vance
7 Levi Goodrich	Elnathan Strong	Timothy P. Fuller	Orra Crosby	"
8 Ebenezer Damon	Orin Carpenter	"	"	"
9 Job Randall	"	"	"	"
10 Eleazer Packer	Philomen Hartwell	"	Obed Johnson	"
11 Josiah Shedd	"	Jacob Blanchard	"	Hazen Merrill
12 William Gray	"	James Neilson jr	"	"
13 Jos. H. Ingalls	"	James Townsend	Stephen Drown	"
14 Ariel Aldrich	"	"	"	David Goss jr
15 John Beckwith	Thomas True	"	Jacob C. Merrill	"
16 James Bell	Nath'l Farrington	N. Farrington jr	"	"
17 S. Hemingway	"	"	Robert Taggard	"
18 Josiah Lane	Abner Morrill			Israel Porter

REPRESENTATIVES, AD., BEN., CAL., CONTINUED.

ADDISON CO.	1832	1833.	1834.	1835	1836
1	Henry Smith	"	Lyman Clark	Heman Converse	"
2	Paris Fletcher	"		Seneca Austin	"
3	Danl E. Parmelee	Abraham Gaige	"	Horatio Needham	"
4	Wm. Hamilton	Asahel Bingham	"	"	Jesse Ellsworth
5	David Hazard	Zuriel Walker	"	"	Luther Carpenter
6	Nathan Capen	"	"	"	"
7	Isaac Parker	"	"	Solon Clark	"
8	Josiah P. Brooks	John Hackett	Josiah P. Brooks	Charles G. Robbins	"
9	John Bullook	William Gile	"	"	Otis Capron
10	Isaac Houstin	Daniel Varney	John Bush	"	William W. Pope
11	Edw'd D. Barber	"	Elisha Brewster	"	"
12	George E Stone	"	Milo W. Kinsley	"	Luman B. Smith
13	Bela Eldridge	Adin Hall	"	"	William Nash
14	T. D. Hammond	"	"	Linus Wilcox	"
15	Jesse Grandey	Enoch Kent	"	Putnam Bishop	"
17	Eben. N. Briggs	"	Ebenezer N. Briggs	Ebenezer N. Briggs	Aaron Barrows
18	John S. Hunsden	"	Isaac Chipman	"	"
19	Theron Downey	"	William Worth 2d.	"	John Hill 3rd.
20	John H. Sherrill	"	E. D. Woodbridge	Jahazel Sherman	"
21	William Barton	George Fisher	"	Josiah Bailey	Joseph Everts
22	Benjamin Wales	"	"	"	Lauren Drake
23	John Branch	Benjamin Needham	"		Moulton Needham
BENNINGTON CO.					
1	Asahel Hurd	"	"	Galen Canfield	"
2	John S. Robinson	John Robinson	John Norton	Jedediah Dewey	Stephen Dewey
3	Sylvanus Sykes	"	Paddock Gray	"	Robert Bloomer
4	Glastenbury		Mark Hotchkiss	Asa G. Hewes	"
5	Joshua Marsh	"	Cephas C. Tuthil	Amori Benson	"
6	Aaron Baker	John S. Pettibone	Elijah Collins	Aaron Baker	Leonard Sargeant
7	Peter Dudley	"	Benja'n Barnard jr.	"	Mark Batchelder
8	Jacob Peck	Reynolds Carpenter	Benjamin Stevens	John Mooar	B'nj'min F. Morgan
9	Elijah Bailey	William Sanford	"	Wm. Strafford	"
10	Silas Harwood	"	Joseph Parker	Simeon Rising jr.	"
11	Ezra West	Joseph Tuttle	Theod'e Sanderson	"	Joseph Tuttle
12	Searsburgh	Luther Park	"	John Knapp	Joshua Morse jr.
13	Nathan L Cross	Artemas Mattison	Jesse Blackmer	"	"
14	Ste'n C. Millard	"	Alonson Cowles	"	James Houghton
15	Noah Landon	Joel Kinney	Wm. Landon	Ethan Bradley	"
16	Reuben Brooks	Nathaniel Mellen	"	"	Francis Kidder jr.
17	William Weed	Joseph Knapp	"	"	Simeon Morse
CALEDONIA CO.					
1	Cloud Harvey	"	Wm. Shearer	Hugh Somers	William Shearer
2	Elam White	Sheldon Coe	"	Benjamin F. Belden	"
3	Nathan Wheeler	Tristram C. Hoit	Oliver A. Warner	"	John W. Dana
4	Augustine Clark	"	Salma Davis	Lewis Fisher	James M. Morrill
6	David Vance	"	John Darling jr.	Isaac N. Hall	"
7	Joseph Patch	Silas Underwood	Timothy P. Fuller	Isaac Pennock jr.	Ethan H. Nichols
8	Joseph Joslin	"	"	Orin Carpenter	James Church
9	Job Randall	"	E—— B. Chase	George C. Cahoon	Elias Bemis jr
10	Rufus Kinney	"	Alpheus Stoddard	"	James Dexter
11	Hazen Merrill	Asa Skeele	"	"	"
12	John Cameron	James Neilson jr.	"	Alonson Stevens	"
13	Jam's Townsend	Ezekiel Miles	"	Robert Whitelaw	"
14	David Goss jr.	"	"	Sewell Bradley	Samuel Bean
15	Jacob C. Morrill	Thomas True	Jonas Flint	David Goss jr.	E. Fairbanks jr
16	Daniel Wooster	"	"	Martin Way	"
17	Robert Taggart	Jonat'n D. Stoddard	"	Wheat'n Livingston	N. Farrington jr
18	Benjamin Conner	"	"	Sylva's Hemingw'y	Lyman Buck
					William Sanborn

REPRESENTATIVES, AD., BEN., CAL., CONTINUED.

ADDISON CO. 1837	1838	1839	1840	1841
1 Lyman Clark	Joseph Hayward	"	Hyder Barnes	"
2 Luther Corey	"	Hiram Smith	"	Abel P. Skiff
3 H. Needham	Philo S. Warner	H. Needham	Philo S. Warner	Winter H. Holley
4 Jesse Ellsworth	"	"	Ebenezer Mathews	"
5 L. Carpenter	William Hazzard	"	Benjamin Ferris	"
6 Francis Brown	"	Elnathan Knapp	"	Justus N. Dart
7 David Eaton	"	Charles Lamb	"	Joseph P. Ball
8 C. G. Robbins	"	Zerah Barnes	"	Charles G. Robbins
9 Otis Capron	James S. Messer	"	Moses Wright	
10 Wm. W. Pope	"	John Bush	William W. Pope	Isaac F. Caldwell
11 E. Brewster	Ralph Gowdy	"	Samuel Swift	
12 L. B. Smith	Lyman Smith	"	Russel Eastman	"
13 Osmond Dond	"	Eras's D. Warner	"	Alfred P. Roscoe
14 J. H. Chittenden	"	Ira Young	"	Horace Wilcox
15 Silas Pond		Silas Tappan	"	Silas Pond
17 Aaron Barrows	Mark R. Weeks	"	"	Franklin Bump
18 Davis Rich	"	Elisha Bascom	"	"
19 Ira Bushnell		Almon Atwood	Benj. L. Knight	"
20 Belden Seymour	For'ce Huntington	"	William T. Parker	John Pierpoint
21 Joseph Evarts	George Fisher	Elijah Benton	"	Charles Bacon
22 Lauren Drake	Sol. W. Jewett	"	Milo Stow	Elijah G. Drake
23 S, T. Walker	Harman Strong	Abel Walker	"	Justus F. Brown
BENNINGTON CO.				
1 Julius Beebe	"	Samuel Canfield		Harman Canfield
2 George Briggs	S. H. Blackmer	Elijah Fillmore	Isaac Weeks	Asa Doty
3 Robert Bloomer	Abiel Blanchard	Chauncey Green	Heman Morse	W. L. Martindale
4 Asa G. Hewes	"	"	"	"
5 David Willey		"	Calvin P. Mead	
6 Aaron Baker	Ahiman L. Miner	"	Aaron Baker	Leonard Sargeant
7 Israel Batchelder	"	Benj. Barnard	John Davison	"
8 Elijah Barber	David Gardner	Elijah Barber	Sebastian Wagar	B. E. Brownell
9 Jacob Hicks	Waters Gillet	"	Joel Houghton	"
10 Sterl'g Sherman	"	Joseph Hastings	"	Seth Sheldon
11 Saml. Cogswell	"	Theo. Sanderson	Roswell Tuttle	"
12	Joseph Eames		Ashley Stone	"
13 Jared Hayward	"	"	Simeon Martin	"
14 James Houghton	Elisha Lake		Ransom O. Dwyer	Ira Stroud
15 F. M'Laughlin	Edmond A. Graves	F. M'Laughlin	Edmond A Graves	"
16 F. Kidder jr	"	Beriah Wheeler	"	Francis Kidder
17 H. Harwood	Joseph Knapp	William Alverson	William Park	William Alverson
CALEDONIA CO.				
1 Walter Harvey	"	"	James Gilchrist	"
2 Joel Trull	Asahel Burrington	"	Geo. H. Denison	Lucius Denison
3 Jeremiah Atkins	"	Robert Lance jr	Robert Lance	Alpha Webster
4 Andr. M'Millen	Saml. B. Mattocks	"	"	Ebenezer Eastman
6 John Darling	"	Isaac N. Hall	"	Jonathan Welch
7 Levi Gooodrich	"	Silas Underwood	Daniel W. Aiken	Samuel Davis jr
8 James Church	Seth Burroughs	Nathabiel Willis	Jos. W Carpenter	"
9 Elias Bemis jr	Benjamin Walker	"	Stephen McGaffy	"
10 Phil'n Hartwell	Alpheas Stoddard	"	John Sleeper	"
11 Moses Martin	"	Simeon Harvey	Saml A. Chandler	"
12 Thomas Nelson	Robert Whitelaw	James Hall 2d	"	"
13 Harris Smith	"	John P. Ingalls	James Townshend	John P. Ingalls
14 E. Fairbanks	"	"	Lambert Hastings	"
15 W. Hutchinson	"	Jacob Blake	Thaddeus Curtis	"
16 N. Farrington jr	Hiram Perkins	Merrill Foster	Hiram Perkins	"
17 Lyman Buck	James Works	"	Richard F. Rowell	"
18 Jonathan Nelson	William Sanborn	Samuel Bigelow	"	E. M. Magoon

REPRESENTATIVES, AD., BEN., CAL., CONTINUED.

	ADDISON CO. 1842	1843.	1844.	1845.	1846.
1	Jonas N. Smith	"	Gideon Segar	"	Carlton E Miles
2	Abel P. Skiff	Joel Rice	"	Joseph Frost	"
3	Royal W. Peake	Titus B. Gaige	"	William C Warner	"
4	Daniel Sanford	Calvin G. Tilden	"	Abram Foot	"
5	Nathan L. Keese	"	Noah P. Porter	D Middlebrooks	"
6	Rufus Towle	"	Reuben Allen	"	Francis Brown
7	Joseph P. Ball	Alonzo G. Allen	Joseph Lamb	"	Hiram Ford
8	C. G. Robbins	Zerah Barnes	"	"	John Hackett
9	John G. Perry	"	Leonard D Jenny	"	John Bullock
10	I. F. Caldwell	Wm. W. Pope	Josiah O. Johnson	Wm W Pope	"
11	Joseph Warner	"	"	Samuel Swift	Harry Goodrich
12	Nathan Smith	"		John A Beers	
13	A. P. Roscoe	Oliver Smith	"	Seth Langdon jr	"
14	Ros'll Bottum jr	Absolum Fuller	"	Chaun'y H Conkey	"
15	Silas Pond	George Spencer	"	Stephen Holland	"
16	Ripton	Saml H. Hendrick	Frederick Smith	"	Saml H Hendrick
17	Franklin Bump	Sumner Briggs	"	Samuel S Crook	"
18	Kent Wright	"	Bela Howe	"	M W C Wright
19	Theron Kidder	Ansel S. Hawkins	"	Isaiah L Strong	"
E.	D. Woodbridge	Geo. W. Grandey	"	Villie Lawrence	"
21	Charles Bacon	Nathan Griswold	John P Strong	"	Charles Bacon
22	Philo Jewett	"	Milo Stow		L D Gregory
23	J F Brown	Samuel T. Walker	Linus Needham	Alvin B Needham	"
	BENNINGTON CO.				
1	Harman Canfield	Samuel Buck	"	Anson Buck	E M Aylesworth
2	P. Harwood jr	Calvin Gilson	Elijah D Hubbell	Norman Blackmer	Perez Harwood jr
3	W. S. Martindale	"			
4	J. H. Mattison	John Elwell	Ishmael R Elwell	"	John Elwell
5	David Willey	Gideon Davis	"	Wm W Martin	"
6	J. S. Pettibone	"	Aaron Baker	Solomon Bentley jr	Ahiman L Miner
7	Freeman Lyon	"	George Batchelder	"	Jesse Rider
8	Noel Barber	Wm. R. Blanchard	Homer O Merchant	David Gardner	Barber Thompson
9		Jason P. Lord	Daniel Carpenter	Joy Bishop jr	D P Carpenter
10	Seth Sheldon	John Harwood	"	Simeon Rising	David Sheldon
11	Roswell Tuttle		Augustus C Beebe	"	Heman Tucker
12	Joseph Eames	Solomon Rich	John N Squires	Alfred Williams	Solomon Rich
13	N. Wheelock	David G. Cole	Nelson Johnson		Dennis J George
14	Jas. Houghton	Jencks Phillips	Thomas Bratten	"	John Pratt
15	Michael Judson	F. M'Laughlin	Michael Judson		F M'Laughlin
16	Beriah Wheeler	Walter Williams	"		Walter Williams
17	William Park	"	William Wood	Anthony Stetson	Lyman Bowles
	CALEDONIA CO.				
1	William Lackie		Walter Harvey	Lloyd Kimball	"
2	Lucius Denison	Ebenezer Darling	"	Charles C Newell	"
3	Alpha Webster	Caleb Fisher	Salem Goodnough		Allen Perry
4	Asa Morrill	"	Theron Howard	Moses Wesson	
6	Jonathan Welch	Hugh Dunn	Moses Buchanan	Jonathan Welch	Moses Buchanan
7	John L. Pope	Amasa Goodrich	William Blair	"	David W Aiken
8	Nathaniel Willis	A. W. Burroughs	Benjamin Nutter	"	Charles H Graves
9	Benaiah Sanborn	"	Asaph Wilmarth	"	Lucius Kimball
10	Alph's Stoddard	James Dexter	Eleazer Davis	"	Jabez Smith
11	E. Chamberlain	"	Simon Blanchard	"	Schuyler Merrill
12	Robert Whitelaw	"	"	Thomas Nelson jr	John Cameron
13	John P. Ingalls	"	"		Caleb Miner
14	H. Paddock	John Bacon	"	Joseph P Fairbanks	"
15	Stephen Eaton	David Giffin	"	Wm Hutchinson	John Ladd jr
16	N. Perkins jr	Nathaniel Perkins	Wm Farrington	Nathaniel Perkins	"
17	Royal Ross	"	"	Dennis May	"
18	Hiel Bradley	Sewall Bradley	"	Nathaniel Hart	Richard Stevens

REPRESENTATIVES, AD., BEN., CAL., CONTINUED.

ADDISON CO. 1847	1848.	1849.	1850.	FIRST TOWN CL'K
1 Carlton E Miles	John W. Strong	"	George Wilmarth	
2 John B. Huntley	"	Simon Z. Walker	"	J. N. Bennett, 1784
3 H. Needham	"	Datus R. Gaige	"	H. M'Laughlin, 89
4 Calvin G. Tilden	"	Rollin J. Jones	"	Joel Linsley '84
5 Hartwell Powers	"	Ira Tupper	"	Jonath'n Saxton, 86
6 William Carlyle jr	John Capen	Wm. Carlyle jr.	John Capen	
7	Alonzo G. Allen	Joseph P. Ball	"	Joseph Patrick,
8 Horace Robinson	Charles G. Robbins	Robert Clafflin	"	Zenus Robbins, 92
9 John Bullock	William F. Wright	Ira B. Farr	William F. Wright	Ebenezer Child, 86
10 Almon C. Allen	Andrew Mitchell	Almon C Allen	Wiliam W. Pope	
11 Harry Goodrich	Ira Allen	"	Joseph Warner	Joshua Hyde, 86
Gilbert D. Eastman		Lewis L. Beers		
13 Elias Bottum	Alfred P. Roscoe	William Nash	Julius L. Eldredge	Luther Everts, 85
14 Albert L. Catlin	"	Nathan Gale	"	David Leonard, 87
15 John D. Smith	"	Loyal Kent	"	Elijah Grandey, 84
16 Saml H. Hendrick	Charles L. Atwood	"	John R. New	Daniel Chipman
17 John Prout	"	John Colby	"	Eleazer Claghorn88
18 Alonzo Birchard	"	Kent Wright	Bela Howe	Eliakim Culver, 87
19 David Ferguson	"	Pearley Hill	"	Warner Pierce, 96
Edward Seymour	"	Fred E Woodbridge	George W. Grandey	Sam'l Chipman jr89
21 Josiah Parker	"	Newton Rose	"	Andrew Barton, 97
22 Sardis Dodge	"	Philo Jewett	Edwin Hayward	
23 W. F. M'Allister	Allen Ketchum	"	Linus Needham	John Wilson, 85
BENNINGTON CO.				
1 Cyrus Hills	Curtis Hawley	John B. Lathrop	Samuel Benedict	RememberBaker 68
2 James P. Godfrey	Morton Brock	Paul M. Henry	Henry G Root	Moses Robinson, 62
3 James Curtis	"	Jarvis Andrus	Daniel G Williams	Asa Baldwin, 69
4 John Elwell	William M'Donald	Asa G. Hewes	Jeremiah M'Daniel	'uman Hewes. 1834
5 David Willey	William W Martin	James Martin	"	Daniel Tuthl, 1800
6 Johnson R Burrett	Aaron Baker	Augustus C. Clark	Amos S. Bourn	Stephen Mead,1766
7 Ezra Dodge	"	Ira K. Batchelder	Edward Batchelder	John Brock, 1802
8 Jona N Carpenter	"	Reynolds Carpenter	Green Brimmer	
9 John Runyen	William M Stafford	Benjamin S. Battles	Elias B. Flint	
Joseph P Harwood	"	David S. Sheldon	Thomas S. Bebee	
11	Charles Sayre	Burton Still	"	
12 Solomon Rich		Timothy G. Crosier		Joseph Eames, 83
13 Dennis J George	Charles E Houghton	Philomon Bates	Freeborn Johnson	Thomas Mattison,
14 John Pratt		Ira Whitney	Ira Stroud	
15 William Kelly	Daniel King	"	Ira McLaughlin	Gid'n Brownson,69
16 Francis Kidder	Silas Eddy	"	Seth Taylor jr.	Asa Beebe jr., 1796
William Alverson	"	Lewis Fox	Alonzo Fox	
CALEDONIA CO.				
1 Obed S. Hatch	John Harvey	Bartholo. Gilkerson	"	Walter Brock, 83
2 Daniel Beckwith	"	Erastus Humphrey	"	Lemuel Walter, 96
3 Allen Perry	Thomas Lyford jr.	"	Daniel Gould	
4	John A. Page	Harvey T. Moore	"	Abram. Morrill, 87
6	James Renfrew jr.		Daniel Coffrin	Nathaniel Knight87
7 David French	"	Dustin Grow	Daniel W. Aiken	Paul Spooner, 95
8 Arunah Leach	Charles H Graves	Arunah Leach	Merit Newhall	Jonathan Lewis, 07
9 Lucius Kimball	Stephen McGaffy	"	Thomas Bartlett jr.	
10 Jabez Smith	Hiram Allard	"	Jabez Smith	
		William Mattocks	"	James Bailey, 83
12 John M'Clure	"	Robert Cockran	"	
	James Roberts	Moses Cheney	"	
14 Moses Kittridge	"	Jerry Dickerman	"	Jonathan Arnold,90
15 Jona'n Pillsbury	John Ladd jr	Nehemiah Shaw	Lorenzo D. Hall	
Sere'o M'ntgomery	"		Isaac Eastman	Natha'l Perkins, 94
17 Joseph Ide	"	Barron Moulton	"	Selah Howe, 1793
18 Nathaniel Hart	Jefferson Cree	"	Edward M, Magoon	

REPRESENTATIVES, CHIT., ES., FRAN., G. ISLE, LAM.

	1788	1789	1790	1791
CHITTENDEN CO.				
1 Bolton				Samuel Bell
2 Burlington	Samuel Lane	Samuel Hitchcock	"	"
3 Charlotte	John M'Neil	"	"	Daniel Hosford jr
4 Colchester	Ira Allen	"	"	"
5 Essex	Timothy Bliss	Joel Woodworth	"	"
6 Hinesburgh		Lemuel Bostwick	"	Elisha Barber
7 Huntington				Jehiel Johns
8 Jericho	Lewis Chapin	Mathew Coles	Martin Chittenden	"
9 Milton	Aaron Mathews	Amos Mansfield	Abel Waters	"
11 Shelburne	Charles Smith	Wm C. Harrington	"	"
15 Williston	Amos Brownson	Jonathan Spafford		Amos Brownson
ESSEX CO.				
8 Guildhall		Benoni Cutler	David Hopkinson	"
10 Lunenburgh	Amasa Grout	"	Samuel Gates	Samuel Phelps
11 Maidstone		David Gaskill	John Rich	"
FRANKLIN CO.				
4 Fairfax	Josiah Safford	Nathan Spafford	"	James Farnsworth
5 Fairfield			Smithfield	Clark Burlingame
8 Georgia	James Everts	Daniel Stannard	John White	Benjamin Holmes
9 Highgate			John Knickerbocker	"
12 Sheldon				Samuel B. Sheldon
13 St. Albans	Jonathan Hoit	Silas Hathaway	"	Jonathan Hoit
14 Swanton			Daniel Stannard	
GRAND ISLE CO.				
1 Alburgh	William Coit			
3 Isle La Mott				Nathaniel Wales
4 North Hero	Ebenezer Allen			Nathan Hutchins jr
5 South Hero			Colonel Pearl	Ebenezer Allen
LAMOILLE CO.				
2 Cambridge	John Fassett	Amos Fassett	John Fassett	"
6 Johnson		Noah Smith	Jonath'n M'Connell	"

FIRST APPOINTED OFFICERS OF VERMONT NOW LIVING.

The first Governor of Vermont, living in 1851, is Cornelius P. Van Ness, chosen in 1823.

" Lieut. Gov.	"	David M. Camp,	" 1836
" Treasurer,	"	Allen Wardner	" 1837
" Secretary of State,	"	Wilham Slade	" 1815
" Speaker of the House,	"	George E. Wales	" 1823
" Clerk of the House,	"	Samuel C. Crafts	" 1798
" Engrossing Clerk,	"	Orsamas C. Merrill	" 1808
" Preacher of Election Sermon	"	Jeremiah Atwater	" 1802
" Secretary to Gov. and Council	"	Samuel Swift	" 1813
" Members of the Council,	"	Samuel C. Crafts & Horatio Seymour	" 1809
" Judge of the Supreme Court	"	William A. Palmer	" 1816
" " Orleans County Court	"	Samuel C. Crafts	" 1800
" " Essex "	"	Mills De Forest	" 1801
" " Rutland, "	"	Caleb Hendee jr	" 1806
" " Franklin "	"	J. D. Farnsworth	" 1807
" " Chittenden "	"	Heman Allen of Col.	" 1808
" " Windham "	"	Jairus Hall	" 1810
" " Addison "	"	Samuel Shepherd	" 1812
" " Washington "	"	Joseph Howes	" 1818
" " Orange "	"	William Spencer	" 1820
" " Grand Isle "	"	Samuel Adams	" 1823
" " Bennington "	"	Myron Clark	" 1824
" " Caledonia "	"	Wm. A. Palmer	" 1826
" " Windsor "	"	Samuel W. Porter	" 1828
" Senator to Congress	"	Wm. A. Palmer	" 1818
" Representative to Congress	"	Wm. C. Bradley	" 1813
" Member of Council Censors	"	Joshua Y. Vail	" 1820

REPRESENTATIVES, CHIT., ES., FRAN., G. ISLE, LAM.

CHITTENDEN	1792	1793	1794	1795.	1796.
1		Samuel Bell	Jabez Jones	"	Robert Kennedy
2	Sam'l Hitchcock	"	William Coit	Wm. C. Harrington	Elnathan Keyes
3	John M' Neil	"	David Hubbell	"	John M'Neil
4	Ira Allen	John Law	Ira Allen	Joshua Staunton jr.	Joshua Staunton
5	Timothy Bliss	Joel Woodworth	Robert Spelman	"	Timothy Bliss
6	Lemuel Bostwick	Thaddeus Munson	Lemuel Bostwick	"	Nath'n Leavenworth
7	James Hall	Jehiel Johns	Amos Brownson	Jehiel Johns	Sylvester Russell
8	M Chittenden	"	"	"	Noah Chittenden
9	Abel Waters	Amos Mansfield	"	Mathew Cole	
10	*Richmond*				Jona'n Chamberlin
11	W C Harrington	"	"	Timothy Hurlburt	"
13	*Underhill*			William Barney	
14	*Westford*	Jeremiah Stone	"	John Seeley	Jeremiah Stone
15	Amos Brownson	Jonathan Spafford	"	"	"
ESSEX CO.					
5	*Concord*		Elijah Spafford	Jonathan Lewis	"
8	David Hopkinson	Benoni Cutler	David Hopkinson	"	"
10	Samuel Phelps	"	Samuel Gates	Amasa Grout	Zerubbabel Eager
		Haines French	"	James Lucas	Haines French
FRANKLIN CO.					
1	*Bakersfield*				Jonas Brigham
2	*Berkshire*				Stephen Royce
4	Thomas Russell	Jonathan Danforth	"	"	Ross Coon
5	David Davis	Edmond Town	"	"	Hubbard Barlow
6	*Fletcher*				
7	*Franklin*		Samuel Peckham	Samuel Hubbard	Samuel Peckham
8	Daniel Stannard	Levi House	John White	Benjamin Holmes	Reuben Everts
9		Jonathn Butterfield	"	Orange Smith	Jonathan Butterfield
11	*Richford*				Benjamin Barnett
12	Elisha Sheldon		Elisha Sheldon	"	"
13	Jonathan Hoit	Noel Potter	Silas Hathaway	"	"
14	Tho. Butterfield	"		Asa Holgate	John Pratt
GRAND ISLE CO.					
1	David Staunton	Elisha Reynolds	Benjamin Marvin	"	"
3	Nathaniel Wales	"	William Utley	"	William Goodrich
4	Enos Wood	Nathan Hutchins jr	Nathan Hutchins	"	"
5	Samuel Mix	Ebenezer Allen	"	William Hazen	"
LAMOILLE CO.					
2	Prince B. Hall	Jonathan Fisk	James Gillmore	Solom'n Walbridge	"
6		Jonathan M'Connel	"	"	"

REV. AARON LELAND,

Was settled over the Baptist society in Chester in 1788, and continued as their Pastor, till his death in 1833. He took an active part in politics as well as religion, being of the Jefferson school, was frequently elected to the offices of Selectman, Town Clerk, &c. He was chosen to represent the town in 1801, and was chosen nine years after, making ten years a member of the House, three years of which he was chosen Speaker, and was four years a Councillor, and five years was chosen Lieutenant Governor by the people. He was eighteen years one of the Assistant Justices of the County Court.—The Parson was fond of a good joke, and he had one neighbor, Hugh Henry, who was a match for him. On a Saturday evening, a young man, and moneyless, called at the Parson's house for supper and lodging. The Parson did not see fit to comply with the request, and sent him to his neighbor Henry, and assured him that he would be well provided for, but still the man will refuse you at first, but you stick to him and he will accommodate you. The young man called as diirected, and was refused. I was told you would refuse to keep me unless I stuck to you, which I shall do· Who told you that? said Mr. Henry, a large man at such a house. Well, if Parson Leland sent you here you shall stay, and what would you like for supper? O most any thing that comes handy, for I have no money to pay you. But what would you choose if you had money? I should like a good warm supper had I wherewith to pay you, for to be honest with you, I have had very little food to-day. A warm supper was soon provided, to which the young man paid his best respects, nor was he allowed to depart the next morning till he had done justice to a good breakfast. The young man was going to try his fortune in the western wilderness, and had a small dog with

REPRESENTATIVES, CHIT., ES., FRAN., G. ISLE, LAM.

CHITTENDEN	1797	1798	1799	1800	1801
1	Robert Kennedy	Jabez Jones	"	"	"
2	Elnathan Keyes	Wm. C. Harrington	Elnathan Keyes	"	"
3	John Thorp	Hezekiah Barnes	"	Nathaniel Newell	"
4	Joshua Staunton	Joshua Staunton jr	"	"	John Law
5	Abel Castle	Nathan Castle	Timothy Bliss	"	"
6	Lemuel Bostwick	Wm. B. Marsh	N. Leavenworth	"	Lemuel Bostwick
7	Sylvester Russell	John Fitch	Sylvester Russell	"	Elias Buel
8	M. Chittenden	Thomas D. Rood	"	James A. Potter	"
9	Abel Waters	"	William Parish	Abel Waters	William Parish
10	J. Chamberlin	"	Joel Brownson	Josh. Chamberlain	"
11	Tim Hurlburt	Sturges Morehouse	"	Benj. Harrington	"
13		Udney Hay	"	"	"
14	John Seeley	"	Martin Powell	John Seeley jr	Martin Powell
15	Solomon Miller	Lemuel Bottum	"	"	"

ESSEX CO.					
3 *Brunswick*		Joseph Wait			John Merrill
4 *Canaan*		James Chamberlin			Samuel Beach
5 Saml. Wetherbee		John Frye	Saml. Wetherbee	"	"
7 *Granby*		Clark Curtis			James Elliott
8 David Hopkinson		Ezekiel May	Hezekiah May	Daniel Dana	"
9 *Lemington*		Mills De Forrest			Mills De Forrest
10 Samuel Phelps		"	"	"	Smith Williams
11 Haines French		James Lucas	Jacob Rich	Joseph Worcester	Isaac Stevens

FRANKLIN CO.					
1		Jonas Brigham	Stephen Maynard	Jonas Brigham	"
2		Stephen Royce	"	"	Abel Johnson
3 *Enosburgh*		William Barber	"	"	
4 Jona. Danforth		"	"	Joseph Beeman jr	"
5 Edmond Town		Hubbart Barlow	"	"	Jos. D. Farnsworth
7 Daniel Bayley		Lemuel Scott	"	"	"
7		Samuel Hubbard	"	"	Samuel Peckham
8 Benj. Holmes		Step'n Fairchild jr	Francis Davis	John White	Benjamin Holmes
9		Sylvester Cobb	John Croye	Sylvester Cobb	Mathew Sax
11			Jonathan Janes	"	"
12		Elisha Sheldon	"	"	Saml. B. Sheldon
13 Levi House		Silas Hathaway	"	Seth Pomeroy	"
14 John Pratt		"	James Brown	John Pratt	James Brown

GRAND ISLE CO.					
1 Benjamin Marvin		Timothy Sowles	John Babcock	"	Samuel Mott
3 Wm. Goodrich		Daniel Baker		Daniel Baker	Truman Clark
4 N. Hutchins jr		"	Ezekiel Taylor	Nathan Hutchins	Stephen Kingsley
5 Timothy Pearl		Ebenezer Allen	Asa Lyon	"	"

LAMOILLE CO.					
2 John Fassett			David Safford	"	Solom'n Walbridge
3 *Eden*					
6 John M'Connell		Robert Balch	Jona. M'Connell	Wm. H. Larrabee	"
10 *Stowe*					Nathan Robinson
12 *Wolcott*					Thomas Taylor

him. Just before he was ready to start. and being near meeting time, Mr. Henry informed his guest, that his dog was not a proper one to go into the wilderness with. and that he had a neighbor who had a large dog, and just the one for the woods among the wild animals, and he would like to exchange him for a small one, but no doubt he will refuse at first, and tell you to go about your business, I do not swap dogs on Sunday, and the like, but you stick to him and you will get his dog. The young man went to the house just as the Parson was starting for meeting and informed him that he had come to swap dogs, and received the answer that Mr. Henry predicted. Well I was told you would make such excuses, but that in case I stuck to you I should get your dog, and that, sir, you may rest assured I shall do, and went with the Parson to the steps of the meeting house. The Parson finding the man to be as good as his word, told him to go and take the dog, and be off in a hurry, and never trouble me again in this way. Mr. Henry outlived the Parson a few years, but their remains are both in one grave yard in Chester, and not far distant from each other as their grave stones show.

REPRESENTATIVES, CHIT., ES., FRAN., G. ISLE, LAM.

CHITTENDEN 1802	1803	1804	1805	1806
1 Jabez Jones	"	"	John Pineo	Augustus Levake
2 W. C. Harrington	Thaddeus Tuttle	Wm. C. Harrington	Stephen Pearl	Wm. C. Harrington
3 Nath'l Newell	Samuel Rich	Nathaniel Newell	Ezra Meach	Nathaniel Newell
4 John Law	Joshua Staunton jr	Benj. Boardman	Simeon Hinds	William Munson
5 Simeon Tubbs	Timothy Bliss	John Johnson	Simeon Tubbs	"
6 N. Leavenworth	"	"	"	"
7 Elias Buel	Jesse P. Carpenter	Elias Buel	John Fitch	"
8 M. Chittenden	James A. Potter	"	Thomas D. Rood	
9 John Jackson	"	Moses Davis	John Jackson	"
10 Joel Brownson	"	Jacob Spafford	Joel Brownson	Nathan Fay
11 Joshua Isham	"	Benj. Harrington	Jedediah Boynton	Timothy Hurlburt
13 Udney Hay	"	William Barney	"	"
14 Samuel Mower	Martin Powell	"	Daniel Hazeltine	Ebenezer Bowman
15 Nathan Allen	Giles Chittenden	Jeremiah French	"	Lemuel Bottum
ESSEX CO.				
1 *Bloomfield*		"	"	
3 John Merrill	Ithiel Cargill		Ithiel Cargill	David Hyde
4 Samuel Beach	"	"	"	
5 Saml. Wetherbee	"	David Hibbard	"	Saml. Wetherbee
7	Joseph Herrick			James Elliott
8 Daniel Dana	"	"	"	"
9	Mills De Forrest	"	"	
10 Smith Williams	Levi Barnard	Samuel Phelps	"	"
11 Haines French	"	"	"	Jesse Hugh
FRANKLIN CO.				
1 Jonas Brigham	"	"	"	"
2 Abel Johnson	Amh't Willoughby	Elam Jewett jr	Stephen Royce	Elijah Littlefield
3 Stephen House	"	"	"	"
4 Joseph Beeman jr	"	Erastus Safford	Asa Wilkins	"
5 J. D. Farnsworth	Hubbard Barlow	Sol. Bingham jr	Bradley Barlow	Samuel Barlow
6 Lemuel Scott	"	John Wheeler	Lemuel Scott	John Wheeler
7 Samuel Hubbard	Samuel Peckham	"	Samuel Hubbard	Salmon Warner
8 Francis Davis	Benjamin Holmes	"	John White jr	Sardius Blodgett
9 Mathew Sax	Sylvester Cobb	Mathew Sax	"	Peter Sax
10 *Montgomery*	Joshua Clapp	"	"	"
11 Jonathan Janes	"	Joseph Parker	Robert Kennede	"
12 S. B. Sheldon	"	"	"	"
13 Levi House	Seth Pomeroy	"	"	Nathan Green
14 Silas Hathaway	Ezra Jones	Joseph Robinson	"	James Brown
GRAND ISLE CO.				
1 Samuel Mott	Elisha Reynolds	"	Lewis Sowles	"
3 Samuel Fisk	Seth Emmons	"	John Borden	"
4 Stephen Kingsley	N. Hutchins jr	"	Nathan Hutchins	"
5 Asa Lyon	Timothy Allen	Asa Lyon	"	
LAMOILLE CO.				
2 Solo'n Walbridge	Elias Fassett	Solo. Walbridge	"	"
3 Thos· H. Parker	"	"	"	Jeduthan Stone
6 Samuel Eaton	Samuel Eaton jr	George Westgate	"	"
8 *Morristown*		Elisha Boardman	"	"
10 Nat'n Robinson	"	"	Nehemiah Perkins	Nathan Robinson
12 Thomas Taylor	"	"	Thomas Taylor	

HON. SAMUEL SAFFORD

Was an early settler in Bennington, and among the early patriots who espoused the cause of Vermont in her controversy with New York, and the cause of the union in her revolutionary struggles with Great Britain. He was a Major in Col. Seth Warner's regiment, and served through the war, except he found time to represent the town of Bennington in the Legislature in 1781-2. In 1783 he was chosen a member of the Council and was annually chosen to that office for twenty-two years

38 REPRESENTATIVES, CHIT., ES., FRAN., G. ISLE, LAM.

CHITTENDEN 1807	1808	1809	1810	1811
1 Eliakim Howe	"	Augustus Levake	John Levake	John Pineo
2 Geo. Robinson	"	"	"	"
3 Ezra Meach	Nathaniel Newell	Hezekiah Barns	"	Nathaniel Newell
4 Simeon Hine	Francis Child	Simeon Hine	"	Roger Enos
5 Simon Tubbs	"	"	Timothy Bliss	"
6 Wm. B. Marsh	"	N. Leavenworth	"	"
7 John Fitch	"	"	"	"
8 Salmon Fay	James A. Potter	Arther Bostwick	Eleazer Hutchins	"
9 Moses Davis	Marshall Smith	"	Heman Allen	"
10 Joel Brownson	Abel Cooper	Nathan Fay	Joel Brownson	James Butler
11 T. Hurlburt	Joshua Isham	Frederick Mack	"	Joshua Isham
13 William Barney		"	"	Luther Dixon
14 E. Bowman	Samuel Mower	"	Amos Partridge jr	Samuel Rice
15 T. Chittenden	Jeremiah French	Lemuel Bottum	Isaac French	Lemuel Bottum
ESSEX CO.				
1	Gaias Kibbe			John French
3 Ithiel Cargill	"	"	"	John Walls
4 Micajah Ingham	Oliver Ingham	Micajah Ingham		Oliver Ingham
5 David Hibbard	S. Wetherbee jr	Richardson Graves	"	
7	Joseph Herrick	"	"	Enos Cook
8 Elijah Foot	Daniel Dana	Elijah Foot	"	"
9	Mills De Forrest	"	"	"
10 Thomas Slade	Levi Barnard	Ebenezer Clark	Azariah Webb jr	"
11 Haines French	Jesse Hugh	Moody Rich	"	Jesse Hugh
FRANKLIN CO.				
1 Silas Hazeltine	"	Jonas Brigham	"	"
2 Elam Jewett jr	Elijah Shaw	Elijah Littlefield	Solo. Bingham jr	"
3 Stephen House	Martin D. Follet	William Barber	Martin D. Follet	John Adams
4 Erastus Safford	"	"	"	Benjamin Gale
5 J. D. Farnsworth	"	"	"	Joseph Bowdish
6 John Wheeler	Lemuel Scott	"	Joseph Robinson	"
7 S. Hubbard	"	S. Peckham jr	"	Hezekiah Wead
8 S. Blodgett	"	Benjamin Holmes	"	Elijah Dee
9 Peter Sax	Benjamin Going	Simeon Hungerford	"	"
10 Henry Marble	Joshua Clapp		Joshua Clapp	Henry Marble
11 R. Kennedy	Amherst Willoby	John Powell	"	William Rogers
S. B. Sheldon died	Ebenezer Marvin jr	Ebenezer Marvin	"	David Sanderson
13 Lewis Walker	Asa Fuller	Carter Hickok	Nathan Green	Jonathan Hoit
14 James Brown	George W. Foster	"	Benjamin Fay	Theo's Mansfield
GRAND ISLE CO.				
1 James W. Wood	Alexander Scott	Lewis Sowles	Philyer Loop	Alexander Scott
2 *Grand Isle*			Asa Lyon	"
3 John Borden	"	"		William Wait
4 Jona. Haynes	Nathan Hutchins	Jedediah P. Ladd	Simeon Robinson jr	N. Hutchins jr
5 Timothy Allen	Asa Lyon	Alpheas Hall	"	"
LAMOILLE CO.				
2 S. Walbridge	"	"	Salmon Green	James Gilmore
3 J. Stone	"	Abel Smith	Jeduthan Stone	
5 *Hydepark*				
6 A. Waterman	"	"	"	"
8 E. Boardman	"	Samuel Cook	"	"
10 N. Robinson	Thomas B. Downer	"	N. Robinson	"
12 Thomas Taylor	"	"		Thomas Taylor

in succession, which, added to the two years he was Representative makes twenty-four years that he was a member in succession, which is serving longer in succession than any other person in the State. He was Chief Judge of the County Court from 1786 to 1807, when by his advanced age he declined any further promotion.

REPRESENTATIVES, CHIT., ES., FRAN., G. ISLE., LAM.

CHITTENDEN,

	1812	1813.	1814.	1815.	1816.
1	John Pineo	Samuel Webster	"	John Pinco	"
2	George Robinson	"	"	"	Luther Loomis
3	Nathaniel Newell	Zadock Wheeler	"	"	Hezekiah Barnes
4	Heman Allen	"	"	"	"
5	Daniel Clark	"	"	Richard Lamson	Samuel Bliss
6	N. Leavenwort h	"	Edmond Baldwin	Nat'n Leavenworth	Edmond Baldwin
7	James Amblerjr.	"	Elias Buel	Benjamin Derby	"
8	Noah Chittenden	"	"	Heman Lowry	Thomas D. Rood
9	Heman Allen	"	"	Lemuel B. Platt	Heman Allen
10	James Butler	Joel Brownson	William Rhodes	"	John Fay
11	Joshua Isham	"	Joshua Morgan	"	Ziba Pierson
12	*St. George*	Lewis Higbee	Reuben Lockwood	Jared Higbee	"
13	Luther Dixon	Caleb Sheldon	"	Peter Martin	Caleb Sheldon
14	Samuel Rice	Amos Patridge jr.	Samuel Rice	"	Ebenezer Bowman
15	Lemuel Bottom	Jeremiah French	Lemuel Bottum	Jeremiah French	"

ESSEX CO.

	1812	1813.	1814.	1815.	1816.
1	John French	Gaius Kibbe	Joseph Clough	"	Daniel Holbrook
3	John Walls	"	"	Thomas Schoff	Haines Schoff
4	Daniel Goss	Oliver Ingham	"	Moses Morrill	Oliver Ingham
5	Robert Taggard	Richardson Graves	"	Cornelius Judevine	
7		Elijah Bugbee	Samuel Hart		
8	Calvin Perkins	Elijah Foot	David Denison	Chester Thayer	Joseph Berry
9	Mills De Forest	"	"	Abraham Boynton	Harvey Johnson
10	Levi Barnard	"	"	"	"
11	Jesse Hugh	"	Moody Rich	Richard Stevens	S. G. Hinman

FRANKLIN CO.

	1812	1813.	1814.	1815.	1816.
1	Jonas Brigham	"	"	"	Samuel Maynard
		William Hamilton	Wm. C. Ellsworth	Harvey Clark	"
3	John Adams	"	"		Nathaniel Griswold
4	Samuel Ufford	"	Joseph Holmes	Stephen Holmes	"
5	Elijah Foot	Bates Turner	Joab Smith		Jos'h D. Farnsworth
6	Joseph Robinson	Samuel Scott	Nathan L. Holmes	Reuben Armstrong	Daniel Bailey
7	Samuel Hubbard	"		"	"
8	Benjamin Holmes		Elijah Dee jr.		
9	Abel Drury	Anthony Rhodes	"	Hira Hill	Solomon Bliss
10	Seth Goodspeed	"	"	Simeon Hungerford	
11	William Rogers	Joseph Parker	William Rogers	John Powell	James Upham
12	DavidSanderson	Chauncey Fitch	"	Stephen Royce jr.	"
13	Abner Morton	Benjamin Swift		Abner Morton	N. W. Kingman
14	Jareb Jackson		"	"	James Brown

GRAND ISLE CO.

	1812	1813.	1814.	1815.	1816.
1	Alexander Scott	Stephen Pettis		Lewis Sowles	Ephraim Mott
2	Asa Lyon	"	"	Enoch Allen	
3	William Wait	Caleb Hill	Charles Carron	William Wait	Jesse A. Clark
4	Nathan Hutchins	"	Dan Hazen	Nathan Hutchins	Dan Hazen
5	Alpheas Hall	"	D. G. Sawyer	Alpheas Hall	"

LAMOILLE CO.

	1812	1813.	1814.	1815.	1816.
2	James Gillmore	Truman Powell	Frederick Hopkins	John Fassett	Enoch Carlton
3	Abel Smith	"	"	Jeduthan Stone	"
4	*Elmore*		Martin Elmore		
5	N. P. Sawyer	"	"	"	Joshua Sawyer
6	David Boynton	"			"
7	*Mansfield*			Daniel Dodge	
8	Samuel Cook	"	"	Peter C. Lovejoy	"
10	Asa Raymond	Nathan Robinson	"	Robert Kimball	"
12	Thomas Taylor		Thomas Taylor	"	

CHITTENDEN 1817	1818	1819	1820	1821.
1 John Pineo	James Whitcomb	"	William Evarts	James Whitcomb
2 Charles Adams	C. P. Van Ness	"	"	"
3 Hezekiah Barnes	Nathaniel Newell	Ithiel Stone	Nathaniel Newell	"
4 Nathan Bryan	William Hine	Jabez Penniman	"	
5 Ezra Slater	"	"	"	Roswell Butler
6 N. Leavenworth	"	Erastus Bostwick	"	N. Leavenworth
7 James Ambler jr	B. Derby	James Ambler jr	Benjamin Derby	
8 W. P. Richardson	"	Thomas Chittenden	"	Thomas D. Rood
9 Heman Allen	Moses Davis	John Jackson	Moses Davis	Jesse P. Carpenter
10 Joel Brownson	John Fay	"	Eli Brownson	Edward Jones
11 Zeba Pierson	Burgess Hall	"	Levi Comstock	"
12 Lewis Higbee				
13 Peter Martin	"	Luther Dixon	Peter Martin	William Barney
14 Eben'r Bowman	"	Amos Partridge	Ebenezer Bowman	Amos Partridge
15 Roswell Morton	M. Chittenden	Chauncey Brownall	"	Martin Chittenden
ESSEX CO.				
1	Daniel Holbrook		Chauncey Curtis	
3 Thos. G. French	"	"	William Marshall	Haines Schoff
4 Oliver Ingham	"	"	"	"
5 J. Woodbury jr	David Hibbard	Jesse Woodbury jr		James May
7				
8 Joseph Berry	Seth Cushman	"	"	David Hopkinson
9 Mills De Forest		Mills De Forest		Mills De Forest
10 Levi Barnard	Azariah Webb	Azariah Webb jr	Azariah Webb	Azariah Webb jr
11 Moody Rich	"	"	Daniel Rich	
FRANKLIN CO.				
1 Joseph Barrett	"	"	"	Silas B. Hazeltine
2 Amherst Willoby	Harvey Clark	Nathan Hamilton	Wm. C. Ellsworth	"
3 N. Griswold	Martin D. Follet	"	"	"
4 Erastus Safford	Samuel Parmalee	Elias Bellows	"	Joseph Beaman
5 J. D. Farnsworth	"	"	"	"
6 R. Armstrong	Zerah Willoby	"	"	"
7 S. Hubbard	William Felton	Samuel Hubbard	"	Joshua Peckham
8 Solomon Bliss		Frederick Bliss	Joel Barber	Elijah Dee jr
9 Abel Drury	Needham Drury	Abel Drury	John Averill	"
10 Jonah Johnson	J. Goodspeed	Henry N. Janes	Jonathan Janes	
11 John Powell	Hezekiah Goff jr	John Powell	"	"
12 Samuel Wead	"	James Mason	"	"
13 J. K. Smedley		Samuel Barlow	Silas Hathaway	Asa Fuller
14 Wm. Brayton	James Brown	"	Daniel B. Meigs	Timothy Foster
GRAND ISLE CO.				
1 Robert Ransom	Joseph Sewell	L. Sowles	Truman A. Barber	Joseph M. Mott
2	James Brown	"	"	"
3 Jesse A. Clark	Truman Clark	"	"	William Wait
4 Jonathan Haynes	"	Dan Hazen	Solomon Hazen	Nathan Hutchins
5 Stephen Davison	Timothy Allen	Benjamin Adams	"	Nathaniel Healey
LAMOILLE CO.				
2 John Wires	"	"	"	"
3				
4				
5 Joshua Sawyer	"	"	"	"
6 Daniel Dodge	"	"	"	"
7	Ivory Luce	"	"	"
8 Samuel Cook	Robert Kimball	Samuel Cook	"	Luther Bingham
10 N. Robinson	Riverius Camp	"	"	Asa Raymond
12			Thomas Taylor	

REPRESENTATIVES, CHIT., ES., FRAN., G. ISLE, LAM. 41

CHITTENDEN 1822.	1823.	1824.	1825.	1826.
1 James Whitcomb	William Everts	James Whitcomb	"	"
2 George Robinson	Eben'r T. Englesby	Charles Adams	Benjamin F. Bailey	"
3 Jeremiah Barton	"	"	Nathaniel Newell	William Noble
4 Nathan Bryan	"	"	Jabez Penniman	"
5 Roswell Butler	"	"	Bille B. Butler	"
6 N. Leavenworth	Mitchell Hinsdell	"	John M. Eldridge	"
7 Benjamin Derby	James Ambler jr.	"	Benjamin Derby	James Ambler jr.
8 Oliver Lowrey	Wm. P. Richardson	Gideon O. Dixon	"	"
9 Heman Allen	Moses Davis	Heman Allen	"	"
10 Edward Jones	Amos B. Cooper	William Rhodes	"	"
11 Levi Comstock	Garrad Burrett	"	Burgess Hall	"
12				Reuben Lockwood
13 William Barney	"	"	"	"
14 William Wood	"	Amos Partridge	"	Ziba Woods
15 Simeon Lee	"	Chauncey Brownell	Selah Murry	Harry Bradley
ESSEX CO.				
1 Joseph Stevens	"			John M. French
3 Daniel Smith	William Marshall		Thomas G. French	"
4 Jesse Cooper	Daniel Goss		"	
6 David Hibbard jr.	"	Oliver Ingham		Caleb Ingalls
7		Dyer Hibbard	Joel Bassett	"
8 D. Hopkinson		"	Erastus Cutler	David Hopkinson
9 Ed. C. Spaulding	Mills De Forest		Noyes Denison	Mills De Forest
10 William Gates	"	"	"	Stephen Howe jr.
11 Moody Rich	"			Moody Rich
FRANKLIN CO.				
1 Silas B. Hazeltine	"	Thomas Child	"	"
2 Penuel Leavens	Geo. w. Woodworth		Cromwell Bowen	Brainard Bradley
3 Martin D. Follett	"	Austin Fuller	"	Thomas Fuller
4 Luther B. Hunt	"	"	Reuben Wood	Luther B. Hunt
4 Joab Smith	Jos'h D. Farnsworth	Joab Smith	"	"
6 Zerah Willoughby		Elias Blair	"	Reuben Armstrong
7 Reuben Fowler	Reuben Towle	William Felton	"	
8 Elijah Baker	Ira Hinkley	Elijah Dee jr.		
9 John Averill	Abel Drury	"	Joel Barber jr.	Alvah Sabin
10 Samuel Lusk		"	John Averill	Thomas Best
11	Sterling Parker	"	"	Alvin House
12 James Mason	"	"	"	"
13 Stephen Royce jr	"	Joshua W. Sheldon	"	"
14 Jonathan Berry	"	"	Benjamin Swift	"
GRAND ISLE CO.			Stephen S. Brown	James Platt
1 John M. Mott		"		
2 James Brown	Joel Allen		Thomas Mott	"
3	Charles Carron	Jedediah Hyde	Melvin Barnes	"
4 Irad Allen	"	"	William Wait	Ezra Pike jr.
5 Elisha Boardman	"	"	Abner Ladd	Irad Allen
LAMOILLE CO.			Benajah Phelps	
1 Belvidere				
2 James B. Gilmore	Moody Shattuck			
3	John Warner	"	Nathan Smilie	"
4				
5 Abner Flanders	"	"	"	"
6 Tho's Waterman	"	"	"	"
7 Ivory Luce	"	Daniel Dodge	"	Solomon Balch
8 Luther Bingham	"	"	"	"
10 Riverius Camp	"	"	"	"
12		"	"	Benjamin Chapman
		Ephraim Ladd		

#	1827	1828	1829	1830	1831
CHITTENDEN					
1	John Pirco	"	"	James Whitcomb	Moses L. Colton
2	Benj'n F. Bailey		"	Timothy Follett	"
3	William Noble	Nathaniel Newell	William Pease	"	"
4	Noah Wolcott	"	"	"	Udney H.Penniman
5	Marshall Castle	Samuel Bliss	Marshall Castle	Roswell Butler	"
6	N. Leavenworth	"	Naum Peck	"	Joseph Marsh
7	James Ambler jr	John Judson	"	"	Selah Ambler
8	Truman Galusha	"	William A Prentiss	Truman Galusha	"
9	Phelps Smith	Levi Smith	Lemuel B. Platt	"	A. G. Whittemore
10	Nathan Fay jr.	"	"	William Rhodes	Edward Jones
11	Levi Comstock	Hyman Holabird	"	Heman Barstow	"
	Reuben Lockwood	Horace Ferris	"	Lewis Higbee	Reuben Lockwood
13	Cyrus Birge	William Barney	"	John H. Tower	"
14	Ziba Wood	Danforth Wales	David Hazelton	Danforth Wales	"
15		Truman Chittenden	"	"	Alexander Lee
ESSEX CO.					
1	John M. French	Adin Bartlett	"	Martin French	Arad Silver
2	*Brighton*				
3	David Hyde	"	Haines Schoff	"	Thomas G. French
4	Oliver Ingham	Jesse Cooper	James Steele		William Morrill
5	Dyer Hibbard	Archibald Taggard	"	"	"
7	Joel Gleason	Joel Bassett		Elijah Baker	Benjamin S. Clark
8	Seth Cushman	John Dewey	David Hopkinson jr	John Dewey	Horace Hubbard
9	Zebina Blodgett	Joseph Downer	Noyes Denison	"	Abdiel Blodgett
10	Azariah Webb jr	John Chandler	Jonah Brooks jr.	"	"
11	Jesse Hugh	"	Moody Rich	Daniel Rich	"
FRANKLIN CO.					
1	Silas B. Hazeltine	Azariah Corse jr.	"	Thomas Child	Harry Reynolds
2	Cromwell Bowen	"	Wm. C. Ellsworth	"	Nathan Hamilton
3	Jehiel R. Barnum	"	Horace Eaton	"	Oliver H. Robinson
4	Erastus Safford	James Farnsworth	James Bellows	Joseph Kingsbury	James Bellows
5	Joab Smith	"	Benjamin Wooster	Joab Smith	Joel Barber jr.
6	Elias Bingham	Ira Armstrong	"	"	Ira Scott
7	Zeri Cushman	"	William Felton	Philip S. Gates	William Felton
8	Joel Barber jr	Elijah Dee	"	Decius R. Bogue	"
9	Thomas Best	John Averill	John Barr	"	
10	Henry N. Janes	Samuel Lusk	"	Selah B. Upham	Daniel Barrows
11	Sterling Parker	Jonathan Carpenter	"	William Rogers	Caleb Royce
12	James Mason	"	Alfred Keith	"	Levi Hapgood
13	John Smith	"	"	"	John Smith
14	Timothy Foster	"	Stephen S. Brown	James Platt	Ruluff W. Green
GRAND ISLE CO.					
1	Thomas Mott	William L. Sowles	"	"	"
2	James Brown	Samuel Adams	"	"	"
3	Ezra Pike jr.	Ira Hill	Harry Hill	"	Charles Carron jr.
	Benjamin Butler 2d	"	"	Joel Allen	Uriah Hazen
5	Benajah Phelps	Bird Landon		Benajah Phelps	Calvin Fletcher
LAMOILLE CO.					
1					
2	Nathan Smilie	"	"	"	"
3	Jonas Stone	Eli Hiads jr.	"	Clark Fisk	"
4	Jonathan Bridge	"	Abner Doty	"	Martin Elmore
5	Abner Flanders	Theophilus W Fitch	Breed Noyes	"	Theophilus W Fitch
6	David Boynton	Solomon Balch	Daniel Dodge	Israel O. Andrews	"
7			Ivory Luce	"	George Town
8	Asa Cole	Luther Bingham	"	"	"
10	B. Chapman	Daniel Moody		Philo G. Camp	Luther Poland
11	*Waterville*	Luther Poland	Amos Willey		Jesse Whitney
12	Ephraim Ladd	"	Jonathan Smith	"	

REPRESENTATIVES, CHIT., ES., FRAN., G. ISLE., LAM. 43

CHITTENDEN 1832	1833	1834	1835	1836
1 M. L. Colton	Almond Whitcomb	"	Samuel B. Kennedy	"
2 T. Follett	Samuel Nichols	John Van Sicklen jr	Nathan B. Haswell	"
3 Myron Powell	"	Noble Lovely	"	Pitt E. Hewitt
4	C. H. Penniman	John W. Weaver	Thomas Brownell	
5 Amasa Bryant	"	Albert Stevens	Thad's R. Fletcher	Albert Stevens
6 Joseph Marsh	Amos Clark	"	Nathaniel Miles	"
7 Selah Ambler	James Ambler jr	Benjamin Allen	"	
8	Thomas Chittenden	"	Erastus Field	"
9 Joseph Clark	"	"	Arthur Hunting	"
10 Edward Jones	John Fay	William Rhodes	John Fay	Artemas Flagg
11	John Tabor	"	Horace Saxton	"
12 Horace Ferris	Sherman Beach	Lewis Higbee	Sherman Beach	"
13 John H. Tower	Henry Oaks	"	William Barney	Reuben Parker
14 John Allen	David Hazelton	John Allen	"	"
15 David French	"	"	Nathan Stearns	Ezbon Sanford
ESSEX CO.				
1 Arad Silver	Martin French	Jeremiah Jourdin		Daniel Holbrook
2 Timothy Corey	William Washburn	Timothy Corey	"	Harvey Coe
3 Benjamin Brown	Haines Schoff	Thomas G. French	"	John Schoff
4 Samuel B. Cooper	Caleb Ingalls	William Morrill	"	Samuel R. Dennett
5 Archi'l Taggard	"		"	Moses Hill
7 Benjamin S. Clark	Joel Bassett	"		Ashley Appleton
8 John Dewey	"	Henry Hall	Reub. W. Freeman	John Dewey
9 Noyes Denison	Abdiel Blodgett			
10 Jonah Brooks jr	Chapin K. Brooks	Stephen Howe	"	"
11 Joseph Gleason	"	Daniel Rich	Gustavus A. Hall	"
FRANKLIN CO.				
1 Harry Reynolds	Silas B. Hazeltine	Thomas Child	Azariah Corse	"
2 Nathan Hamilton	"	M. C. Stone	Mitchell Stone	John S. Webster
3 O. H. Robinson	John Adams	"	Horace Eaton	"
4 J. Bellows	Joseph Larned	Joseph Larned jr	Alonson Webster	Alfred Wheeler
5 Joel Barber jr	Joseph Sowle	Joel Barber jr	Joseph Soule	"
6 Guy Kingsley	Ira Armstrong	"	Guy Kinsley	"
7 Philip S. Gates	"	William Felton	Elisha Bascom	"
8 Solomon Bliss			Alvah Sabin	Elijah Dee
9 Jesse Carpenter	"	Robert L. Paddock	Chas. H. Jenison	"
10 Daniel Barrows	Rufus Hamilton	Samuel Lusk	Richard Smith jr	Rufus Hamilton
11 William Rogers	John Huse	John Huse	"	Alden Sears
12 Levi Hapgood	William Green	Joshua W. Sheldon	"	Fred. W. Judson
13 *John Smith*	*John Smith*	Lawrence Brainard	John Smith	"
14 George Green	"	Lewis Janes	Bradford Scott	"
GRAND ISLE CO.				
1 Giles Harrington	Joseph Sewall	"	John M. Sowles	Geo. W. Goodrich
2 H. C. Boardman	"	Samuel Adams	"	"
3 C. Carron jr	Reuben Pike	"	Minus M'Roberts	William Dawson
4 Joel Allen	Angustus Knight	Benjamin Butler	"	Elijah Haynes
5 Bird Landon	Benajah Phelps	Samuel Boardman	"	
LAMOILLE CO.				
1 Josiah W. Potter	Alva Chaffee			Alva Chaffee
2 N. Smilie	James B. Gillmore	Nathan Smilie	Harry Reynolds	Isaac Griswold
3 Luther H. Brown	Martin Wheelock	Luther H. Brown	Walter Wheelock	"
4 Abner Doty	Martin Elmore	"	"	Jonathan Bridge
5 Joshua Sawyer	"	"	"	"
6 Thos. Waterman	Moses Morse jr	"	"	Levi B. Vilas
7	George Town	N. Butts	Ivory Luce	Elisha A. Town
8 David P. Noyes	"	"	"	Joseph Sears
9 *Sterling*		Asaph Kentfield		
10	Uriah Wilkins	U. Wilkins 2d	Joseph H. Bennett	Elisha Cady
11 Jesse C. Holmes	"	"	"	"
12	Jesse Whitney	Nathaniel Jones		Ephraim Ladd

REPRESENTATIVES, CHIT., ES., FRAN., G. ISLE, LAM.

CHITTENDEN

#	1837	1838	1839	1840	1841
1	John Pineo	"	Joseph Smith	"	Moses L. Colton
2	Harry Bradley	"	Carlos Baxter	"	Wm. A. Griswold
3	P. E. Hewett	Samuel H. Barnes	"	Aaron L. Beach	"
4	T. Brownell	Arad Merrill	"	John Lyon	John T. Webster
5	Byron Stevens	"	Daniel Littlefield	"	Elijah G. Staunton
6	Steph'n Byington	"	Jedediah Boynton	"	Heman R. Smith
7	John Snyder	John Judson	"	Alex'r Ferguson	"
8	Lyman Field	"	Andrew Warner	"	Zebina Bliss
9	George Ayres	"	Daniel H. Onion	"	Samuel Boardman
10	Artemas Flagg	James Humphrey	"	Ransom Jones	"
11	Samuel Fletcher	"	Elnathan W. Spear	"	Robert White
12	Reub. Lockwood	"	Sherman Beach	Silas Isham	"
13	Reuben Parker	Peter Martin	E. F. Hutchins	"	H. A. Narramore
14	William Wood	"	Artemas Allen	"	Daniel Jackson
15	David French	William H. French	Nathaniel Parker	Alson Landon	"

ESSEX CO.

#	1837	1838	1839	1840	1841
1	Martin French	Arad Silver	"	Seldon Burbank	Henry Fuller
2	Harvey Coe	Elias Aldrich	"	"	John Stevens
3	John Schoff	Thomas G. French	Haines Schoff	"	Isaac Richardson
4	William Morrill	Joshua Morrison	"	Alex. H. Morrill	"
5	Moses Hill	David Hibbard 3d	"	"	Nathan J. Graves
7	Ashley Appleton	"	"	Abram W. Rice	"
8	John Dewey	"	R. W. Freemen	Horace Hubbard	John Dewey
9	John Bailey 2d			Mills De Forest	
10	Stephen Howe	Jonah Brooks jr	"	Charles Ames	"
11	Joseph Rich	"	Moody Rich	Samuel D. Merrill	"
12	Victory				Loomis Wells

FRANKLIN CO.

#	1837	1838	1839	1840	1841
1	Silas B. Hazeltine	Azariah Corse	"	"	Charles C. Stone
2	J. S. Webster	Joseph Smith	"	Nathan Hamilton	"
3	Jonas Boutell	"	Samuel Kendall	"	H. N. Barber
4	A. Wheeler	James Bellows	Lyman Hawley	"	J. H. Farnsworth
5	Joab Smith	Joseph Soule	"	Wakefi'ld W. Thorp	"
6	John Kinsley	D. H. Watkins	John Kinsley	"	John Kinsley jr
7	Henry Bowman	"	Jona. H. Hubbbard	"	"
8	Elijah Dee	Alvah Sabin	William R. Warner	Alvah Sabin	Ira Hinckley
9	John Barr	Luther K. Drury	Joseph B. Cutler	"	William Skeels
10	B. W. Fuller	"	"	Asa Wheeler	"
11	Alden Sears	John Huse	"	Nathaniel Sears	Jay Powell
12	Cyrus Keith	J. J. Beardsley	Alfred Keith	Alonson Draper	"
13	John Smith	A. G. Tarlton	Stephen S. Brown	Isaiah Newton	Cornelius Stilphen
14	Geo. W. Foster	Joseph Blake	John S. Foster	"	John Barney

GRAND ISLE CO.

#	1837	1838	1839	1840	1841
1	G. G. Goodrich	Frederick Hazen	"	"	Nathan Kinsley
2	Samuel Adams	"	Lewis Ladd	"	Jabez Ladd
3	William Dawson	Enoch Hall	"	Martin Reynolds	"
4	Benjamin Butler	Horace Wadsworth	"	"	Jedediah Hazen
5	David Corbin	"	"	Hector Adams	"

LAMOILLE CO.

#	1837	1838	1839	1840	1841
1		Moody Shattuck	"	Stickney Hodgkins	R. P. Tillotson
2	Oel Safford	Willard Griswold	"	Nathan Smilie	Joseph Baker
3	Luther H. Brown	Edmond Clark	Clark Fisk	"	Eli Hinds jr
4	Peleg Schofield	Samuel Bailey	Jesse N. Perley	George W. Bailey	Seth Town
5	Levi Edgerton	"	Lucius H. Noyes	"	Almond Boardman
6	Levi B. Vilas	Albert Stone	"	John B. Downer	Asa Andrews
7	Elisha A. Town	Ivory Luce	Joshua Luce	"	James Harris
8	Joseph Sears	David P. Noyes	John Ferrin	"	George Small
9					
10	Elisha Cady	Orion W. Butler	"	Nathan Robinson jr	"
11	Moses Fisk	"	"	"	D. H. Hulburd
12	Isaac Pennock jr	George H. Whitney	Isaac Pennock	Porter Crane	"

REPRESENTATIVES, CHIT., ES., FRAN., G. ISLE, LAM.   45

CHITTENDEN 1842.	1843	1844	1845	1846
1 Moses L. Colton	Jesse Jewell jr.	John Bedee	"	Samuel Morse
2 John V,n Sicklen	Henry B. Stacy	"	Charles Russell	"
BurkeLeavenworth	"	William R. Pease	"	Abner Squire
4 John S: Webster	Joseph E. Rhodes	"	Jacob Rolfe	"
5 ElijahG Staunton	Joseph B. Weed	Alonson Bliss	"	Samuel Thrasher
6 Heman R. Smith	John S. Patrick	"	Lyman Dorwin	"
7 Selah Ambler	"	George Eddy	"	John Snyder
8 Zebina Bliss	Albert Lee	"	David Fish	"
9 Sam'l Boardman	Alb't GWhittemore	"	Benjamin Fairchild	"
Sylvanus Douglass	"	Nathan Fay	"	
11 Robert White	Ira Andrews	"	William Harmon	"
12 R. Lockwood	Silas Isham	William M Sutton		Reuben Lockwood
13 H. A.Narramore	John Story	Frederick Fletcher	"	
14 Daniel Jackson	Noah Tyler	Amos Hobart	Reuben Farnsworh	Amos Hobart
15 NathanielParker				William H. French
ESSEX CO.				
1 Henry Fuller	Jeremiah Wright	Selden Burbank	"	Jeremiah Wright
2 Elias Aldrich	John Stevens	"	Isaac W. Aldrich	
3 George Marshall	"	Royal C. Belknap	"	Joel B. English
4 William Morrill	Mathias Weeks	"	Harvey Hinman	"
5 Nathan J. Graves	David Hibbard jr.	"	Harvey G. Fry	"
6 Easthaven			John Walter jr.	"
7 Henry Hartshorn	"	Jonathan Mathews	Jona'n Mathews jr.	Charles Cheney
8 Allen Gould	"	Oramel Crawford	"	Stephen Ames
9 John Bailey		William C. Simms		Richard Morgan
10 Jonah Brooks jr.	Stephen Howe	"	"	Reuben C. Benton
11 Leonard Walker	"	James Follansbee	"	Moody Rich
12 Loomis Wells	Ransom Hall	"	Harlon Keyes	James Towle
FRANKLIN CO				
1 H. T, Brigham	Holloway tBrigh'm			
2 Joseph Smith	Henry Follett	Elias Babcock	Arza Andrus	Homer E. Royce
3 H N Barber	Bennett Eaton	"	Charles B. Maynard	"
4 Asa S Gove	Joseph Learned	"	Reuben Dewey	"
5 Joseph Soule	Jonathan Sherwood		Bradley Barlow	
Joseph Ellsworth jr	"	Ebenezer Bailey	Lucas Holmes	"
7 Dolphus Dewing	Philip S. Gates	Isaac Warner	Peter Chase	Jona'n H Hubbard
8 Lorenzo Janes	Solomon Bliss	"	Isaac P. Clark	"
9 John Barr	Luther Meigs	Luther K. Drury	Philo F. Drury	"
10 Joshua Clapp	"	John L. Clapp	"	Daniel H. Bailey
11 Jay Powell	Josiah Blaisdell	Alden Sears		Harvey D. Farrar
12 Elihu Goodsill	"	Jacob Wead	Lloyd Mason	
Cornelius Stilphen	John Gates		Orlando Stevens	William Bridges
14 John Barney	"			James Platt
GRAND ISLE CO.				
1 Nathan Kinsley	William A. Ladue	"	Solomon J. Davis	"
2 Jabez Ladd	Bemjamin Griffith	Guy Reynolds	Samuel Adams	Guy Reynolds
Eph'm A Holcomb	"	Elihu Holcomb	"	Hiram Hall
4 Jedediah Hazen	John Martin	"	John Hazen	William Wilsey
5 Wallis Mott	Lorenzo Hall	"	Abner B. Landon	Henry Robinson
LAMOILLE CO.				
1 Jerre Shattuck		A. K. Whittemore	Allen Chaffee	Phinehas Carpenter
2 Joseph Baker	Joseph B. Morgan			Nathan Smilie
3 Eli Hinds jr.	"			
4 George W Bailey	Seth Town		Heman H. Elmore	"
Almond Boardman	Levi Edgerton		Nathaniel P. Keeler	"
6				
7 James Harris	Albert Luce	"	Amander Peterson	"
8 George Small	Moses Terrill	Ver. W Waterman	Vernon W. "	Moses Terrill
Zebina W Bennett	"	Samuel Benson ?	"	Nathaniel Russell
11 O. M'Farland	William Wilber	"	William Page	
12 Ephraim Ladd			Phin's S Benjamin	"

	CHITTENDEN 1847	1848	1849	1850	FIRST TOWN CL'K
1	Heman H. Pinney	"	John D. Stone	Daniel Colton	
2	Wyllys Lyman	David K. Pangborn	"	Henry Leavenworth	Samuel Lane 1787
3	Abner Squier	Elanson H. Wheeler	John Sherman	"	John M'Neil
4	Jacob Rolfe	A. C. Richardson	Andrew J. Merrill		Ira Allen 91
5	S. Thrasher	Warren Williams	Josiah Tuttle	Holman Bates	Elkanah Billings 86
6	Bial Boynton	"	Rufus Patrick	"	Elisha Berben 87
7	John Snyder	William S. Hurlbut	"	George W. Bromley	Chas. Brewster 90
8		Hiram Day	"	Lucius S. Barney	Lewis Chapin 86
9	Hector Adams	A. G. Whittemore	Rhodo's Sanderson	"	Enoch Ashley 88
10		Iddo Green	"		J. Chamberlin 95
11	Elijah Root	Henry S. Morse	"	Elijah Root	Caleb Smith 87
12	Colonel Smith	William M. Sutton	"	Nathan Lockwood	Jared Higbee 1813
13	John Story	Hiram H. Dixon	"	Martin Wires	William Barney 95
14	Jonas Hobart	Hosea B. Bates	Artemas Allen	"	
15	Wm. H. French	Rufus Walston		Roswell B. Fay	Rob't Donnelly 86
	ESSEX CO.				
1	Jeremiah Wright	Julius J. Holbrook	"	Samuel N. Silver	
2	Harris Brown	Elias Aldrich	"	Welcome F. Fisher	Wm. Malada 1832
3	Joel B. English	Elisha Webster	"	John D. French	
4	Stilman Blood	"	William Morrill	William Trask	
5	William B. May	"	Jenneson Carruth	"	Elijah Spafford 94
6	Abraham Powers	"	Horatio L. Walter	Horace B. Root	
7	Charles Cheney	Gershom Carpenter	"	Loomis Wells	Jos. Herrick 1802
8	Stephen Ames	Jonathan Benjamin	John P. Denison	Jonathan Benjamin	
9	Richard Morgan				M. De Forest 1802
10	Stephen Howe	Mitchel Silsby	"	Reuben C. Benton	David Hopkins 81
11	Charles Stevens	Moody Rich	Charles Stevens	Daniel C. Kimball	
12	James Towle	Jonathan Hill	James Towle	"	Loomis Wells 1841
	FRANKLIN CO.				
1	Earl Smilie		Charles C. Stone		
2	Homer E. Royce		Paschal P. Leavens	"	David Nutting 94
3	Caleb E. Brewer	James M. Dean	"	Henry Walbridge	Isaac B. Farrar 98
4	H. E. Hubbell	"	"	"	Thomas Russell 87
5	William Sherman	Albert G. Soule		Bradley Barlow	Edmond Town 90
6	Joseph King	"		Guy Kinsley	
7				Lathrop Marsh	Eben'r Sanders 93
8	Alvah Sabin	"	"	Isaac P. Clark	Reuben Evarts
9	Daniel Watson		Jesse Cutler	Arwin P. Herrick	
10	D. H. Bailey	Bethuel W. Fuller	"	John L. Clapp	Saml. Barnard 1802
11	H. S. Farrar	Silas P. Carpenter	"	Caleb Royce	Charles Wells 99
12	William Green	"	"	Alfred Keith	S. B. Sheldon 91
13	Wm. Bridges	H. R. Beardsley	Benj. B. Newton	William Bridges	
14	H. W. Barney		George Bullard	Isaac B. Bowdish	T. Butterfield 90
	GRAND ISLE CO.				
1	S. J. Davis	Albert C. Butler	"	Job Babcock jr	T. C. Reynolds 92
2	Abel Brown	"	Samuel B. Gordon	William Brown	James Brown 1809
3	Simeon Cooper	"	Dyer Hill	"	Abraham Knapp 90
4	Wm. Wilsey	David Harvey	Asa Mooney	"	Nathan Hutchins
5	Lewis Mott	"	George Landon	"	
	LAMOILLE CO.				
1	A. K. Whittemore	Merritt W. Powers	Moses Phelps		John Brown 1815
2		Jason Crain			John Fassett 85
3	Philo A. Mathews	"	David Randall	"	M. Wentworth 1802
4	Joseph C. Bailey	"	Crispus Shaw	"	Joseph Leach 92
5	John C. Page	"	Carlos Noyes		Jabez Fitch 91
6		Jonathan C. Dodge			
7	Ivory Luce	Noah C. Butts	Annexed to Stowe		J. C. White 1814
8		Julius P. Hall		Julius P. Hall	Comfort Olds 96
9			Arad Baker		John Boyce 1819
10	N. Russell	Luke J. Town	"	Jared D. Wheelock	Joseph Hurlbut 97
11	Jos. D. Freeman	Elias Willey	"	Eliphalet Brush	Moses Fisk 1827
12	Dan G. Pennock	Lyman Titus	"	Samuel Pennock	

REPRESENTATIVES, ORANGE, ORLEANS, RUTLAND

ORANGE CO.	1788	1789	1790	1791
1 Bradford	John Barron	Ashur Chamberlain	"	John Barron
2 Braintree				Isaac Nichols
3 Brookfield		Abel Lyman	Daniel Kingsbury	"
4 Chelsea				Theo's Huntington
5 Corinth		Peter Sleeman	"	"
6 Fairlee	Israel Morey	"	"	Samuel Smith
7 Newbury	Thomas Johnson	"	"	Joshua Bayley
9 Randolph	Asa Edgerton	Israel Converse	"	"
10 Strafford	Alex'er Pennock	"	William Denison	"
11 Thetford	Beriah Loomis	"	Israel Smith	"
13 Tunbridge	Seth Austin	"	"	"
14 Vershire		Andrew Peters	Ebenezer West	Thomas Porter
17 Williamstown	Elijah Paine	"	"	Cornelius Lynde
ORLEANS CO.				
6 Craftsbury				
RUTLAND CO.				
1 Benson	Asahel Smith	"	"	"
2 Brandon	Nathan Daniels		Nathan Daniels	Jacob Simonds
3 Castleton	Eli Cogswell	Noah Lee	Eli Cogswell	"
4 Chittenden		Nathaniel Ladd	"	"
5 Clarendon	Daniel Marsh	Elihu Smith	"	Abel Spencer
6 Danby	Peter Lewis	Lemuel Griffith	Wing Rogers	"
7 Fairhaven	Mathew Lyon	Simeon Smith	Mathew Lyon	"
8 Hubbardton	Nathan Rumsey			James Whelpley
9 Ira	George Sherman	Cephas Carpenter	"	George Sherman
11 Middletown	John Burnham	Ephraim Carr	"	"
13 Mt. Tabor	John Stafford		John Jenkins	John Stafford
14 Pawlet	Lemuel Chipman	"	"	"
16 Pittsford	Noah Hopkins	"	Benjamin Cooley	"
17 Poultney		James Brookins	William Ward	Thomas Ashley
18 Rutland	Samuel Williams	"	"	"
20 Shrewsbury	Ichabod Robinson	"	Nathan Finney	Emanuel Case
21 Sudbury		John Hall	"	"
22 Tinmouth	Ebenezer Marvin		"	John Spafford
23 Wallingford	Joseph Randall	Abraham Jackson	"	Thomas Randall
24 Wells	Abel Merriman	Samuel Lathrop	"	"

COUNCIL OF CENSORS.

1st 1785	2d 1792	3d 1799	4th 1806	5th 1813
In'se Moseley, Pres	Saml. Knight pres	"	Apollos Austin	Nathaniel Chipman
Ebenezer Curtis	Daniel Buck	Benjamin Emmons	Ezra Butler	Isaac Tichenor
Eben'r Walbridge	Orl'do Bridgeman	Elias Buel	Loyal Case	David Edmonds
Benj. Carpenter	Benjamin Burt	Noah Chittenden	Isaac Clark	Daniel Farrand
Stephen Jacob	Elijah Dewey	"	Josiah Fisk	Ebenezer Clark
Jonathan Hunt	Jonas Galusha	David Fay	Thomas Gross	Isaac Bailey
Ebenezer Marvin	Anthony Haswell	Lott Hall	Udney Hay	Nicholas Baylies
Elijah Robinson	Beriah Loomis	Jonathan Hunt	Wm. Hunter	Solomon Bingham
Joseph Marsh	Samuel Mattocks	John Leaverett	S. Huntington	William Hall jr
John Session	Elijah Paine	Nathaniel Niles	John Noyes	Luther Jewett
Lewis Beebe	Isaac Tichenor	Moses Robinson		Charles Marsh
Jonathan Brace	John White	"	Mark Richards	Elijah Strong
M. Townsend Sec	Ros'll Hopkins Sec	John Willard	James Tarbox	Robert Temple

The Council of Censors chosen in 1799, and 1806, did not order any convention to be holden, and no alterations were made in the Constitution by any convention between 1793 and 1829. The convention of 1829 made an amendment in relation to the voting of Foreigners, that made it necessary for them to become naturalized before they were allowed to vote in freemen's meeting. The convention of 1836 changed the old Council of 12, to a Senate of 30. The convention of 1843 made no alteration. The convention of 1850 changed the mode of electing County Court Judges, Sheriffs, High Bailiffs, State's Attornies, Judges of Probate, and Justices of the Peace, giving the appointment of those officers to the people of their several districts.

REPRESENTATIVES, ORANGE, ORLEANS, RUTLAND.

ORANGE CO.

	1792	1793	1794	1795	1796
1	Nathaniel White	John Barron	"	Micah Barron	"
2	Isaac Nichols		Isaac Nichols	John French	"
3	Experience Fisk	Elisha Allis	Experience Fisk	Elisha Allis	"
4	Theo. Huntington	Samuel Badger	"	Joshua Elderkin	Stephen Buchanan
5	Sam'l Hazletine	"	"	"	Mansfield Taplin
6	Samuel Smith	Israel Morey	"	"	"
7	Daniel Farrand	"	Joshua Bailey	Thomas Johnson	Daniel Farrand
9	Josiah Edson	"	"	Abner Weston	Josiah Edson
10	Wm. Denison	"	Herber Gilbert	William Denison	Asahel Chamberlin
11	Israel Smith	Oramel Hinckley	Ashur Chamberlin	"	"
13	Reuben Hatch	"	Nathan'l Kingsbury	Reuben Hatch	Elias Curtis
14	Thomas Porter	"	"	"	"
15	*Washington*		Thaddeus White	Jedediah S. Skinner	Thaddeus White
17	Cornelius Lynde	"	"	Joseph Crane	"

ORLEANS CO.

| 6 | Ebenezer Crafts | " | Joseph Scott | | Samuel C. Crafts |
| 9 | *Greensboro'* | | | Timothy Stanley | Aaron Shepherd |

RUTLAND CO.

1	Asahel Smith	"	Chauncey Smith	Asa Furnam	Chauncey Smith
2	Jacob Simonds	John Mott	"	Hiram Horton	"
3	Eli Cogswell	"	Noah Lee	"	Isaac Clark
4	Nathaniel Ladd		John Bancroft	Nathan Nelson	
5	Abel Spencer	"	Abel Cooper	Theop. Harrington	Abel Spencer
6	Wing Rogers	"	Elihu Sherman	Abel Horton	Daniel Sherman
7	Simeon Smith	Mathew Lyon	"	"	"
8	James Whelpley	"	Nathan Rumsey	James Whelpley	Nathan Rumsey
9	George Sherman	"	"	"	"
11	Jona. Brewster	Nathaniel Wood	Jonathan Brewster	John Burnham	Jonathan Brewster
12	*Mount Holly*	Abraham Jackson	"	Stephen Clark	"
13	John Stafford	"	"	Gideon Tabor	Palmer Stafford
14	Lemuel Chipman	"	Joseph Haskall	Nathaniel Smith	"
15	*Pittsfield*				Thomas Hodgkins
16	Benjamin Cooley	"	Thomas Hammond	Amos Kellogg	"
17	Thomas Ashley	"	Isaac Hosford	"	Jonas Safford
18	Samuel Williams	"	"	"	Nathan Osgood
20	Emanuel Case	"	"	"	"
21	John Hall	Timothy Miller	Amasa Blanchard	"	Timothy Miller
22	Orange Train	Samuel M'Clure	Orange Train	"	"
23	Joseph Randall	Asahel Jackson	Joseph Randall	William Fox	Samuel M'Clure
24	Joseph Button	Samuel Lathrop	Joseph Button	Samuel Lathrop	"

COUNCIL OF CENSORS, CONTINUED.

6th 1820.	7th 1827	8th 1834	9th 1841	10th 1848
Wm. Hunter, Pres.	Asa Aiken, Pres.	Joel Doolittle Pres.	J. D. Farnsworth p	C.K Williams, Pres
Charles Rich	Wm. A. Griswold	Stephen Robinson	Peter Starr	"
Joel Brownson	Daniel Kellogg	Wm. Strong	John A. Pratt	Keyes P. Cool
Joseph Scott	John W. Dana	John Phelps	Wallis Mott	David Crawford
Augustine Clark	Jedediah H. Harris	Nathan el Harmon	Austin Birchard	Salmon F. Dutton
Isaac N. Cushman	Obadiah Noble jr.	Joseph Reed	Martin C. Deming	William Hebard
William Nutting	William Gates	Alvin Foote	Luther Carpenter	Henry F. Janes
John Phelps	William Howe	Robert Harvey	Gordon Newell	James Bell
Joel Pratt	Bates Turner	E. H. Starkweather	Heman Allen	Augustus Burt
Amos Thompson	Samuel S. Phelps	Joseph Smith	Alvah H. French	Ira H. Allen
Asa Aldis	Leonard Sargeant	David Hibbard jr	Ephraim Paddock	Henry Stowell
Jedediah Hyde	Joel Allen	Samuel W. Porter	David Hibbard jr	John Dewey
Joshua Y. Vail Sec.	E. P. Walton, Sec.	William Hebard S	Hez. H. Reed Sec.	John N. Pomeroy S.

REPRESENTATIVES, ORANGE, ORLEANS, RUTLAND.

ORANGE CO 1797	1798	1799.	1800	1801
1 Micah Barron	Andrew B. Peters	"	William Simpson	Andrew B. Peters
2 John French	Isaac Nichols	John Hutchinson	Isaac Nichols jr.	John Hutchinson
3 Elisha Allis	"	Daniel Kingsbury	"	Nathaniel Wheatley
4 Reuben Hatch	"	Theop. Huntington	"	Reuben Hatch
5 Mansfield Taplin	Samuel Hazletine	Mansfield Taplin	Samuel Hazletine	Mansfield Taplin
6 Israel Morey	Samuel Smith	"	Nathaniel Niles	"
7 Thomas Johnson	Daniel Farrand	Thomas Johnson	"	"
8 *Orange*	Ezra Goodell	"	Thomas S. Paine	Ezra Goodell
9 James Tarbox	Aaron Storrs	"	James Tarbox	"
Asahel Chamberlin	Benjamin Preston	"	"	"
11 Oramel Hinckley	Israel Smith	"	J. P. Buckingham	Elijah Hammond
12 *Topsham*				William Thompson
13 James Tyler	"		Elias Curtis	
14		Thomas Porter	"	Asa Smith
15 Elisha Smith	Thaddeus White	Elisha Smith	Stephen Strong	Thaddeus White
17 Joseph Crane	Jonathan Fisk	"	"	"
ORLEANS CO.				
2 *Barton*				
3 *Brownington*		Elijah Strong	"	"
6 Joseph Scott	"	"	Samuel C, Crafts	"
7 *Derby*	Timothy Hinman	John Ellsworth	"	"
9 Timothy Stanley	"		Timothy Stanley	"
15 *Newport*			Luther Chapin	"
17 *Troy*				
18 *Westfield*				
RUTLAND CO.				
1 Chauncey Smith	Simeon Goodrich	"	Reuben Nash	Chauncey Smith
2 Hiram Horton	"	"	Benajah Douglass	"
3 Isaac Clark	"	"	Samuel Shaw	"
4 John Cowee	"	"	"	"
5 *Abel Spencer*	Theoph. Harrington	"	"	"
6 Daniel Sherman	Abel Horton	"	Abel Norton	Edward Vail
7 Simeon Smith	James Witherill	"	"	"
8 Theophilas Flagg	Nathan Rumsey	Theophilas Flagg	"	"
9 George Sherman	Cephas Carpenter	"	John Anderson	"
11 John Burnham	"	Nathaniel Wood jr.	"	Nathaniel Wood
12 Stephen Clark	Abraham Jackson	Stephen Clark	Samuel Shaw	Stephen Clark
13 John Moseley	Gideon Tabor	"	"	"
14	Gideon Adams	"	"	"
15		Thomas Hodgkins	"	"
16 Benjamin Cooley	Amos Kellogg	Thomas Hammond	"	"
17 William Ward	"	"	Thomas Ashley	"
18 Israel Smith	Samuel Williams	"	Jonathan Wells	Darius Chipman
19	John Anthony	"	"	"
20 Emanuel Case	William Marsh	"	"	"
21 Timothy Miller	"	"	"	"
22 Orange Train		"	"	"
23 William Fox	Samuel M'Clure	"	"	"
24 Samuel Lathrop	Simon Francis	"	"	"

HON. GAMALIEL PAINTER.

Came into Middlebury, from Salisbury, Conn., in company with John Chipman, from the same place, early in the year 1773, with a view of making a permanent settlement. Before they arrived, a Mr. Benjamin Smalley had come into town with his family for the same object, and built a small house, the first erected in town. They settled near together in the south west corner of the town. Chipman had commenced a clearing of six or eight acres in 1766 and abandoned it, as no one lived within many miles of him. When he returned he settled on the same lot that he first began upon, and where Jonathan Seeley now resides. Painter settled near a mile south of him on the south line of the town, as the lines are now established, and Smalley about half a mile west of Chipman. Thus the settlement continued to increase till the ravages of the war caused them all to abandon their homes in June, 1776, except Benjamin Smalley and a Mr. Daniel Foot, and they followed in September after. After the close of the war, in 1783, many of those who had left in 1776, with others returned to the town, and became permanent settlers. Thompson's Vermont, does not inform us whether Painter or Chipman returned or not. Gamaliel Painter and John Chipman re-

	1802	1803	1804	1805	1806
ORANGE CO.					
1	Daniel Kimball	Andrew B. Peters	"	Arad Stebbins	Daniel Kimball
2	John Hutchinson	"	"	Lyman Kidder	John Hutchinson
3	Nath'l Wheatley	"	"	"	"
4	Theo. Huntington	Josiah Dana	Elihu Hyde	Theop. Huntington	Josiah Dana
5	Samuel Hazletine	"	Daniel Cook	Joshua Tenney	"
6	Nathaniel Niles	Elisha Thayer	"	"	"
7	Joshua Bailey	"	"	Isaac Bayley	James Spear
8	Thomas S. Paine	John Stacy	"	David Rising	John Stacy
9	Abner Weston	James Tarbox	"	Dudley Chase	"
	Asahel Chamberlin	"	"	"	"
11	Elij'h Hammond	"	J. P. Buckingham	"	William Childs
12	Wm. Thompson	H.E.G. M'Laughlin	"	"	"
13	Seth Paine	"	John Riddall	Nathaniel King	"
14	Thomas Porter	"	"	"	"
15	Daniel Peaslee	"	"	"	"
17	Jonathan Fisk	"	"	"	"
ORLEANS CO.					
2	Jonathan Allyn	"	"	Joseph Owen	"
3	William Baxter	Elijah Strong	"	Luke Gilbert	William Baxter
4	*Charleston*				
5	*Coventry*	Joseph Marsh	"	John Ide jr.	
6	Daniel Davison	Samuel C. Crafts	Royal Corbin	Samuel C. Crafts	Royal Corbin
7	Timothy Hinman	"	"	"	"
8	*Glover*	Ralph Parker	"	"	"
9	Timothy Stanley	"	"	"	John Ellsworth
10	*Holland*				Eber Robinson
11	*Irasburgh*	"	Caleb Leach	"	"
15	Luther Chapin		"		
17	Alpheus Moore	Stephen Underhill	"	"	Josiah Lyon
18	Jesse Olds	"	Anthony Burgess	"	Asa Hitchcock
RUTLAND CO.					
1	Chauncey Smith	Reuben Nash	Chauncey Smith	"	"
2	Benajah Douglass	"	Uriah Horton	Penuel Childs	"
3	Samuel Shaw	"	"	"	"
4	John Cowee	"	"	"	"
5	Theo. Harrington	Theoph's Harrington	Daniel Dyer	"	James Harrington
6	Edward Vail	"	Abel Horton	John H. Andrus	"
7	James Witherill	Oliver Church	Isaac Cutler	"	Oliver Church
8	Theophilas Flagg	"	Elisha Walker	"	"
9	John Anderson	"	"	Preserved Fish	"
10	*Mendon*				
11	Nathaniel Wood	Nathaniel Wood jr.	John Burnham	Dyer Leffingwell	"
12	John Shaw	Jedediah Hammond	"	"	"
13	Gideon Baker	Gideon Tabor	"	"	"
14	Gideon Adams	John Sargeants	Ephraim Fitch	"	"
15	Isaac Eddy	"	"	"	Zebedee Sprout
	Thomas Hammond	Caleb Hendee jr.	"	Thomas Hammond	Caleb Hendee jr.
	Tim'y Cruttenden	"	Amos Thompson	"	"
18	*Abel Spencer*	Abel Spencer	Ezekiel Porter	"	Abel Spencer
19	*Sherburne*		John Fuller	"	"
20	William Marsh	"	"	David Holden	"
21	Timothy Miller	"	"	Joseph Warner	"
22	Zenas Allen	"	Ziba Hamilton	Nathaniel Chipman	"
23	Samuel M'Clure	Lent Ives	"	William Fox	"
24	Simon Francis		Andrew Clark	Simon Francis	Andrew Clark
0	*Philadelphia*				Elijah Segar

turned in 1784, and took possession of their old lots, where Chipman remained till his death in a good old age. Painter removed into the village in 1787 and built a saw mill and grist mill on the east side of the creek on the site of Wood's grist mill and the cotton factory. Judge Painter represented the town in 1786, 7, 8, 9, 90, 1, 2, 3, 6, 1801, 3, 5, 9 and 10 and was elected Councillor in 1813 and 14. He was a Judge of the County Court in 1785, 7, 8, 9, 90, 1, 2, 3 and 5, and Sheriff in 1786. He was a delegate to the Dorset Convention in 1777 that declared the independence of Vermont at an adjourned meeting at Westminster.

He was a public spirited man and made many donations for various purposes. He took an ac-

REPRESENTATIVES, ORANGE, ORLEANS, RUTLAND.   51

ORANGE CO. 1807	1808	1809	1810	1811
1 Daniel Kimball	"	"	"	"
2 John Hutchinson		Jonathan Bass	John Hutchinson	"
3 Natha'l Wheatley	"	"	Barnabas Bigelow	"
4 Elisha Hotchkiss	Josiah Dana	"	Benjamin H. Oaks	Elisha Hotchkiss
5 Joshua Tenney	Joseph Ormsbee	Nicholas Hale	William Spencer	"
6 Elisha Thayer	Samuel Smith	Elisha Thayer	"	"
7 James Spear	"	Joshua Bayley		Benjamin Porter
8 John Stacy	"	"	Timothy Thurston	"
9 Dudley Chase	Dudley Chase	Dudley Chase	Dudley Chase	Dudley Chase
10 Asa'l Chamberlin	"	"	Jediah H. Harris	"
11 William Childs	"	"	"	Lyman Fitch
H.E.G M'Laughlin	"	"	"	Samuel Butterfield
13 Nathaniel King	"	"	"	Nath'l Kingsbury jr
14 Asa Smith jr.	"	"	"	"
15 Daniel Peaslee	Jacob Burton	"	"	"
17 Jonathan Fisk	Cornelius Lynde	John Campbell jr.	Jared Kimball	Jonathan Fisk
ORLEANS CO.				
1 Albany	Thomas Cogswell			
2 John Kimball	"	"	Oliver Blodgett	Jonathan Allyn
3 William Baxter	"	"	"	"
4 Abner Allyn	"	Robert H. Hunkins	"	Abner Allyn
5 John Ide jr.	"			
6 Jesse Olds	Royal Corbin	"	"	"
7 Timothy Hinman	"	"	Timothy Hinman	Charles Kingsbury
8 Ralph Parker	"	"	"	"
9 Eli Austin	Timothy Stanley	Eli Austin	"	Timothy Stanley
10				Eleazer B. Wilkins
11 Caleb Leach	"	Reuben Willey	"	"
13 Lowell				
14 Morgan				
15	Amos Sawyer	"		Rufus Stewart
17 Thomas Wallace	"	"	James C. Adams	"
18 Medad Hitchcock	"	"	"	Jonathan Simpson
				Asa Hitchcock
RUTLAND CO.				
1 Reuben Nash	Chauncey Smith	"	Asa Standish	Putnam Gleason
2 Peauel Childs	Joel Green	John Conant	"	John Arnold
3 Samuel Shaw	John Mason	"	David Sanford	Ebenezer Langdon
4 John Cowce	Samuel Cooley	"	"	Thomas Manley
5 James Harrington	Eleazer Flagg	"	Thomas Stewart	"
6 John H. Andrus	"	"	"	"
7 Oliver Church	Salmon Norton	"	Oliver Church	"
8 Elisha Walker	"	"	Gideon Horton	Elisha Walker
9 Preserved Fish	"	"	"	Isaiah Mason
10 Benj'n Farmer	"	"	Philip Perkins	Johnson Richardson
11 John Burnham	Jonas Clark jr.	"	Jacob Burnham	Orson Brewster
12 Stephen Clark	John Crowley	"	"	"
13 Gideon Tabor	"	"	"	"
14 James Leach	"	"		"
15 Nathan Eddy	"	Asa Gaines	Benjamin Fitch	"
16 Caleb Hendee jr	Thomas Hammond	Caleb Hendee jr	"	Thomas Hammond
17 Amos Thompson	"	John Stanley	"	Asahel Pond
18 Abel Spencer	Ezekiel Porter	Charles K. Williams	Chauncey Thrall	Charles K. Williams
19 John Fuller	"		Nathaniel M Fuller	"
20 David Holden	"	"	"	"
21 Joseph Warner	"	"	"	"
22 Nath'l Chipman	"	"	"	Obadiah Noble jr.
23 William Fox	"	"	Eliakim H. Johnson	William Fox
24 Andrew Clark	Samuel Mix	Ira Mix	William Potter	Joseph Button
0			Elijah Segar	

tive part in all the improvements of the village, and to his influence more than any other person, are the friends of Literature indebted for the establishment of the College in Middlebury; and to his generosity are the town indebted, by a free gift of the common on the east side of the creek, and the Congregational Church are under a debt of gratitude to him for the assistance and funds he furnished in erecting their house of worship.

ORANGE CO.	1812	1813	1814	1815	1816
1	D. Kimball	"	John H. Cotton	"	"
2	Lyman Kidder	"	"	William Ford jr	Lyman Kidder
3	Barna Bigelow	Elisha Allis	David Bigelow	"	Noah Paine
4	Elisha Hotchkiss	"	"	Elihu Hyde	Daniel A. A. Buck
5	William Spencer	Nicholas Hale	Daniel Cook	Joseph Ormsby	John B. Corliss
6	Nathanel Niles	"	"	Asa May	Elisha Thayer
7	Benjamin Porter	Asa Tenney	Isaac Bayley	"	Benjamin Porter
8	Luther Carpenter	"	"	Mason Bill	Thaddeus Clapp
9	*Dudley Chase*	James Tarbox	Ezekiel Story	"	William Nutting
10	J. H. Harris	Asah'l Chamberlain	J. H. Harris	Daniel Cobb	"
11	Lyman Fitch	Elijah Hammond	Joseph Reed	"	"
12	Saml Butterfield	Jonathan Jenness	"	Gilman White	"
13	Nathaniel King	"	"	Samuel Austin	"
14	Asa Smith jr	"	"	"	"
15	Stuart Brown	Daniel Peaslee	"	"	Stuart Brown
17		Thomas Howe	Abiel Smith	"	Robert Seaver
ORLEANS CO.					
1	Eli Chamberlain		John Skinner	"	Daniel Skinner
2	Joseph B. Leland	Samuel Works	Ellis Cobb	John Kimball	F. W. Adams
3	William Baxter	"	"	"	"
4	Ebenezer Cole	"			Jonas Warren
5	Peleg Redfield	"	"	"	"
6	Royal Corbin	"	"	Joseph Scott	Royal Corbin
7	Luther Newcomb	William Howe	"	"	"
8	Ralph Parker	"	John Boardman	"	Charles Hardy
9	Timothy Stanley	"	Willard Lincoln	Peleg Hill	"
10	Eber Robinson		Jason Hinman		Parmenas Watson
11	Roger Enos	Nathaniel Killam	Joshua Johnson	John Killam	Samuel Conant
13	Asahel Curtis	"		John Harding	"
14	Rufus Stewart	Ira Leavens	Jotham Cummings	"	"
14	James C. Adams	Amos Sawyer	Martin Adams	Amos Sawyer	Daniel Warner
17	Jona'n Simpson	Thomas Wells	"	"	"
18	Thos. Stoughton	Walter Stone	Medad Hitchcock	"	"
RUTLAND CO.					
1	Chauncey Smith	"	Allen Goodrich	Samuel Howard	Chauncey Smith
2	Joel Green		"	"	Samuel Burnell
3	Eben'r Langdon	Chauncey Langdon	"	Willard Pond	"
4	Thomas Manly	Jonas Wheeler	"	Thomas Manley	Wolcott H. Keeler
5	Thomas Stewart	Seba French	"	David Tinkham	Thomas Stewart
6	John H. Andrus	"	Zoheth Allen	"	John H. Andrus
7	Tilly Gilbert	Ethan Whipple	Tilly Gilbert	James W. Rosman	Thomas Christie
8	Elisha Walker	David Barber	"	"	"
9	John Anderson	"	Isaiah Mason	Math. Anderson 2d	Preserved Fish
10	J. Richardson	Zidon Edson	John Shaw	Rufus Richardson	John Shaw
11	Jacob Burnham	Jonas Clark jr	D, Leffingwell	Jonas Clark jr	"
12	Jed. Hammond	John Crowley	Jedediah Hammond	"	Nathan T. Sprague
13	Gideon Tabor	"	John Sweet	Jonathan Hulett	Gideon Tabor
14	Benjamin Fitch	"	"	"	Innet Hollister
15	Asa Gaines	"	"	"	Erastus Holt
16	Thos. Hammond	Caleb Hendee jr	Wm. Harrington	Caleb Hendee jr	Wm. Harrington
17	Asahel Pond	Amos Thompson	"	John Stanley	Amos Thompson
18	James D. Butler	"	Charles K. Williams	"	William Denison
19	R. Estabrooks	Josiah Wood jr	"	Nathl. M. Fuller	"
20	Philo'en Adams	"	David Holden	Bart. Chadwick	"
21	Joseph Warner	"	"	"	"
22	O. Noble, jr	Thomas Porter jr	"	Obadiah Noble jr	"
23	William Fox	"	E. H. Johnson	William Fox	"
24	Aaron Mosher	"	"	Shubael Lamb	Aaron Mosher
	Wolcott H. Keeler		Howard Mitchell	" annexed to	Goshen & Chit'n

He had buried two wives, and his third one survived him a few years. He had two sons by his first wife, and one daughter by his second, all of which were taken from him by death before his decease; his youngest son was drowned in June, 1797, aged 24. The Judge died May 21, 1819, leaving no heirs. In his will he left a few legacies to his wife, and faithful servants, and the remainder from 10 to $15,000 to Middlebury College.

REPRESENTATIVES, ORANGE, ORLEANS, RUTLAND.

ORANGE CO. 1817	1818	1819	1820	1821
1 John H. Cotton	"	John Picket	"	"
2 John Hutchinson	William Ford jr.	Lyman Kidder	"	William Ford jr.
3 Freder'k Griswold	"	Moses Hubbard jr.	"	"
4 Daniel A. A Buck	"	"	*Daniel A. A. Buck*	*Daniel A. A. Buck*
5 Peter Eaton	"	"	William Spencer	"
6 Elisha Thayer	"	Solomon Mann	"	Elisha Thayer
7 Simeon Stevens jr	Asa Tenney	Simeon Stevens jr.	James Spear	Levi Rogers
8 Thaddeus Clapp	Luther Carpenter	"	"	Daniel Nelson
9 William Nutting	"	Timothy Baylies	"	Abner Weston
10 Daniel Cobb	Jedediah H. Harris	"	"	"
11 Beriah Loomis	Joseph Reed	"	Lyman Fitch	"
Jonathan Jenness	"	"	"	"
13 Eli Austin	Samuel Austin	"	"	Samuel Austin
14 Asa Smith jr.	Simeon Bacon	"	"	Nathaniel Jones jr.
15 Stuart Brown	Jacob Burton	Stuart Brown	"	
17 Robert Seaver	Enoch Burnham	Robert Seaver	Jonathan Fisk	Abiel Smith
ORLEANS CO.				
1 William Rowell	"	Simeon Spaulding	William Rowell	"
2 John Kimball	Ellis Cobb	John Kimball	Ellis Cobb	"
3 William Baxter	"	William Baxter	"	"
4 Jonas Warren	"			
5 Peleg Redfield	"	"	"	John Ide
6 Joseph Scott	William Scott	"	Hiram Mason	Augustus Young
7 William Howe	"	"	Benjamin Hinman	"
8 Charles Hardy	"	"		"
9 Levi Stevens	Peleg Hill	"	Levi Stevens	Stephen Sherman
10 Parmen's Watson				
11 Joshua Johnson	Ira H. Allen	"	"	Roger Enos
13 John Harding	Asahel Curtis		John Harding	
14	Jotham Cummings			Ira Leavens
15 Daniel Warner	"		"	Josiah Rawson
17		Samuel H. Hovey	Thomas Wells	George Flint
18 Walter Stone	James Brown	Jairus Stebbins	James Brown	Jairus Stebbins
RUTLAND CO.				
1	Chauncey Smith	"	Reuben Nash	"
2 Samuel Burnell	John Conant	Samuel Burnell	Samuel Buel	John Conant
Chauncey Langdon	John Mason	Chauncey Langdon	"	Reuben Moulton
4 Thomas Manley	Howard Mitchell	Jonas Wheeler	Wolcott H. Keeler	"
5 Horatio Beal		Henry Hodges	"	"
6 William Hitt	Zoheth Allen	William Hitt	"	James M'Daniels
7 Moses Colton	Erastus Coleman	Oliver Church	John P. Colburn	"
8 Samuel Cheaver	"	"	"	"
9 Preserved Fish	"		"	"
10 William Sabin		Elisha Estabrooks	"	"
11 Jonas Clark	"	"	"	"
Nathan T. Sprague	Abel Bishop	"	"	"
13 Gideon Tabor	"		Caleb Buffum	Gideon Tabor
14 Innet Hollister	"	Phinehas Strong	"	Benjamin Fitch
15 Erastus Holt	"	"	"	"
16 Caleb Hendee jr.	Gordon Newell	"	Caleb Hendee jr.	"
17 Joel Beaman	"	Asahel Pond	"	Harvey D. Smith
18 Moses Strong	Chauncey Thrall	Robert Pierpoint	Charles K Williams	
19 -	Josiah Wood jr.			Josiah Wood jr.
20 Bart. Chadwick	John White	"	Elijah Holden	David Holden
21 Joseph Warner	Barnard Ketcham		"	"
22 Elias Post	Eastus Barker	Elias Post	Obadiah Noble jr.	Wait Rathbone
23 William Fox	"	Eliakim H. Johnson	"	William Fox
24 Shubael Lamb	Ansel Goodspeed	"	"	"

Judge Painter was born at New Haven, Conn., May 22d, 1743. He was a Captain in the Revolutionary war, and a member of the Convention that formed the present Constitution at Windsor, July 4th, 1793.

REPRESENTATIVES, ORANGE, ORLEANS, RUTLAND.

ORANGE CO.	1822	1823	1824	1825	1826
1	Geo. W. Prichard	John Picket	Jesse Merrill 2d	"	"
2	John Hutchinson	William Ford jr	John Hutchinson	William Ford	Lyman Kidder
3	Fred. Griswold	Abel Lyman	"	John Whealey	"
4	*Dan'l A. A. Buck*	H.E G.M'Laughlin	Benjamin Rolfe	Daniel A. A. Buck	Daniel A. A. Buck
5	Richard Smith	"	"	"	William Spencer
6	Solomon Mann	Jesse Stodard	Moulton Morey	"	Phinehas Bailey
7	Charles Johnson	John L. Woods	"	"	Charles Johnson
8	Luther Carpenter	"	"	"	"
9	Shubael Converse	Dudley Chase	"	Lebbeus Edgerton	"
10	Martin Barrett	"	Daniel Cobb	"	Nathan Young
11	Joseph Reed	Lyman Fitch	"	"	Israel H. Smith
12	Jona'n Jenness	"	James Petrie	"	Jonathan Jenness
13	Samuel Austin	Nathaniel King	Samuel Austin	"	James Hutchinson
14	Nath'l Jones jr	"	"	George W. Maltby	"
15	Stuart Brown	Jacob Bliss	Stuart Brown	William Kimball	Daniel Peaslee
16	*West Fairlee*	Samuel Graves	"	Elisha Thayer	"
17	Robert Seaver	Bradford Newcomb	Darius Pride	Bradford Newcomb	Darius Pride
ORLEANS CO.					
1	E. Chamberlain jr	William Rowell	Eli Chamberlain	J. B. Chamberlain	"
2	Ellis Cobb		Saml. Chamberlain	John Kimball	Fred. W. Adams
3			William Baxter	Jasper Robinson	William Baxter
4				Jonas Allen	"
5	John Ide	"	"	"	"
6	Agustus Young	"		Joseph Scott	Agustus Young
7		Benjamin Hinman	"	David M. Camp	"
8	John Boardman	Charles Hardy	"	"	John Boardman
9	Stephen Sherman	"	"	"	Samuel Hill
10		Jason Hinman		Jason Hinman	
11	Ira H. Allen	"	Roger Enos	Joshua Johnson	Ira H. Allen
13	John Harding		John Harding	"	"
14	Ira Leavens				
15	Josiah Rawson			Nathaniel Daggett	Samuel Warner
16	*Salem*				
17	Reub. Washburn	Samuel H. Hovey	"	"	
18	Jairus Stebbins	"	"	Thomas Hitchcock	Jairus Stebbens
RUTLAND CO.					
1	John Kellogg	Samuel Howard	John Kellogg	"	Isaac Norton
2	Asahel June	Daniel Pomeroy	"	"	"
3	Chau'y Langdon	Reuben Moulton	"	"	"
4	James Wheeler	Wolcott H. Keeler	"	Warren Barnard	Wolcott H. Keeler
5	Henry Hodges	Lindsey Round	Silas W. Hodges	"	Thomas Stewart
6	James M'Daniels	Rufus Bucklin jr	James M'Daniels	David Young	"
7	Artemas Wyman	John P. Colburn	"	"	George Warren
8	Seth Wallace	"	"	David Barber	"
9	Daniel Graves	Josiah Mason	Preserved Fish	"	Leonard Mason
10	E. Estabrooks	Rufus Richardson	Nathan Fisher	"	"
11	Jonas Clark	David G. M'Clure	"	Jonas Clark	"
12	N. T. Sprague	"	"	"	Isaac Dickerman
13	Gideon Tabor				
14	Benjamin Fitch	Oliver Hanks	"	"	"
15	Warner Durkee	"	Erastus Holt	"	Warren Durkee
16	Caleb Hendee jr	Jonathan Warner	"	"	Lyman Granger
17	Harvey D. Smith	John Ransom	"	Harris Hosford	"
18	Edm'd Douglass	Robert Pierpoint	Robert Temple	"	"
19	Albro Anthony	Josiah Wood	.	Josiah Wood	"
20	Zidon Edson	Benj. Needham jr	"	Zidon Edson	"
21	Barn'd Ketchum	"	Mason Knapen	Joseph Warner	Barnard Ketchum
22	Wait Rathbone	Eastus Barker	Theophilus Clark	"	Paine Gilbert
23	John Fox	"	"	Eliakim H. Johnson	Alexander Miller
24	Jared Francis	"	Seth Blosson	"	Shubael Lamb
25	*Westhaven*	Josiah Bascomb	Artemas Wyman	Oliver Hitchcock	Artemas Wyman

GRANGE CO 1827	1828	1829	1830	1831
George W Pritchord	Jesse Merrill 2d	Joseph Clark jr.	Jesse Merrill 2d.	John B. Pickett
2 R. Huntington	William Ford	Jonathan Bass	Seth Riford	"
Frederick Griswold	"	John Wheatley	Frederick Griswold	Nathaniel Wheatley
H.E.G.M'Laughlin	Harry Hale	Daniel A. A. Buck	Daniel A. A. Buck	H.E.G M'Laughlin
5 William Spencer	Stephen Eaton	"	Winthrop Green	"
6 Phinehas Bailey	"	"	Isaac Farrington	"
7 Timothy Shedd	"	Peter Burbank	"	"
8 Luther Carpenter	"	Nathan Foster	Luther S. Burnham	Nathan Foster
9 Jacob K. Parish	"	Belcher Salisbury	"	Martin Flint
10 Nathan Young	Martin Barrett	Eleazer Baldwin	Martin Barrett	"
11 Israel H. Smith	Simeon Short	"	"	"
12 Jonathan Jenness	"	James Petrie	"	Jonathan Jenness
James Hutchinson	Eli Austin	Nathaniel King	"	Elijah Dickerman
Nathaniel Jones jr.	George W. Maltby	Simeon Bacon	"	"
15 Asa Burton	"	"	"	"
16 Isaac Lyon	"	Jabez Lamphear	"	"
17 Darius Pride	Abijah White	"	Darius Pride	Jedediah Smith
ORLEANS CO				
1 William Rowell	Dyer Bill	"	John Fairman	"
2 Ellis Cobb	John Kimball	"	Ellis Cobb	John Kimball
3 Jasper Robinson	"	George C.West	"	Jasper Robinson
4 Jonas Allyn	Elisha Bingham	"	Tyler Bingham	"
5 John Ide	Calvin Harmon	Philip Flanders	Calvin Harmon	Isaac Parker
6 Hiram Mason	Augustus Young	"	"	Royal Corbin
7 Benjamin Hinman	Charles Kingsbury	"	Benjamin Hinman	Jacob Bates
8 John Boardman		Charles Hardy	"	"
9 Samuel Hill	"	Marvin Grow	"	Samuel Hill
Truman Fairchild jr	"	Isaiah Emerson	"	Ezra Hinman
11 Ira H. Allen	E. H. Starkweather	"	"	"
12 Jay	Madison Keith	"	"	Ebenezer Sanborn
13 John Harding	William Colby	Thomas Proctor	Henry Smith	"
14 Ira Leavens	John Harding			Ira Leavens
15 Israel H. Scott	Elias Eastman	Samuel Warner	"	"
16 Ephraim Blake	Noyes Hopkinson	Josiah Lyon	"	"
17 Frederick Fuller	Samuel H. Hovey	Frederick Fuller	"	"
18 Jairus Stebbins		Silas Lamb		
RUTLAND CO.				
1 John Kellogg	"	"	"	"
Mathew w. Birchard	"	Edward Jackson	John A. Conaut	"
3 Reuben Moulton	"			Selah H. Merrill
Wolcott H. Keeler	Jonas Wheeler	"	"	John Woodbury
5 Oziel H. Round	"	Frederick Button	Linsey Round	Lewis Walker
6 David Young	James M'Daniels	Ira Edmonds		Seeley Vail
7 John P. Coburn	Ira Leonard	"	John Jonas	Wm. C. Kittredge
8 Samuel Cheever	"	Ira Jennings	"	"
9 Leonard Mason	Joshua Harrington	"	Whipple Martin	"
10 Nathaniel Fisher	Amos Robinson	Nathan Fisher	Edward Mussy	"
Orson Brewster	Allen Vail	"	Eliakim Paul	"
12 Isaac Dickerman	"	"	Nathan T. Sprague	Marvel Johnson
	Samuel Baldwin jr			Silas Hathern
14 Return Strong	"	"	Milton Brown	"
15 Erastus Holt	William R Blossom	"	"	Ira Parsons
16 Lyman Granger	Germon Hammond	Jirah Barlow	"	"
17 Almon Warner	"	Daniel Mallary	Joel Beaman	"
18 Geo. T. Hodges	"	"	Rodney C. Royce	"
19 Josiah Wood	R. Eastabrooks jr.	"	Rich'd Eastabrooks	R. Eastabrooks jr
20 Elijah Holden	John Buckmaster	"	"	"
Barnard Ketchum	Joseph Warner	"	"	"
22 Paine Gilbert	Thomas Porter jr	"	Obadiah Noble	Noah W. Sawyer
23 Amos Bucklin	"	"	Thomas Hulett	"
24 Seth Blossom	"	Ansel Goodspeed	Seth Blossom	William Potter jr.
25 Artemas Wyman	Erastus Coleman	Artemas Wyman	David B Phippeney	"

56 REPRESENTATIVES, ORANGE, ORLEANS, RUTLAND.

ORANGE CO. 1832	1833	1834	1835	1836
1 Jesse Merrill 2d	"	Arad Stebbins	"	"
2 Daniel Wait jr	"	Nathan Harwood	"	Isaac Nichols
3 John Wheatly	Thomas Kingsbury	"	Justis Edson	John W. Hopkins
4 Harry Hale	Daniel A. A. Buck	"	"	Harry Hale
5 Winthrop Green	"	Plant Sawyer	William Spencer	George Sleeper
6	Phinehas Bailey		Stephen Jenkins	
7 A. B. W. Tenney	"	"		Simon Stevens jr
8 Nathan Foster	Luther S.Burnham	"	"	Luther Carpenter
9 Martin Flint	"	"	William Hebard	Sylvanus Blodgett
10 Lyman Benson	Eleazer Baldwin	Albigence Pierce	"	Royal Hatch
11 Israel H. Smith	Presbury West jr	J. C. Hammond	Lyman Fitch	"
12 JonathanJenness	"	James Petrie	Samuel Bachelder	"
13 Samuel Austin	Elijah Dickerman	Ebenezer Hackett	"	Philip Farnam
14 RufusBlanchard	"	Simeon Bacon	Stephen F. Spencer	Simeon Bacon
15 Wm.Huntington	Stephen Burton	"	Wm. Huntington	John Colby
16 Wm.L Churchill	Phinehas Kimball	"	"	George May
17 Jedediah Smith	Enoch Howe	"	William S. Beckett	John Poor
ORLEANS CO.				
1 Jabez Page	"	John N. Hight	Rufus B. Hovey	John N. Hight
2 Harry Baxter	"	Asa Kimball	Richard Newton	"
3 George C. West	Elijah G. Strong	Gilbert Gross	"	Alex. L. Twilight
4 Silas Gaskill	"	Ebenezer Cole	"	Elisha Bingham
5 Charles Storey	Isaac Parker	Charles Storey	Holland Thrasher	Argulas Harmon
6 Agustus Young	Joseph Scott jr		Joseph Scott jr	William J.Hastings
7 Jacob Bates	Orin Newcomb	David M. Camp	"	Lemuel Richmond
8 Charles Hardy	John Crane	Charles Hardy	"	Joseph H. Dwinnell
9 Ezekiel Rand	George A. Morey	"	Stephen Sherman	Willard Lincoln
10 Isaiah Emerson	Joshua French			Jason Hinman
11 Joseph Wiggins	Moody B. Kimball	"	Ira H. Allen	Sabin Killam
12	Ebenezer Sanborn			Ebenezer Sanborn
13 John Harding	Silas Lamb			
14	John Bartlett	"	Shubael Farr	John Bartlett
15 Samuel Warner	Asa B. Moore	Jonathan Frost	"	Asa B. Moore
16 Nathaniel Cobb		Noyes Hopkinson		
17 SamuelH.Hovey	Ezra Johnson		Curtis Phelps	Frederick Fuller
18 Guy Stoughton	Chester Coburn			
19 *Westmore*	John C. Page	"	"	David Wilson
RUTLAND CO.				
1 Joseph Bascomb	"	Rowland P. Cooley	"	Milo W. Smith
2 C. W. Conant	"	"	"	"
3 Selah H. Merrill	Nehemiah Hoyt	John Meacham		
4 Jonas Wheeler	John Woodbury	Jonas Wheeler	Thomas J. Leonard	"
5 Lewis Walker	Daniel S. Ewings	A. F. Campbell	Chapman Giddings	Jonathan W. Shaw
6 Benjamin Barnes	"	Daniel Bartlett	"	Rufus Bucklin jr
7 Tilly Gilbert	Wm. C. Kittredge	Ira Leonard	Barnabas Ellis	"
8 Ira Jennings	"	"	David Barber	"
9 Whipple Martin	John Mason	"	P. W. Wilkinson	"
10 Edward Mussey	"	"	Timothy Gibson	Edward Mussey
11 Merritt Clark	"	Orson Clark	"	Eliakim Paul
12 Marvel Johnson	"	David French	"	Rufus Crowley
13 Silas Hathern	Gsdeon S. Tabor			
14 Milton Brown	Elisha Allen	"	Sheldon Edgerton	"
15 Ira Parsons	Levi Rix	"	Eleazer B.Rockwell	
16			German F. Hendee	Samuel H. Kellogg
17 W. L. Farnham	"	Almon Warner	"	Joel Beaman
18 RodneyC.Royce	Solomon Foote	Ambrose L. Brown	"	Solomon Foote
19 Silas Colton	"		"	R. Eastabrooks jr
20 JohnBuckmaster	"	"	Harry Holden	John Buckmaster
21 John C. Sawyer	James K. Hyde	"	"	Isaac Ketchum 1st
22 Paine Gilbert	Noah W. Sawyer	Eliada Crampton	"	Jeffrey Ballard
23 Amos Bucklin	Saml. M. Edgerton	"	Amos Bucklin	Howard Harris
24 Caleb Monroe	William Potter jr	Joseph Parks	"	"
25 Orin Church	Willard Hitchcock	John Offensend	"	Horace Adams

REPRESENTATIVES, ORANGE, ORLEANS, RUTLAND. 57

ORANGE CO. 1837	1838	1839	1840	1841
1 J. W, D Parker	Arad Stebbins	J. W. D. Parker	Adams Preston	Alvan Taylor
2 Elijah Flint	Charles Brackett	John Waite	Charles Brackett	Jabez Smith
	Abel Bigelow	"	A Cleavland jr.	
4 Thomas Winslow	"	"	Levi B. Vilas	"
5 George Sleeper	"	Richard Smith	David Dearborn	"
6 Samuel Moore	"	Alexan'r H Gilmore	"	Zebulon Norris
7 Lincoln Stevens jr	Moody Chamberlin	A. B, W. Tenney	"	"
Louis F, Peabody	Carlos Carpenter	Louis F. Peabody	Carlos Carpenter	Horace Fifield
9 Sylvanus Blodgett	Seth Washburn	Loren Griswold	William Hebard	"
10 Royal Hatch	William Sanborn	"	"	Daniel Cobb
11 Henry Gillett	"	Morrill J. Walker	"	Harry H. Niles
12 David Corliss	"	James F. George	"	Charles Grow
Charles B. Chandler	"	John E, Dodge	Joseph Foster	"
14 Simeon Bacon	"	Rufus Blanchard	"	S T. Wiggins
15 John Colby	"	Philip Sargeant	John Colby	John Emery
16 George May	Stephen Thomas	"	David Robinson	George May
William S. Beckett	Robbins Dinsmore	William S, Beckett	Enoch Howe	
ORLEANS CO.				
1 Rufus B. Hovey	Wells Allen	"	Simeon S. Hovey	"
2 Amos C. Robinson	"	Horace Pierce	Harry Baxter	Horace Pierce
3 Jeremiah Huntoon	"	Elijah G. Strong	Elisha White	"
4 Elisha Bingham	Silas Gilkey	Stephen Cole	Ebenezer Cole	Stephen Cole
5 Argalus Harmon	Samuel S. Kendall	Elijah Cleveland	"	"
William J Hastings	"	George H. Cook	"	Daniel Dustin
7 Lemuel Richmond	Charles Kingsbury	"	John G. Chandler	"
8 Charles Hardy	Willard Leonard	Joseph H. Dwinnell	Willard Leonard	William H. Martin
9 George H. Page	"	L. F. Waterman	George H. Page	"
10 Jason Hinman	"	Ezra Hinman	"	"
11 Ira H. Allen	"	Timothy P Redfield	Ira H. Allen	Charles W Prentiss
	George Flint	Walter Charlton	"	"
13 Herod Farnum	Sabin Scott	"	"	Benjamin F Pickett
Jotham Cummings	Ira Leavens	John Bartlett	Cyrus Hemengway	"
15 Asa B. Moore	Sumner Frost	"	William Moon	"
Noyes Hopkinson	Samuel Blake	"	Jos.ah Lyon	"
Horace A. Warner	David H. Bard	"	"	Joseph Burnham
	Jere Hodgkins	"	Nathan H. Downs	"
19 David Wilson	Peter Gilman	"	Ethan Blodgett	Peter Gilman
RUTLAND CO.				
1 William Field	"	Isaac Norton	Horace King	"
Franklin Farrington	"	Edward Jackson	Nathan T. Sprague	"
3 Hyde Westover	"	Erastus Higley	"	William Sanford
4 Capen Leonard jr	"	"	"	"
5 Enoch Smith	Joseph A. Hays	"	"	Enoch Smith
6 Rufus Bucklin jr	"	Timothy Reed	"	Ira Edmonds
Wm. C. Kittredge	Adams Dutton	Ira Leonard	Joseph Sheldon jr.	"
8 Seth St John	"	Chaun'y S. Rumsey	"	James Flagg
9 Leonard Mason	"	Oriel H. Round	"	Russel Fish
10 Timothy Gibson	James K. Pearson	"	Timothy Gibson	Samuel Caldwell
11 Eliakim Paul	Jonathan Morgan	Merritt Clark	Eliakim Paul	"
12 Rufus Crowley	Chauncey Cook	"	John Bryant	"
	Caleb Buffam	"	"	"
14 Joshua Potter	David Blakeley	"	Horace Wilcox	"
Eleazer B Rockwell	Amos Holt	"	Levi Rix	Daniel Bowe
Samuel H. Kellogg	"	"	Henry Simonds	"
17 W. L. Farnham	Amon Bailey	"	Joel Beaman	William P. Noyes
18 Solomon Foot	Solomon Foot	George T. Hodges	"	Francis Slason
19 Silas Colton	"	George W. Topliff	"	So'omon W Adams
20 Harry Holden	Elisha Johnson jr.	"	John Buckmaster	Benja'n T Needham
Isaac Ketchum 1st	John C. Sawyer	"	James K. Hyde	Asher Moon
22 Jeffrey Ballard	Calvin Brewer	"	Harvey Shaw	"
23 Dennis Hulett	John Fox	Dennis Hulett	John Fox	"
24 Samuel Culver	Allen Grover	"	David B. Lewis	"
25 Horace Adams	James Forbes	"	Hiram Coleman	"

8

REPRESENTATIVES, ORANGE, ORLEANS, RUTLAND.

ORANGE CO, 1842	1843	1844	1845	1846
1 Alvan Taylor	George P. Baldwin	"		Arnold Stebbins
2 Elijah Flint	Ira Kidder	"	Joseph Riford	
3				
4 Levi B. Vilas	"		Perley C. Jones	"
5 Reuben Page jr.		Samuel Darling	"	Ephraim Ward
6 Zebulon Norris	John W. Lane	Dyer Waterman	Jerome B. Bailey	"
7 William H Carter	Simeon Stevens jr.	John Atwood	James Buchanan	"
8 Carlos Carpenter	Timothy Hancock	"	Artemas Houghton	"
9 William Hebard				
10 Daniel Cobb	William Sanborn			
Harry H. Niles	William Kingman	"	Joseph Gillett	"
12 Charles Grow	Moses Jones	"	Carlos P. Bill	"
13 Elizur H. Foster	"	"	John Lougee	
14 S, T. Wiggins	Jacob Church			Elizur H. Foster
15 John Emery	"	B. W. Bartholomew	Stephen Burton	Daniel Fitts
16 Elisha May		Elisha May	Stephen Thomas	"
17 Enoch Howe	Asa Howe		William S. Beckett	
ORLEANS CO,				
1 William Rowell	"	William A. Boyce		
2 Harris Smith	Benjamin Smith	"	Harris Smith	Luther Merriam
3 Gilman Esty	"	Elisha White	William Joslyn	
4 Isaac Brackett	Amos Parlin	"	Gardner Gage	"
5 Thomas Guild	"	Josiah B. Wheelock	"	Elijah Cleveland
6 Daniel Dustin				
Stoddard B. Colby	Abel Wilder	"	William Nelson	"
8 James Simonds	Amos P. Bean	Isaac B. Smith		
9 N W. Scott	Jabez Pinney			
10 Joshua French	Jason Hinman	Richard P. Goodell	"	Jason Davis
Charles W Prentiss	Alexand'r Jameson	George Bryant	"	Henry M. Bates
12 Walter Charlton		Bradley Sanborn		
13 William S. Flint	"		Amos Paine	"
14 Charles Cumings	"	Zenas Bartlett	"	Simeon Albee
15 Asa B. Moore	Orville Robinson	Samuel B. Rider jr		Roswell Prouty
16 Samuel Blake		Josiah Lyon		Samuel Blake
17 Curtis Phelps		Hubbard Hastings	Robert Kay	
18 Jere Hodgkins	"	Arad Hitchcock	"	Jere Hodgkins
19 John M. Kibbey	Ethan Blodgett	Carlton Cheney		John M. Kibbey
RUTLAND CO.				
Edward S. Howard	John Dickinson	"	Philo Wilcox	"
2 Nathan T Sprague			Ebenezer N. Briggs	"
3 William Sanford	Oliver R. Harris	"	Samuel Cheever	"
Dan'l B. Bogue	"	"	Capen Leonard jr.	Thomas Manley
5 Philip Briggs		Franklin Billings		Franklin Billings
6 Ira Edmonds	Albert Bucklin	"		Isaac M'Daniels
7 Barnabas Ellis	Asahel H. Kidder	"	Jonathan Capen	
8 James Flagg	James W. Barber	"	Reuben Balis	
9 Russel Fish	Leonard Mason	James L. Gilmore		Amos Tower
10 Saml. Caldwell	Leland Houghton	"	Ethan Temple	
Caleb B. Harrington	"	Horace Clark	"	Caleb B. Harrington
12 Russell Barber	John Crowley	"	"	Abijah Cole
13 R. H. F. Hill	David Bolster	"	Azel Kelly	
14 Hiel Hollister	Ira Marks	Charles F Edgerton	"	Ira Marks
15 Daniel Bowe	Free'n F Mathews	"	Lyman Gibbs	
Samuel H. Kellogg	"	"	Thomas F. Bogue	Jeffrey Barnes
William P. Noyes	Henry G. Neal	"	Adin Kendrick	
18 Luther Daniels	"	William Gilmore	"	Joel M. Mead
Solomon W Adams		Benjamin Maxham	"	
Benj. T. Needham	Wm. Mathewson	"	Elisha Johnson	William B. Brown
21 Asher Moon	Thomas J Goodrich	"	Charles W. Horton	"
22 John Cobb	"	Sampson Allen	Royal Coleman	"
23 John Fox	Samuel M Edgerton	Harvey Burton	"	
24 John Barden	"	"	"	John S. Hulett
25 William H Green	"	Salmon P. Abel	Horace Adams	Seneca Field

REPRESENTATIVES, ORANGE, ORLEANS, RUTLAND.

ORANGE CO. 1847	1848	1849	1850	First Town Ck't.
1 Geo. P. Baldwin	Hubbard Wright	"	"	S. M'Connell 1773
2	John S. Nichols	"	Joseph Riford	Elijah French 68
3		Homer Hatch		Timothy Cole
4		Elihu Hyde	"	Enos Smith 88
5 Ephraim Ward	John A. Tenney			George Bondfield
6 Lewis Jenkins	"	Stephen Chapman	William Child	Samuel Smith 75
7 Samuel Grow	"	A. B. W. Tenney	"	Jacob Kent 63
8 David Holbrook	"		Orange Fifield	John Sloan 96
9		Benj. T. Blodgett	Ammi Burnham	J. Woodward 83
10		Royal Hatch		D. Chamberlain 79
11 Joseph Matson	"	Roger S. Howard	Josiah Coburn	Abner Howard 63
12 J. W. Batchelder		Hale Grow	"	Lemuel Tabor 90
13 .	Jeremiah Foster	"	William Putnam	A. Stedman 36
14 Rufus Blanchard			James Matthews	Andrew Peters 83
15 Daniel Fitts	"	Elisha Tracy	"	Jacob Burton
16 JeromeB Slayton	Alvah Bean	"	J. P. Southworth	Elisha Thayer 97
17	Porter Martin	"	Milton Martin	Cornelius Lynde 87

ORLEANS CO.				
1	George Putnam	"	William Rowell	Benj. Neal 1806
2 Lyndon Robinson	Benj. F. Robinson	John Evans	"	Abner Allyn 98
3 John Bryant	"	L. Chamberlain	Thomas C. Stewart	
4 Winthrop Cole	"	Jacob Richards		Abner Allyn 1806
5 Isaac Parker	"	Wm. M. Dickerman	"	Joseph Marsh 1803
6	William J. Hastings	"		Saml. C. Crafts 92
7 Aaron Hinman	"	Levi L. Collier	"	Tim. Hinman 93
8 Lyndal French	"	Isaac N. Cushman	Willard Leonard	
9 Ezekiel Rand	Jabez Pinney	"	Eben'r R. Randall	
10 Micah Ferrin	"	Henry Pinney	"	Eber Robinson 1805
11 Henry M. Bates	"	"	Geo. Worthington jr	Samuel Conant 1803
12	Orin Emerson		Willard Walker	
13 John D. Harding	"			Asahel Curtis 1812
14 Simeon Albee	"	Marson Leavens	"	C. Bartlett 1807
15 Roswell Prouty	William Moon jr	Jonathan Frost	Freeman Miller	
16	Calvin S. Grow	"	Samuel Blake	Samuel Blake 1822
17 Curtis Elkins			William C. Gilman	Curtis Elkins 1802
18	George Stoughton	David F. Boynton	"	Jesse Olds 1802
19	David Giltillan		Calvin Gibson	

RUTLAND CO.				
1 Loyal C. Kellogg	Isaac Dickinson	"	Loyal C. Kellogg	Allen Goodrich 86
2 Nat'n T. Sprague	"	William M. Field		Gideon Horton 84
3 Timothy W. Rice	"	Ezra S. Carr	William B. Colburn	Jesse Belknap 77
4 Wm. H. Harrison	Reuben Harris	Wm. H. Harrison	Saml. W. Harrison	
5 Walter Ross	Calvin Spencer	Green Arnold	Joseph Congdon	Stephen Arnold 78
6 Galen J. Locke	William Otis	Harris F. Otis	Azariah Hilliard	Thomas Rowley 69
7 Wm C. Kittredge	Wm. C. Kittredge	Wm. C. Kittredge	Abram Graves	Eleazer Dudley 83
8 Pliny Holmes	"	Justin Jennings	"	David Hickock 85
9 Amos Tower	Lester Fish	"	Erwin Collins	Isaac Clark 79
10 Jared Long	William Harkness	"	John Osborn	John Page 1806
11 Harris G. Otis	William N. Gray	"	Roswell Buel jr	Joseph Rockwell 86
12 Abijah Cole	John Crowley	John Ackley	"	Stephen Clark 92
13 David Bolster	Benjamin B. Britton	"	David Stimson	John Jenkins 88
14	Sheldon Edgerton	"	Robert H. Smith	Simeon Burton 69
15 Calvin Joslyn	Orton Hatch	Nahum E. Green	Orton Hatch	Thos. Hodgkins 93
16 Jeffery Barnes	David Hall	"	Simeon Gilbert	Benj. Cooley 70
17 Amon Bailey		"	Joseph Joslin	Heber Allen 74
18 So'omon Foot	Edwin L. Griswold	Charles K. Williams	Martin G. Everts	
19 R. Richardson jr	"	Benjamin Maxham	Amial Johnson	Albro Anthony
20 David B. Jones	"	Elisha Johnson	William B. Brown	
21 John C. Sawyer	Henry H. Merritt	"	Henry J. Horton	
22 Dexter Gilbert	"	George Capron jr	"	Charles Brewster 77
23 Stephen Hyde	Isaac B. Munson	"	Robinson Hall	Abra'm Jackson 73
24 John S. Hulett	Harvey Parks	"	C. Hopson jr	John Ward 73
25 Seneca Field	Harvey Howes	"	John H. Wyman	William Wyman 93

	1788	1789	1790	1791
WASHINGTON CO.				
8 Middlesex				Samuel Harris
9 Montpelier				Jacob Davis
16 Waterbury				
WINDHAM CO.				
1 Athens	Joseph Bullen	Elijah E'mer	James Shafter	Joseph Bullen
2 Brattleboro'	Israel Smith	Samuel Knight	Gardner Chandler	"
5 Dummerston	William Sargeants	Thomas Clark	"	Jason Duncan
6 Grafton	William Stickney	Charles Perkins	Henry Bond	Stephen Hayward
7 Guilford	Benjamin Carpenter	William Bigelow	Peter Briggs	William Bigelow
8 Halifax	Hubbel Wells	Benjamin Henry	"	"
9 Jamaica		Silas Hayward	"	
10 Londonderry	Edward Aiken	"		Edward Aiken
11 Marlboro'	Phinehas Freeman	"	Benjamin Olds	Jonas Whitney
12 New'ane	Luke Knowlton	"	Calvin Knowlton	"
13 Putney	Daniel Jewett	"	John Campbell	"
14 Rockingham	Jonathan Holton	Samuel Cutler	Jehiel Webb	Samuel Cutler
17 Townshend	Joshua Wood	"	"	John Hazletine
18 Vernon		Arad Hunt	"	"
19 Wardsboro'		Asa Wheelock	"	"
20 Westminster	Stephen R. Bradley	Lot Hall	Stephen R. Bradley	Lot Hall
21 Whitingham	James Roberts	Isaac Lyman	"	Jabez Foster
22 Wilmington	Jesse Cook	Chipman Swift	"	"
WINDSOR CO.				
1 Andover		"	"	"
3 Barnard	Frederick Rogers	"	Aaron Barlow	"
4 Bethel	Joseph Foster	"	Michael Flynn	Nathaniel Throop
5 Bridgwater	Nathaniel Throop	"	"	Benjamin Perkins
6 Cavendish	John Hawkins	Asaph Fletcher	"	John Russell
7 Chester			"	"
8 Hartford	David Heald	Elisha Marsh	Joshua Hazen	"
9 Hartland	Joshua Hazen	George Denison	Oliver Gallup	Roger Enos
11 Norwich	William Gallup	"	Joseph Hatch	Paul Brigham
13 Pomfret	Elisha Barton	Abida Smith	Barius Green	Abida Smith
14 Reading	John Throop	"	Elkanah Day	"
15 Rochester	John Weld	"	"	"
16 Royalton	Enoch Emmerson	"	Daniel Tuller	Benjamin Eastman
17 Sharon	Calvin Parkhurst	"	"	Calvin Parkhurst
18 Springfield	Joel Marsh	Anthony Morse	"	Daniel Gilbert
19 Stockbridge	Abner Bisbee	Jotham White	"	Nathaniel Weston
20 Weathersfield		"	"	"
23 Windsor	Joseph Hubbard			"
24 Woodstock	Stephen Jacob	Bryant Brown	Benjamin Greene	"
	Jesse Safford	Warren Cottle	Jesse Safford	Benjamin Emmons

DAVID REDDING AND ETHAN ALLEN.

In the journals of the Legislature held at Bennington, June 6, 1778, may be found the following: *Voted,* that the petition presented to this House by David Redding, be taken into consideration; and that a committee of five be appointed to prepare a bill, in consequence of said petition, &c. Committee chosen, Mr. Webb, Mr. Alverd, Capt. John Fassett, Ensign Harris and Major Olin.

Redding had been convicted of *enemical conduct* towards Vermont which was considered, at that time, unpardonable by the multitude, and sentenced to be executed on the 4th day of June. The curiosity which has ever been manifested on such occasions, was greatly heightened on this, as it was the first public execution ever witnessed in Vermont. To this curiosity was added a strong feeling of indignation which such a crime was calculated to excite in those days. A vast multitude collected to witness the execution. In the meantime, Redding's Council had discovered a very important defect in the proceedings. Redding had been tried by a jury of *six* only, which was not in accordance with the common law of England, which required *twelve*. On application to the Governor and Council, the following reprieve was granted just as the people were assembling to view the execution:

"IN COUNCIL, June 4th, 1778.

To Benjamin Fay, Esq., Sheriff of the County of Bennington —This Council have taken into consideration, this day, the petition of David Redding, now a prisoner, under sentence of death, and do hereby, in Convention, reprieve him, the said David Redding, until Thursday next, the 11th instant, June, precisely at the hour of 2 o'clock, in the afternoon of said day. You are, therefore, hereby ordered to suspend his execution until that time.

By order of Council, THOMAS CHITTENDEN."

WASHINGTON 1792	1793	1794	1795	1796
1 *Barre*	Nathan Harrington	Asaph Sherman	"	"
2 *Berlin*	John Taplin	"	Abel Knapp	"
3 *Calais*			Peter Wheelock	"
4 *Duxbury*		Benjamin Davis	"	Jesse Arms
8 Seth Putnam		Seth Putnam	Josiah Hurlbut	Seth Putnam
9 Jacob Davis	"	"	"	"
10 *Moretown*		Luther Mosely		Wright Spaulding
14 *Waitsfield*			Benjamin Wait	"
16 Daniel Bliss		Ezra Butler	"	"
WINDHAM CO.				
1 James Shafter	"	"	"	"
2 Josiah Arms	"	"	Samuel Warner	Josiah Arms
5 Jason Duncan	"	Daniel Taylor	"	"
6 Henry Bond	Ezra Edson	David Palmer	Enos Lovell	Amos Fisher
7 Wm. Bigelow	"	"	"	Peter Briggs
8 Benjamin Henry	"	"	"	"
9 Silas Hayward	Ezra Livermore	Caleb Hayward	Ezra Livermore	"
10 Edward Aiken	"	"	John Burnap	Samuel Thompson
11 James Whitney	"	"	"	"
12 L. Knowlton	Moses Kenney	Ebenezer Allen	"	"
13 John Campbell	"	"	"	"
14 DavidSanderson	"	"	Samuel Cutler	"
17 E. Wheelock	"	John Hazletine	"	Ephraim Wheelock
18 Arad Hunt		John Bridgman	Jonathan Carver	John Bridgman
19 Asa Wheelock	"	"	"	"
20 Lot Hall	Eliakim Spooner	"	"	Benjamin Burt
21 Jabez Foster	"	James Roberts	Jabez Foster	"
22 Chipman Swift	Timothy Castle	"	Chipman Swift	Timothy Castle
WINDSOR CO.				
1 Moses Warner	"	Frederick Rogers	Moses Warner	"
3 John Foster	Aaron Barber	John Foster	Stewart Southgate	John Foster
4 Elisha Hubbard	Joel Marsh	Joseph Marsh	Michael Flynn	"
5 John Hawkins		Benjamin Perkins	"	"
6 Asaph Fletcher	James Smith	"	Leonard Proctor	"
7 Abner Field	Daniel Heald	Waitstill Ranney	Daniel Heald	"
8 Elisha Marsh	Joshua Hazen	John Clark	"	"
9 Oliver Gallup	"	"	"	"
10 *Ludlow*			Peter Read	Josiah Fletcher
11 Aaron Storrs	Daniel Buck	Daniel Buck	John Bush	Ebenezer Brown
12 *Plymouth*			Moses Priest	Asa Briggs
13 John W. Dana	William Perry	"	"	"
14 John Weld	Aaron Kimball	Abijah Stone	Elijah Stone	David Hapgood
15 Enoch Emerson	"	"	Benjamin Eastman	E. Emerson
16 Elias Stevens	"	"	"	Abel Stevens
17 Joel Marsh	Ebenezer Parkhurst	Reuben Spaulding	James Parker	Ebenezer Parkhurst
18 Daniel Gill	Samuel Cobb	Simeon Stevens	*Lewis R. Morris*	*Lewis R. Morris*
19 John Whitcomb	Elias Keyes	"	"	"
20 Elijah Robinson	"	"	Nath'l Stoughton	"
23 Benj. Greene	Alden Spooner	Stephen Jacob	William Hunter	Zebina Curtiss
24 Benj. Emmons	"	"	Jabez Cottle	Benjamin Emmons

On the reading of the reprieve a clap of thunder would not produced half of the excitement manifested. Reasoning was out of the question. The mass had pronounced him guilty, and were not in a condition to understand how the verdict of the whole could, so easily, be set aside by the Governor and Council. While they were agitating what to do, and greatly excited with indignation, ETHAN ALLEN, suddenly pressing through the crowd, ascended a stump, and waving his hat, exclaimed, "ATTENTION THE WHOLE "—proceeded to announce the reason which produced the reprieve—advised the multitude to depart peaceably to their homes, and return on the day fixed for the execution, in the act of the Governor and Council;—adding with an oath—"You shall see somebody hung at all events, for if Redding is not then hung, I will be hung myself." Upon this assurance, the people became quiet and soon dispersed. Redding was again tried on the 9th and executed on the 11th, so that Allen was spared to show an act of humanity two years afterwards.

---o---

LOST CHILDREN.

In the town of Sunderland, on the 31st. of May, 1780, two daughters of Eldad Taylor, then of Sunderland, but afterwards of Williston, Keziah aged 7, and Betsey aged 4 years, wandered into

REP'S., WASHINGTON, WINDHAM, WINDSOR.

	1797	1798	1799	1800	1801
WASHINGTON					
1	Benj Walker	Nathaniel Killam	Benjamin Walker	James Fisk	"
2	Abel Knapp	"	Eleazer Hubbard jr		Abel Knapp
3	Peter Wheelock	"	"	Abdial Bliss	"
4	Moses Heaton	"	"	Joseph Nash	"
8	Seth Putnam	"	"	"	Henry Perkins
9	David Wing jr	"	Perley Davis	David Wing jr	"
10		Joseph Hazletine		Roswell Smith	Seth Munson
11	*Northfield*				Amos Robinson
12	*Plainfield*			Bradford Kinne	Thomas Vincent
14	Benjamin Wait	"	"	Stephen Pierce	Benjamin Wait
16	Ezra Butler	George Kennan	Ezra Butler	"	"
WINDHAM CO.					
1	James Shafter	"	"	Willard Evans	James Shafter
2	Samuel Knight	John W. Blake	"	Joseph Clark	"
5	Daniel Taylor	Jason Duncan	"	Jonas Walker	Daniel Taylor
6	Amos Fisher	Thaddeus Taylor	William Hall jr	Thaddeus Taylor	"
7	William Bigelow	"	John Noyes	"	"
8	Benjamin Henry	Darius Bullock	Benjamin Henry	"	"
9	Benjamin Muzzy	Ezra Livermore	"	Benjamin Muzzy	"
10	John Woodburn	Samuel Arnold	James Aiken	John Aiken	"
11	Jonas Whitney	Ichabod King	Jonas Whitney	Ichabod King	Sylvester Bishop
12	Ebenezer Allen	"	"	"	"
13	Daniel Jewett	"	"	"	Josiah Goodhue
14	Samuel Cutler	"	"	"	Daniel Sanderson
15	*Somerset*		Daniel Rice	"	"
16	*Stratton*		Samuel Boutell	"	"
17	Ep'm Wheelock	"	"	Ephraim Wolcott	Ephraim Wheelock
18	Arad Hunt	"	"	"	"
19	Daniel Reed	Asa Wheelock	"	"	"
20	Benjamin Burt	"	"	S. R. Bradley	Mark Richards
21	James Roberts	"	"	"	"
22	Timothy Castle	"	Chipman Swift	Jesse Swift	Israel Lawton
WINDSOR CO.					
1	Moses Warner	Alvin Simonds	Moses Rowell	Moses Warner	Alvin Simonds
3	John Foster	Aaron Barlow		Thomas Freeman jr	"
4	Nathaniel Throop	"	Stephen Cleveland	"	
5	John Hawkins	Phinehas Williams	Benjamin Perkins	John Hawkins	James Topliff
6	James Smith	"	"	"	"
7	Daniel Heald	Jabez Sargeant	"		Aaron Leland
8	John Clark	William Strong	"	Benjamin Russ	William Strong
9	Ebenezer Allen	Oliver Gallup	Samuel Perkins	Oliver Gallup	Elihu Luce
10	Josiah Fletcher	Jesse Fletcher	"	Josiah Fletcher	"
11	Roswell Olcott	"	Elisha Burton	"	Peter Olcott
12	Asa Briggs	"	"	"	Elias Williams
13	O. Hutchinson	"	William Perry	"	Jeremiah Conant
14	David Hapgood	Moses Chaplain	"	Solomon Keyes	Elias Jones
15	Enoch Emerson		"	"	"
16	Silas Allen	Jacob Smith	Elias Stevens	Jacob Smith	Abel Stevens
17	Reub. Spaulding	Anthony Morse	Joel Marsh	Reuben Spaulding	Anthony Morse
18	Jotham White	"	Samuel Cobb	"	"
19	Asa Whitcomb	Elias Keyes	"	"	"
20	N. Stoughton	Thomas Prentiss	"	"	"
23	Zebina Curtis	"	"	Alden Spooner	"
24	Jesse Williams		Jabez Bennett	Benjamin Emmons	"

the woods. Not returning, the parents became alarmed and commenced a search, which, with the aid of a few neighbors was continued through the night. The next day a universal turn out renewed, and continued the search till the middle of the afternoon of the third day, when it was unsuccessfully relinquished, and the people assembled who had been out, with a view of returning to their homes. Being about to disperse, a large, stout man ascended a stump, and in a loud voice informed them that the search ought not to be abandoned. Soon every eye was upon him. In the usual manner of the man, after pointing to the father and mother of the children, now overcome with grief and despair, bade each person present, and especially those who were parents, to make the case of those parents their own, and then say whether they would go contentedly home, and not make one more effort to save those dear little ones, who were, probably, now alive, but fast perishing with hunger, and will soon spend their last breath in crying to have father and mother

WASHINGTON 1802	1803	1804	1805	1806
1 James Fisk	"	"	Luther Holton	Nathan Carpenter
2 Abel Knapp	Eleazer Hubbard jr	"	Salvin Collins	"
3 Joshua Bliss	Gershom Palmer	Lemuel Perry	Gershom Palmer	"
4 Joseph Nash	Ebenezer Corse	"	Benjamin Davis	Ebenezer Corse
7 *Marshfield*		Stephen Pitkin	"	"
8 Henry Perkins	Seth Putnam	"	"	Henry Perkins
9 Perley Davis	Joseph Woodworth	Edward Lamb	Cyrus Ware	"
10 Seth Munson	Wright Spaulding	Seth Munson	Cephas Carpenter	"
11 Amos Robinson	"	"	"	"
12 Bradford Kinne	"	"	"	Jonaathan Kinne
13 *Roxbury*		Zebediah Butler		
14 Benjamin Wait	Bissel Phelps	"	"	"
16 Ezra Butler	"	"	George Kennan	"
WINDHAM CO.				
1 James Shafter	"	Thad's Alexander	James Shafter	Thad's Alexander
2 John W. Blake	Lemuel Whitney	"	"	"
5 Samuel Porter	"	"	"	Jason Duncan
6 Thaddeus Taylor	John B. Wheeler	Enoch Hale	"	David Palmer
7 John Noyes	"	"	Gilbert Dennison	"
8 Darius Bullock	"	"	"	"
9 Benjamin Muzzy	"	"	"	"
10 Emerson Hodges	John Aiken	"	Samuel Arnold	"
11 Eli Halladay	Sylvester Bishop	Timothy Mather	Eli Halladay	Timothy Mather
12 Ebenezer Allen	"	"	Luke Knowlton	Luke Knowlton jr
13 James Fitch	Daniel Jewett	"	"	"
14 Daniel Farrand	Levi Sabin	Alex. Campbell	Elijah Knight	Alex. Campbell
15 Daniel Rice				
16 Samuel Boutell	"	"	"	"
17 Ep'm Wheelock	"	John Dyer	"	"
18 Jonathan Hunt	Arad Hunt	"	"	"
19 Asa Wheelock	Abner Perry	"	Daniel Reed	"
20 Mark Richards	Ephraim Ranney jr	Mark Richards	"	William C. Bradley
21 James Roberts	"	Jabez Foster	"	James Roberts
22 Israel Lawton	Timothy Castle	Jairus Hall	"	"
23 *Windham*			John Aiken	
WINDSOR CO.				
1 Moses Rowell		Samuel Burton	Alvin Simonds	William Stevens
3 Benjamin Clapp	"	"	Thomas Freeman	Thos. Freeman jr
4 S. Cleveland	Nehemiah Noble	Stephen Cleveland	Eli Noble	Nehemiah Noble
5 James Topliff	Phinehas Williams	"	"	"
6 James Smith	"	"	"	John G. Wheelock
7 Aaron Le and	"	Aaron Leland	Aaron Leland	Aaron Leland
8 William Strong	William Perry	"	Sherman Dewey	"
9 Elihu Luce	"	"	"	"
10 David Lewis	"	Austin Fenn	"	Asahel Smith
11 Pierce Burton	Hezekiah Goodrich	"	Pierce Burton	Daniel Buck
12 Asa Briggs	"	"	Daniel Brown	"
13 Jeremiah Conant	Joseph Perry	"	"	Elisha Smith
14 Elias Jones	"	"	"	"
15 Enoch Emerson	"	"	"	"
16 Jacob Smith	Elias Stevens	Nathan Page	"	Elias Stevens
17 George Dana	Joel Marsh	Paul W. Brigham	"	Reuben Spaulding
18 Samuel Cobb	Lewis R. Morris	"	Lewis R. Morris	"
19 Elias Keyes	Norman Webber	"	Rufus Lyon	"
20 Nath'l Stoughton	"	Gregory Stone	"	"
21 *Weston*	Alvin Simonds			
23 Alden Spooner	"	Pascal P. Enos	"	Jabez Delano
24 Benj. Emmons	"	Titus Hutchinson	Jabez Cottle	Titus Hutchinson

give them some food to eat. As he spoke, his large frame became agitated, and the tears fast rolling down his cheeks, and in an assembly of several hundred bold men of that day, but few dry eyes were among them. "I'll go! I'll go!" was soon heard from every part of the multitude. They soon took for the woods, and before night they were successful in restoring the lost ones to the arms of their parents. Need I inform you that that large man was any other than the brave and bold officer, ETHAN ALLEN? The first night they laid down by a large tree, and the second on a large rock. They found plenty of water but not much food but leaves, &c.

REP'S., WASHINGTON, WINDHAM, WINDSOR.

WASHINGTON	1807	1808	1809	1810	1811
1	John Dodge	"	James Fisk	"	Nathan Stone
2	Eleazer Hubbard	Abel Knapp	"	Samuel Smith	Abel Knapp
3	Gershom Palmer	"	"	"	"
4	James Smalley	Ebenezer Corse	"	"	Curwin Wallace
7	Stephen Pitkin	"	George Rich	"	"
8	Seth Putnam	"	David Harrington	"	"
9	Cyrus Ware	"	"	Joseph Woodworth	Timothy Merrill
10	Cep's Carpenter	"	Seth Munson	William M. Knight	Joseph Haseltine
11	Amos Robinson	"	"	Gilbert Hatch	Amos Robinson
12	Bradford Kinne	"	"	"	"
13		Samuel Robinson	Rhodolph's Willard	"	"
14	Bissel Phelps	Amos Skinner	Amasa Skinner	"	Stephen Pierce
15	*Warren*		Thomas Gerald	Joseph W Eldridge	"
16	Ezra Butler	George Kennan	Asaph Allen	George Kennan	John Peck
17	*Woodbury*				
18	*Worcester*	James Green	Carpus Clark		"
WINDHAM CO.					
1	T. Alexander		"	Tim'y H. Whitney	"
2	Lemuel Whitney	John Noyes	Jonas Mann	John Noyes	"
4	*Dover*				Amos Rice
5	Jason Duncan	"	"	"	"
6	D. Palmer	Thaddeus Taylor	"	Thomas K. Palmer	John Barrett
7	Gilbert Dennison	"	John Noyes	"	"
8	D. Bullock	Stephen Otis	"	"	"
9	Benjamin Muzzy	"	Amasa Howard 2d	Benjamin Muzzy	"
10	Samuel Arnold		John Gibson	"	"
11	Eli Halladay	"	"	"	Timothy Mather
12	Elijah Elmer	Joseph Ellis	"	Martin Field	Sylvanus Sherwin
13	Daniel Jewett	Daniel Leavitt	"	Willard Taft	"
14	Alex. Campbell	"	Elijah Knight	David Campbell	"
15					
16	Samuel Boutell		"	"	"
17	Samuel Fletcher	Ezekiel Ransom	John Dyer	"	"
18	Arad Hunt	"	"	"	Jonathan Hunt jr.
19	Asa Wheelock	"	"	"	"
20	Wm. C Bradley	Lott Hall	Eleazer May	"	Isaiah Eaton
21	James Roberts	Jabez Foster	"	Amasa Brown	"
22	Jairus Hall	"	"	"	"
23	John Aiken	"	"	"	"
WINDSOR CO.					
1	C. G. Persons	Cyrus Smith	"	Moses Warner	"
3	Thos. Freeman jr	Benjamin Clapp	"	"	"
4	Nehemiah Noble	Joseph Wallace	John Wallace	Nehemiah Noble	Jonathan Marsh
5	James Topliff	"	"	"	James Southgate
6	Randall Lovell	James Smith	Uriel C. Hatch	"	"
7	Aaron Leland	Thos. S. Fullerton	Aaron Leland	"	William Hosmer
8	Sherman Dewey	"	"	Elijah Mason	Nathan Gere
9	Elihu Luce	"	"	Laban Webster	Elihu Luce
10	Asahel Smith	"	"	"	"
11			Pierce Burton		"
12	Daniel Brown	"	Ephraim Moor	"	"
13	Elisha Smith	Daniel Dana	Ignatius Thompson	Daniel Dana	Ignatius Thompson
14	Elias Jones	"	Lemuel Ide	Solomon Keyes	Jonathan Shead
15	Oliver Mason	Enoch Emerson	Lemuel Richardson	"	"
16	Jacob Smith	"	"	"	"
17	Reub. Spaulding	James Parker	"	Oliver Lathrop	James Parker
18	John Davis	Lewis R. Morris	James Davis	Joseph Selden	Asahel Powers
19	Rufus Lyon	"	"	"	"
20	Gregory Stone	Reuben Hatch	Peter Robinson	"	"
21			Cornelius G. Persons	?	Cornelius G Persons
23	William Hunter	"	Jabez Delano	"	Joseph Winslow
24	T. Hutchinson	"	"	"	Joseph Wood

Betsey, the youngest, was married to Capt. John Munson, and is now living in Burlington with her husband. The other was the wife of John Jones, of Williston, who died some years since, at Williston.

WASHINGTON	1812	1813	1814	1815	1816
1 Warren Ellis		"	"	James Fisk	Warren Ellis
2 Eleazer Hubbard	Abel Knapp	"		Jabez Ellis	Abel Knapp
3 Gideon Wheelock		"	Samuel Fay	Benjamin Page	"
4 Ebenezer Corse	James Smalley		Curwin Wallace	Ebenezer Corse	"
7 Stephen Pitkin		"	Stephen Pitkin	"	"
8 David Harrington	Seth Putnam	"	Seth Putnam	"	"
9 Timothy Merrill	Joseph Howes		Edward Lamb	"	Naum Kelton
10 Joseph Haseltine	John Foster		Cephas Carpenter	Seth Monson	"
11 Amos Robinson		"	"	Gilbert Hatch	"
12 Bradford Kinne		"	Joseph Nye	"	Bradford Kinne
Rhodolph's Willard	Darius Spaulding		"	"	"
14 Amasa Skinner		"	Stephen Pierce	Amasa Skinner	Edmond Rice
Joseph W Eldridge		"		"	Amos Rising
16 Sylvester Henry		"	Dan Carpenter	"	"
Elisha Benjamin jr			John Bruce	"	"
18 Elisha B Green	Carpus Clark		Cyrus Brigham	"	
WINDHAM CO.					
1 Thad. Alexander	James Shafter		Thad's Chamberlin	James Bayley	Tim'y H. Whitney
2 John Noyes	Samuel Elliott		"	"	Jonathan Hunt jr.
4 Amos Rice		"	Samuel Clark	Amos Rice	Gardner Howe
5 Jonathan Huntley		"	"	"	"
6 John Barrett		"	"	Nathan Wheeler	John Barrett
7 Aaron Barney	Jonah Cutting		John Phelps	Aaron Barney	Willard Martin
8 Darius Bullock		"		"	"
9 Benjamin Muzzy		"	Ezra Livermore	"	"
10 John Gibson	Abiel Richardson		"	"	Simeon Leland
Sylvester Bishop		"	Joseph Olds	"	Daniel Halladay
12 Luke Knowlton		"	John Brooks	Luke Knowlton	Sylvanus Sherwin
Natha'l Chamberlin		"	David Leavitt	Phinehas White	"
14 Henry Lake	Joseph Weed		Henry Lake	Benjamin Smith jr.	"
16 Samuel Boutell		"	"	"	"
17 Ezekiel Ransom		"	Amzi Doolittle jr.	"	Munnis Kinney
18 Cyrus Washburn	Zadock Wright		Arad Hunt 2d.	"	Israel Johnson
19 Asa Wheelock		"	"	Stephen Presson	"
20 Daniel Mason		"	"	Gideon Warner	"
	Rufus Hosley		"	Ephraim Smith	"
22 Jairus Hall		"	Jesse Swift	"	Jairus Hall
23 John Aiken		"	Luther Stowell	"	Amos Emery
WINDSOR CO.					
1 Joel Manning	John Wait		Samuel Manning	John Wait	Samuel Manning
3 Benjamin Clapp		"	"	"	"
4 Jonathan Marsh		"	"	Samuel Lillie	"
5 James Topliff	James Southgate		" .	James Topliff	James Southgate
6 Uriel C. Hatch		"	"	"	"
7 William Hosmer	Aaron Leland			Joshua Leland	
8 Nathan Gere	Abel Barron		"	William Strong	"
9 Elihu Luce	David H, Sumner		"	Elihu Luce	"
10 Asahel Smith	Ariock Smith		"	Elisha Ives	"
Pierce Burton		"	Israel Newton	Don J. Brigham	"
12 Ephraim Moor		"		"	"
13 John Bridge		"	Ignatius Thompson	"	John Bridge
14 Jonathan Shedd	William L Hawkins		"	Jonathan Shedd	Sewal Fullam
15 Enoch Emerson	Oliver Mason		"		Enoch Emerson
16 Jacob Smith	Rhodolphus Dewey		"	Daniel Rix jr.	Elias Stevens
17 Reub. Spaulding		"	"	Samuel Steele	
18 Asahel Powers	John Holton		"	Leonard Walker	"
19 Rufus Lyon		"	Norman Webber	"	Branch Whitcomb
20 Peter Robinson	Carlos Cowles		Oliver Whipple	"	Lemuel Hitchcock
22 *West Windsor*				Jabez Delano	
23 Joseph Winslow	Jabez Delano		Oliver Farnsworth	Zebina Curtis	Jabez Delano
24 T. Hutchinson	Henry C. Dennison		"	"	Stephen Farnsworth

REP'S., WASHINGTON, WINDHAM, WINDSOR.

WASHINGTON 1817

#	1817	1818	1819	1820	1821
1	Warren Ellis	Phineas Thompson	"	Warren Ellis	Jacob Scott
2	Jabez Iris	Charles Bulkley	Joel Warren	Israel Dewey	"
3	Gideon Wheelock	Caleb Curtis	"		Gideon Wheelock
4	Curwin Wallace	"	Ebenezer Corse	Curwin Wallace	"
7	Stephen Pitkin	"	"	William Martin	
8	David Harrington	Nathan Carpenter	David Harrington	Nath'l Carpenter	David Harrington
9	Naum Kelton	"	Geo. Worthington	Naum Kelton	Arunah Waterman
10	Seth Munson	"	Rufus Clapp	"	Paul Mason
11	Gilbert Hatch	Abram Shipman	"	Josiah B. Strong	"
12	Joseph Nye	"	Benjamin Whipple	"	Bradford Kinne
	JonathanF Ruggles	Charles Samson	"	"	"
14	Mathias S Jones	"	"	"	Ralph Turner
16	Dan Carpenter	Joseph W. Eldridge	Tehan Rising		Joseph W. Eldridge
		John Peck	Dan Carpenter	"	"
	Nathan B. Harvey	Benjamin Fowler	"	Joel Cilley	"
18					

WINDHAM CO.

#	1817	1818	1819	1820	1821
	Timo'y H. Whitney	"	"	"	"
2	Jonathan Hunt jr.	James Elliott	"	Samuel Clark	"
4	Elijah Stearns	"	"	"	"
5	Jonathan Huntley	Thomas Boyden	"	"	Amos Rice
6	Nathan Wheeler	"	John Barrett	Barzilla Burgess	"
7	William Bigelow	John Phelps	Willard Martin	Joseph Boyden	Aaron Barney
8	DariusBullock	Russel Avery	Darius Bullock	Benjamin Henry	"
	Nathaniel Robbins	"	Asa Stevens	Nathaniel Robbins	"
	Abiel Richardson	Samuel Arnold	Luther Stowell	Samuel Arnold	Luther Stowell
11	Dan Halladay jr	Luther Very	"	"	"
12	Horace Dunham	Luke Knowlton	Martin Field	Sylvanus Sherwin	Martin Field
13	Phinehas White	"	"	"	Joseph Winslow
14	Peter Willard	Alex. Campbell	"	Henry Lake jr.	"
					Hazleton Rice
16	Bille Mann	"	"	Abel Groat	Bille Mann
17	Munnis Kinney	Peter R. Taft	Dana Bailey	Peter R. Taft	Munnis Kinney
18	Isaac Johnson	Samuel Sikes	Arad Hunt 2d.	Samuel Sikes	Elijah Stebbens
19	Paul Wheeler	"	Pearley Fairbanks	"	Abner Holbrook
20	Gideon Warner	Benjamin Ranney	William C Bradley	Samuel Mason	Ellery Albee
		Amos Brown	John Roberts	"	"
22	Jairus Hall	"	"	"	"
23	Amos Emery		Benjamin Pierce	"	"

WINDSOR CO.

#	1817	1818	1819	1820	1821
1	Joseph Kirk	Samuel Manning	Oliver Farrar	Joel Balch	Oliver Farrar
3	Thomas Freeman	"	"	Zebina Eaton	"
4	Samuel Lillie	"	Peleg S. Marsh	Daniel Lillie	"
5	James Southgate	James Topliff	"	James Southgate	
6	Uriel C. Hatch	Salmon Dutton jr	Uriel C. Hatch	Asaph Fletcher	Uriel C. Hatch
7	Amos Heald		Abner W. Field	"	"
		William Strong	James Udall	"	George E Wales
9	Elihu Luce	"	Simeon Willard	"	"
10	Asahel Smith	Jesse Bailey	"	Zacha'h Spaulding	"
	Don J. Brigham	"	"	Aaron Loveland	"
12	Ephraim Moor	Asa Briggs	"	Ephraim Moore	"
13	John Bridge	Dexter Hawkins	"	"	"
14	Sewal Fullam	"	"	"	Jonathan Shedd
	Daniel Huntington	Enoch Emerson	William Powers	"	"
16	Daniel Rix jr,	Rhodolphus Dewey	Moses Cutter	Rhodolphus Dewey	Jacob Collamer
17	James Parker	"			
18	Asahel Powers	Leonard Walker	Bezaleel Wood	"	Jonathan Whipple
	Branch Whitcomb	Elias Keyes	Branch Whitcomb	Elias Keyes	Joel Cooper
	Lemuel Hitchcock	Carlos Cowles	Amos Hulett	"	"
23	Jabez Delano	Asa Aiken	Horace Everett	"	Asa Aiken
24	S. Farnsworth	Daniel Dana		Howland Simmons	Titus Hutchinson

WASHINGTON, 1822	1823	1824	1825	1826
1 Warren Ellis	Peter Nichols	Dennison Smith	"	Peter Nichols
2 Abel Knapp	"	Chester Nye	"	Israel Dewey
3 Benjamin Page	Lovel Kelton	"	"	David G. Sheple
4 Edward Crossett	"	Ebenezer Corse	Nathan Huntley	"
5 *Fayston*	Theophilus Bixby			Jotham Carpenter
7 William Martin	Josiah Hollister	"	Alonzo Foster	"
8 Seth Putnam	Josiah Holden		Holden Putnam	
Arunah Waterman	"	Samuel Prentiss	"	Arunah Waterman
10 Paul Mason	John Foster	Barnabas Mayo	"	David Belding
11 Joel Winch	"	Abel Keyes	"	John Starkweather
12 Thomas Vincent	Benjamin Whipple	Joseph Nye	Thomas Vincent	"
13 Robert Cram	"	Charles Sampson	"	Isaiah Shaw
14 Ralph Turner	"	Mathias S. Jones	"	"
15 Amos Rising	James Richardson	Amos Rising	"	"
16 Dan Carpenter	"	"	"	"
17 Joel Cilley	Benjamin Fowler	"	"	Joel Cilley
18 Allen Vail	"	Amos Rice	Samuel Hubbard	
WINDHAM CO.				
0 *Acton*		Eben'r Huntington	Lemuel Farwell	Eben'r Huntington
Timo'y H Whitney	"	Jonathan Hunt	James Bailey	Abraham Ball
2 Samuel Elliott	"	"	Samuel Clark	"
3 *Brookline*	Benjamin Ormsbee		William Perry jr.	Benjamin Ormsbee
4 Amos Rice	Gardner Howe	Ebenezer Jones	David Burr	Ebenezer Jones
5 Jonathan Huntley	"	Marshall Miller		Josiah Taft
6 Barzilla Burgess	"	William Stickney jr	"	Nathan Wheeler
7 Willard Martin	Amos Billings	Joseph Boyden		Dana Hyde jr.
8 George Boardman	James L. Stark		Willard Martin	"
9 Nath'l Robbins	"	Zelotes Skinner	"	Nathaniel Robbins
10 Samuel Arnold	John Gibson	Samuel Arnold		John Gibson
11 Simeon Adams		"	"	
Sylvanus Sherwin	Jason Duncan jr.	"	Sylvanus Sherwin	Wm. H, Williams
13 Joseph Winslow	Theoph's Crawford			Asa Keyes 2d.
14 Eleazer Albee	"	Benjamin Smith jr		William Hall
15		Sam'l Worthington		Ephraim Rice
16 Abel Grout	Billy Mann	Richard Scott	"	
17 Peter R. Taft	Dana Bailey	Peter R. Taft	Luke S. Rand	Epaphro's Ransom
18 Samuel Sikes	"	Benjamin Lee	Samuel Sikes	Nathan Wood
19 Abner Holbrook	Jonathan Robinson		Paul Wheeler	Leland Fairbanks
20 Ellery Albee	Elijah Ranney jr.	Mark Richards	Gideon Warner	Mark Richards
21 John Roberts	"	Amos Brown	Horace Roberts	"
22 Jairus Hall	"	"	"	"
23 Benjamin Pierce	"	"	Amos Emery	Benjamin Pierce
WINDSOR CO.	"			
1 Joel Balch		Edward Simonds	"	"
2 *Baltimore*		Benjamin Page	"	"
3 John Foster	Apollas Warner	"		Joseph Atherton jr
4 Daniel Lillie	"	"	Elijah Aiken	"
5 James Topliff	Isaiah Raymond	"	"	James Wallace
6 Jesse Adams	"	Levi Jackman	"	Edmond Ingalls
7 Abiel Richardson	Stephen Field	"	"	Jabez Sargeant
8 George E. Wales	*George E. Wales*	George E. Wales	Wyllis Lyman	"
9 Simeon Willard	Isaac N. Cushman	"	Robert Bartlett	"
10 Asahel Smith	"	Moses Haven	Asahel Smith	"
11 Aaron Loveland	"	Thomas Emerson	"	"
12 Ephraim Moor	John Lakin	"	"	Joseph Kennedy
13 Eben Snow	Dexter Hawkins	Eben Snow	John Bridge	"
14 Jonathan Shedd		Samuel C. Loveland	"	Abel Gilson jr.
15 Enoch Emerson	Ephraim D. Briggs	"	Lyman Emerson	"
16 Jacob Collamer	Rhodolphus Dewey	"	Oel Billings	Nathan Kimball
17 William Steele	James Parker	"	"	William Steele
Jonathan Whipple	Phinehas T. Wales	"	Bezaleel Wood	Leonard Walker
19 Rufus Lyon	Elias Keyes	"		Dwight Gay
20 Amos Hulett	Daniel Bowen	"	Barnabas Dean	"
	John Wait	"	Amos N. Burton	"
23 Horace Everett	"	Henry Gray	Jabez Delano	Abner Forbes
24 Jasper Hazen	"	Titus Hutchinson	"	Richard M. Rasmon

REP'S., WASHINGTON, WINDHAM, WINDSOR.

WASHINGTON 1827	1828	1829	1830	1831
1 Phino's Thompson	Peter Nichols	Denison Smith	Alvin Carter	Lucius B. Peck
2 James Sawyer	James H. Langdon	"	Jonathan P. Miller	"
3 Lovell Kelton	Pardon Janes	"	"	"
4 Nathan Huntley	Ira Arms	"	"	Samuel Turner
5 Jotham Carpenter	"	Merrill Tyler	"	William Sherman
7 William Martin	"	"	Spencer Lawrence	"
8 Holden Putnam	Josiah Holden	"	John Vincent	William H. Holden
9 William Upham	"	Naum Kelton	William Upham	Azel Spaulding
10 David Belding	John Foster	"	H. W. Carpenter	Stephen Pierce
11 J. Starkweather	Charles Paine	"	Lebbens Bennett	"
12 Jeremy Stone	"	Israel Goodwin	"	"
13 Isaiah Shaw	Charles Samson	Nathan Morse	Charles Samson	Isaiah Shaw
14 Jenison Jones	"	Jason Carpenter	"	"
15 Jas. Butterfield	Joseph A. Hyzer	Moses Sargeant jr	"	"
16 Amasa Pride	"	Dan Carpenter	Charles R. Cleaves	"
17 Benj'in Fowler	"	Joel Cilley	"	Ebenezer Bruce
18 Nathan Adams	"	Milton Brown	"	"
WINDHAM CO.				
0	E. Huntington	Nathan Fisher	"	
1 T. H. Whitney				Micah Davis
2 Lemuel Whitney	Samuel Elliott	"	"	Lemuel Whitney
3 Benj'in Ormsbee	William Perry	Jacob Burditt	"	Samuel Stebbins
4 David Burr	Ebenezer Jones	Wm. H. Hodges	James Miner jr	"
5 Josiah Taft	Joseph Duncan	"	Asa Knight	"
6 John Barrett	William Stickney jr	"	"	"
7 Dana Hyde	Aaron Barney	"	Russel Hyde	Ward Bullock
8 James L. Stark	"	Sanford Plumb	"	Darius Bullock
9 Peter R. Taft	Alpheus Kellogg	Nathaniel Robbins	"	Nathaniel Cheney jr
10 Samuel Arnold	Luther Stowell	Samuel Arnold	"	"
11 Simeon Adams	H. H. Winchester	"	"	"
12	Sylvanus Sherwin	Joseph Ellis	"	Henry Wheelock
13 Asa Keyes 2d	David Crawford	"	John Campbell	"
14 William Hall	Alex. S. Campbell	Manasseh Divoll	"	Alex. S. Campbell
15 S. Worthington	Charles Morse	S. Worthington	"	"
16 Richard Scott	"	"	"	"
17 E. Ransom	William R. Shafter	"	"	John P. Marsh
18 Nathan Wood	Joseph Franklin	Nathan Wood	Eli Lee	Cyrus Washburn
19 Leland Fairbanks	Freeman Holbrook	Nathaniel Ward	"	Silas Dexter
20 Eben'r Goodell	Mark Richards	Daniel Mason	Ellery Albee	John Smith
21 Schuy'r Murdock	Simeon Morse	"	Schuyler Murdock	Amos Brown
22 Ephraim Tyler	Lancy Forbes	"	David Rugg	"
23 Benjamin Pierce	Daniel Cobb	"	"	Harvey Burnap
WINDSOR CO.				
1 Edward Simonds	"	Orin Hazeltine	"	William Warner
2	Benjamin Page			
3 John S. Bicknell	Ebenezer Richmond	"	Levi Belknap	"
4 James Wallace	"	Daniel Lillie	John Woodbury	"
5 I. Raymond	"	David Thompson	"	James H. Munger
6 Edmond Ingalls	James Smith jr	"	Levi Jackman	"
7 Jabez Sargeant	Rufus Bruce	Abel Richardson	"	David Bates
8 Wyllis Lyman	"	"	"	"
9 Albe Lull	Simeon Willard	"	Elihu Luce	"
10 Asahel Smith	Jonas Dunn	"	Asa Fletcher	"
11 Thomas Emerson	"	Cyrus Partridge	Elias Lyman jr	Elias Lyman
12	John Lakin	Samuel Page	Levi Slack	Samuel Page
13 I. Tinkham jr	"	Henry Hewett	Nathan Snow	"
14 S. C. Loveland	"	Simeon Buck		
15 D. Huntington	Lyman Emerson	"	Ephraim D. Briggs	Stilman Emerson
16 Jacob Collamer	Harry Bingham	"	Jacob Collamer	Wm. Woodworth
17 William Steele	"	"	"	"
18 Samuel W. Porter		William Thayer jr	William Thayer	"
19 Dwight Gay	Norman Webber	Daniel Gay jr	"	"
20 John Brown	"	Joshua Upham	"	Cyrus Boynton
21 Henry Gray	John Wilder	Henry Lovejoy	Jonathan Webster	"
22				
23 Abner Forbes	Thomas Leland	"	"	Allen Wardner
24 Billy Brown	Richard M. Ransom	Sylvester Edson	Lysander Raymond	Billy Brown

REP'S., WASHINGTON, WINDHAM, WINDSOR.

WASHINGTON	1832	1833	1834	1835	1836
1	Alvin Carter	"	John Thwing	"	Jacob Scott
2	Josiah Benjamin	Jonathan P. Miller	Orren Smith	"	"
3		Shubael Wheeler	"	Pliny Curtis	"
4	Samuel Turner	Ira Arms	L. C. Turner	Horace Atkins	
5	Peter Drew	"	"	Orin Wheeler	Merrill Tyler
7	William Martin			William Martin	"
8		John Vincent	Holden Putnam	John Vincent	Holden Putnam
9	Azel Spaulding	"	William Billings	"	Lucius B. Peck
10	Calvin Clark	Cephas Carpenter	William Harris		Ira Carpenter
11	John Averill	"	David Robinson	Moses Robinson	Anson Adams
12	John Vincent	"	"	Baxter Bancroft	
13	Isaiah Shaw	"	Nathan Morse	"	"
14	ThomasPrentiss	"	Jason Carpenter	"	"
15	Joseph A. Hyzer			Artemas Cushman	"
16	Amasa Pride	Paul Dillingham jr	"		Thaddeus Clough
17	Ebenezer Bruce	"	"	Luther Morse	Asaph Town
18	Milton Brown	Daniel Adams	Milton Brown	Joel Newton	"

WINDHAM CO.

	1832	1833	1834	1835	1836
0				Nathan Fisher	
1	Joseph Tinkham	"	Tim. H.Whitney	Lyman Alexander	"
2	Lemuel Whitney	Charles Chapin	Lemuel Whitney	Asa Keyes	Lemuel Whitney
3	Samuel Stebbins	Edson Higgins	Thomas Crane	Ephraim H. Mason	"
4	Lyman Howe	"	"	David Dexter	"
5	Enos Leonard	"	Asa Knight	"	Joseph Duncan
6	Erastus Burgess	John Gibson	William Stickney	John Gibson	Ambrose Burgess
7	Ward Bullock	Russel Hyde	Nathan Conant	Ward Bullock	"
8	Sanford Plumb	Benj. Woodward	James L. Stark	B. Woodward	"
9	Nathaniel Cheney	Peter R. Taft	"	Timothy Goodale	"
10	Samuel Arnold	Ruel White	"	Sem Pierce	"
11	H H.Winchester	"	Simeon Adams	Cotton Mather	"
12	HenryWheelock	GeorgeWilliams 2d	"	Roswell M. Field	"
13	David Crawford	"	Alex. Campbell	"	"
14	N. B. Roundy	"	William Henry	"	Mannesseh Divoll
15	Elliott Morse	"	"	Ephraim Rice	"
16	Stephen Ballard		Benjamin Thatcher	"	David Rice
17		Waitstill R.Ranney	Chapin Howard	"	"
18	John Stebbins	"	Eli Lee	"	Ebenezer Howe jr
19	Em'y Wheelock	Silas Dexter			Solomon Newell
20	Mark Richards	John Smith	Mark Richards		Eleazer May
21	John Roberts		Nathan Brown	Obed Foster	"
22		Alonson Parmerlee	"	Charles K. Field	"
23		Timothy Sherwin	Levi Kimball	"	"

WINDSOR CO.

	1832	1833	1834	1835	1836
1	William Warner	Edward Simonds	Jerry Adams	Joel Balch	John B. Manning
2					Jona. Woodbury jr
3	Thomas Freeman	"	S. S. Hemenway	Lorenzo Richmond	"
4	Elisha Fowler	Julius Converse	John Woodbury	"	James Wallace
5	J. H. Munger	Lyman Raymond	"	"	"
6	Levi Jackman	Josiah Gilson	"	Samuel Adams	William Smith
7	David Bates	Stephen Fields	"	Dearborn S. Hilton	Ptolemy Edson
8	Wyllis Lyman	Andrew Tracy	"	"	"
9	L. N. Cushman	Wells Hadley	"	John S. Marcy	"
10	Ariock Smith	Reuben Washburn	Sewall Fullam jr	"	"
11	Elias Lyman	Alden Partridge	"	Cyrus Partridge	"
12	Samuel Page	Cephas Moore	Samuel Page	John S, Fullerton	"
13	Cyrus Snow	"	Isaiah Tinkham jr	"	Otis Chamberlain
14	William Felch	"	Shubael C. Shedd	"	BridgmanHapgood
15	StilmanEmerson	Lyman Emerson	John Trask	"	Joseph F. Tilden
16	CalvinParkhurst	Nathaniel Sprague	Samuel Selden	Oramel Sawyer	"
17			"	John Baldwin	
18	John White	Russell Burke	"	Abner Field	Bezaleel Wood
19	John Leonard	Daniel Ranney	William A. Millett	"	Merrick Gay
20	Barnabas Dean	Jonathan Lawrence	Barnabas Dean	"	Jonathan Lawrence
21	Jona. Webster	Parker Shattuck	Asa B. Foster	"	"
22					
23	Allen Wardner	"	Carlos Coolidge	"	Carlos Coolidge
24	Jason Kendall	"	Daniel Taft	Lysander Raymond	Tracy Bingham

#	1837	1838	1839	1840	1841
WASHINGTON					
1	Jacob Scott jr	"	Newell Kinsman	"	Leonard Keith
2	James Currier	Orren Smith	Wooster Sprague	Isaac T. Davis	"
3	Joseph Lance	"	Alonzo Pearce	"	Abdiel Kent
4	David Belding	Lyman C Turner	"	Samuel Turner	Lyman C. Turner
5	Merrill Tyler	Ira Richardson	"	Jacob Boyce	"
7	Welcome Cole	"	William Martin	Horace Hollister	"
8	John Vincent	William J. Holden	Thomas Stowell	Holden Putnam	Leander Warren
9	Lucius B. Peck	Royal Wheeler	"	Horatio N. Baylies	"
10	Ira Carpenter	Joseph Sawyer	Ira Carpenter	Lester Kinsley	"
11	Jesse Averill	"	"	Lebbeus Bennett	Moses Robinson
12	James Palmer	"	Harvey Bancroft	"	James Palmer
13	Charles Samson	"	"	Isaiah Shaw	Charles Samson
14	R. Richardson jr	"	"	Hiram Jones	"
15	William Cardell	"	William B. Taylor	Franklin A. Wright	"
16	P. Dillingham jr	"	"	William W. Wells	Eliakim Allen
17	Asaph Town	Ebenezer Bruce	Abner Town	"	Ira M'Loud
18	Milton Brown	Jacob Cushman	"	Farris Leonard	"
WINDHAM CO.					
0		Nathan Fisher		Nathan Fisher	Set to Townsend
1	Amos Davis	Comfort Thrasher	"	Tisdale Porter	Mark Bell
2	Calvin Townsley	"	Ebenezer Wells	"	Cyril Martin
3	William Adams	"	Ephraim Park	William Adams	Hiram Whitney
4	James Miner	"	Lewis Hall	"	William H. Jones
5	Joseph Duncan	Clark Rice	Samuel French	"	"
6	Ambrose Burgess	Thomas Hill	B. H. Bridgman	"	"
7	Ward Bullock	"	John Lynde	Ward Bullock	Isaac Brown
8	Isaac Warden	"	James L. Stark	Rufus K. Henry	"
9	Nathan Adams	Timothy Goodale	S. T. D. Cheney	"	"
10	Alfred Pierce	"	Stephen Smith	"	Peter C. Atwood
11	H. H. Winchester	Simeon Adams	Ira Adams	William Newton	"
12	James Elliott	"	Walter Eager	Nahum Eager	"
13		Forris Moore	John Smith		Henry N. Barton
14	John Seaver	Asa Wentworth	A. Wentworth jr	Samuel L. Billings	"
15	Hollis Town	"	Ephraim Rice	"	"
16	David Rice	"	Joseph Blodgett	David Rice	Ashbel Kidder
17	J. H. Bingham	"	"	Saml. H. Thompson	J. M. M. Shafter
18	Eben'r Howe jr	"	John Stebbins	Cyrus Washburn	John Stebbins
19	Em'y Wheelock	"	Solomon Newell	John P. Warren	"
20	David Allen	S. S. Stoddard	Alvin Goodale	John M'Neil	Alvin Goodale
21	William Bond jr	Obed Foster	James Roberts	Elisha Putnam	"
22	Charles K. Field	"	Azor Smith	"	Henry Eastabrook
23	Amos Emery	William Harris	"	"	"
WINDSOR CO.					
1	T. B. Manning	Joseph Dodge jr	"	"	Solomon Howard
2	J. Woodbury jr		Lyman Litch	Levi Harris	William Davis
3	Eben'r Atwood jr	"	Hiram Aiken	Orin Gambell	Hiram Aiken
4	David Woodbury	Thomas P. Russell	James Woodworth	Daniel Lillie	"
5	L. Raymond	Isaiah Raymond	"	"	Alvan Lamb
6	Levi Jackman	Joseph White	Samuel Adams	"	Zenas F. Hyde
7	Abner W. Field	Horace Onion	Hugh H. Henry	Gideon M. Lee	Hugh H. Henry
8	Andrew Tray	John Porter	"	"	"
9	Daniel Ashley	"		Hampden Cutts	"
10	S. Fullum jr	"	"	"	"
11	Alden Partridge	Thomas Hazen	Alden Partridge	Aaron Loveland	Ira Davis
12			Levi Slack		"
13	Henry Hewett	"	Otis Chamberlain	Ora Paul	"
14	B. Hapgood	Solomon Keyes	"	Benoni Buck	"
15	J. P. Tilden	John Trask	Thomas Barnes	"	Barney Cooper
16		David Wheelock	"	Truman H. Safford	"
17	J. Baldwin	A. F. Dean	"	Freeman Holt	Lyman Tyler
18	Bezaleel Wood	Abner Field	Henry Closson	"	O. M. Whipple
19	Samuel Eaton	Merrick Gay	Paul W. Gay	Justin Morgan	"
20	J. Lawrence	Barnabas Dean	"	Stephen Prentiss	"
21	Perkins N. Wiley	"	Thos. B. Wakefield	"	"
22					
23	Charles Hopkins	"	Carlos Coolidge	Carlos Coolidge	Carlos Coolidge
24	John Moulton	"	Oliver P. Chandler	"	

REP'S., WASHINGTON, WINDHAM, WINDSOR.

WASHINGTON	1842	1843	1844	1845	1846
1	Leonard Keith	David D. Wing	"	Webber Tilden	Obadiah Wood
2	Pearley Foster	Osmon Dewey	"	Schuyler Phelps	"
3	Abdiel Kent	Charles Dudley	"	Nelson A. Chese	"
4	L. C. Turner	John Towle	"	Chester Marshall	Ebenezer W. Corse
5	John C. Griggs	"	Eli Bruce	"	Burr Freeman
6	"	"	"	"	"
7	Horace Hollister	Ira Smith	"	Step'n R. Hollister	"
8	Horace Holden	"	Leander Warren	William X. Holden	Joseph Hancock
9	Addison Peck	"	Jerem'h T. Marston	"	Charles Clark
10	Micah B. Taplin	"	Calvin Clark	Daniel Harris	Barnabas Mayo
11	Nathan Morse	David W. Hadley	John L. Buck	David W. Hadley	"
12	Mark M. Page	Ezra Kidder	"	Nath'l Townshend	"
13	Allen Spaulding	"	"	Thomas R. Shaw	"
14	Hiram Jones				Ithamer Smith
15	Artemas Cushman	Thomas Sargeant	Lewis Cardell	Moses Ordway	"
16	Henry Douglass	"	William Carpenter	"	Thaddeus Clough
17	Ira McLoud	"	"	Abner Town	Ira McLoud
18	Moses Folsom	"			Allen L. Vail

WINDHAM CO.					
1	John Austin				
2	La Fayette Clark	"	John R. Blake	Gardner C. Hall	Royal Tyler
3	Hiram Whitney	Hubbard Eastman	John S. Osgood		
4	William H. Jones	Fayette Perry	"	"	
5	Reuben Smead	"			William O. Miller
6	Wm. Whitcomb	"	Abishai Stoddard	"	
7	Elisha Field	"	John Lynde	"	Samuel L. Hunt
8	Wm. H. Stark	Benj. Woodward	Nicholas Clark	William Plumb	Stephen Niles
9	Solomon Newell	Luke Howard			Pliny Barrows
10	Peter C. Atwood	Ezra Dodge	"	Reuben Harrington	"
11	"		Willard Snow	WmW. Winchester	
12	Walter Eager	Otis Warren	"	Oliver P. Morse	
13	Henry H. Barton	Joseph T. Radway	"	James Keyes	W. P. Richardson
14	J. S. Fullerton		Henry Walker	Daniel Kellogg	Royal Earle
15	Ephraim Rice	"	"	"	Hazeltine Rice
16	John H. Glazier	David Rice	Amos Parsons jr	"	Amos Parsons
17	J. M. M'Shafter	Nathan Fisher	Henry L. Aiken	"	A. C. Howard
18	Eben'r Howe jr	Jarvis F. Burrows	"	Eli Lee	
19	L. W. Johnson	"			
20	Joel Page	Ira Goodhue	John M'Neil	Ira Goodhue	Ellery Albee
21	Harvey Brown	"	Rufus Brown	Hosea F. Ballou	Rufus Carley
22		Frederick L. Stanley			
23	William Harris	Amos Emery	"	Jason D. Jones	"

WINDSOR CO.					
1	Solomon Howard	"	Joseph Dodge jr	"	Charles Sherwin
2	William Davis		Jona. M. Boynton		
3	Hiram Aiken	Charles Walcott	"	Joseph B. Danforth	"
4	Thomas P. Russell		David Bosworth		Oliver Hincher
5	Alvan Lamb	Ovid Thompson	"		R. W. Southgate
6	Zenas F. Hyde	William Smith	Christo'r Webber	Joseph Adams	"
7	Hugh H. Henry	"	Haskell Weston	"	"
8	Shubael Ross	"	John Porter	Allen Hazen	"
9	Daniel Dennison	"	Lewis Merritt	"	Henry Shedd
10	Benj. Billings	"	Surry Ross	"	"
11	Ira Davis	"	Ebenezer Spear 2d	Shubael Converse	"
12	Levi Slack	Moses Pollard jr	"	Jared Marsh	"
13	Gard'r Winslow	"	"		Robert Perry jr
14	John Wheeler	"	Rufus Forbush	"	John Wheeler
15	Barney Cooper	Thomas B. Martin	"	Thomas B. Harvey	William B. Henry
16	John L. Bowman	"	Henry Bingham	John L. Bowman	Romanzo Walker
17	Lyman Tyler	Roderick D. Lathrop		Roder'k D. Lathrop	John C. Baldwin
18	O. M. Whipple	Hiram Harlow	"	"	James Whipple
19	Paul W. Gay	John R. Forrest			Asahel Felch
20	Augustus Tuttle	"	John Spafford	"	Hyren Henry
21	Solon Richardson	"	Edward S. Barrett	Jerry Adams	Stephen Smith
22					
23	Allen Wardner	Horace Everett	Thos F. Hammond	"	Dyer Story
24	Andrew Tracy	Andrew Tracy	Andrew Tracy	Nathan T. Churchill	"

REP'S, WASHINGTON, WINDHAM, WINDSOR.

WASHINGTON 1847	1848	1849	1850	FIRST TOWN CL'K.
1 Geo. W. Collamer	"	Harvey Tilden	Warren H. Ellis	Josedh Dwight 1793
2 Asa Andrews	"	Orren Smith	Elijah H. Covell	David Nye 91
3 Shubael Wheele:	Enoch C. McLoud	"	David B Fay	Peter Wheelock 95
4 David Belding	Ebenezer W. Corse	"	Lorenzo Davis	
5 Burr Freeman	Merrill Tyler	Jacob Boyce	"	
6 East Montpelier		Nathaniel C. King	"	Royal Wheeler 1848
7	Enoch D. Putnam		Hiram Potter	
8	Joseph Hancock	John Poor	"	Mr. Wilson 88
9 Charles Clark	Homer W. Heaton	Jackson A. Vail	"	Ziba Woodworth 91
10 R. H. Kimball	Don P. Carpenter	Dennis Childs	"	
11 Hem'n Carpenter	"	George B. Pierce	John Gregory	N. Richardson 94
12 Reuben Huntoon	Daniel A. Perry	Francis B. Hall	Ezra Kidder	Harvey Bancroft 96
13 Benj. Edwards jr	"	Dexter Samson	"	Thos Huntington 96
14 Ithamer Smith	Benjamin Reed jr		Roder'k Richardson	Moses Heaton 94
15 Denslow Upham	William Rankin	"	Gideon Goodspeed	Samuel Lard 98
16 Thad's Clough	Charles C. Arms 2		"	Ezra Butler 90
17 Michael Jackson	"	Benjamin Wells	"	
18	George W. Leavitt		Milton Brown	John Young 1803
WINDHAM CO.				William Beal 81
1	Lyman Alexander	"	Samuel Earl jr	Henry Wells
2 John R. Blake	George Newman	"	Isaac Wellman	John Waters 95
3 Asa Flint	Joel Codding	"	"	Reuben Dean 1811
4 Joel Lyman	James Miner	"	George R. Miller	
5 Wm. O. Miller	Winslow Dutton	"	Ambrose Burgess	Aaron Putnam 80
6 B. H. Bingham	John L. Butterfield	"	"	J. Sheperdson 1772
7 Nathan P. Chapin	"	Aaron C. Barney	"	Sam'l Woodard 72
8 Jonas Scott	"	Joseph Henry	Amos Tucker	Wm. H. Church 81
9	John C. Butler	"	Luke Howard	
10 David Arnold	"	Winfield Wright	Abiel Whitman	Wm. Mather 75
11 Sylves'r Worden	Zebina Wallace	"	John L. Roberts	Luke Knowlton 74
12 Marshall Newton	George Arnold	Sir Isaac Newton	"	Lucas Wilson 70
13 W.P. Richardson	W. B Richardson	"	Mark Crawford	Joshua Webb 60
14 Benjamin Smith	Asa Wentworth jr	"	Russel Hyde	
15 Ephraim Rice	Hollis Town	Ephraim Rice	Joseph Morse	
16 Amos Parsons		John Underwood	Rufus Lyman	
17 A. C. Howard	James H. Phelps	"	William H. Joy	Joseph Tyler 91
18 Jos. E. Franklin	Eli Lee	Joseph E. Franklin	Ebenezer Howe jr	John Bridgman 70
19 Erastus Plimpton	Justice Knowlton	Levi Fitts	"	Aaron Hudson 86
20 Ira Goodhue	Ellery Albee	Alvan Goodell	N. Tracy Sheafe	
21 Waters Gillett	Eli Green	"	"	Eliphalet Hyde 80
22	Stephen P. Flagg	"	"	
23 Simeon Pierce	"	Jason D. Jones	William A. Chapin	
WINDSOR CO.			Solomon Howard	Moses Warner 81
1 John Adams	George W. Stickney	John Adoms	Luther M. Graves	Joseph Artherton 94
2	William Davis	Jona. M. Boynton	"	Thos. H. White 78
3 Hiram Aikens	Sebast'n R. Streeter	"	Almon Durkee	Barnabas Strong 82
4		Aug's P. Hunton	John Osgood	John Hawkins 84
5 R. W. Southgate	Charles S. Raymond	"	William Smith	Josiah Fletcher 77
6 John F. Deane	"		A E. Prescott Heald	Thos. Chandler 67
7 Rodney Sherwin		Allen Hazen	Albert G. Dewey	Elijah Strong 68
8 John Porter	"		Paschal P. Taft	Zadock Wright 67
9 Hampden Cutts	Eben M. Stocker	Ward Cotton	Daniel A. Heald	Jesse Fletcher 92
10 Wm. K. Manning	Darius L. Green		Ebenezer B. Brown	
11 Wm. Loveland		Ebenezer Spear 2d	Abraham S. Day	Adam Brown 87
12 Moses Pollard jr	"	Levi Slack	Elisha Smith	John W. Dana 73
13 Oliver Leonard	Martin D. Follett	Joshua Vail	Luther Carlton	Jed'h Leavens 80
14 Charles Buck		Solomon Keyes	"	
15	James Wing 2d	John W. Chaffee	John Coy	Comfort Seaver
16 R. Walker	James Davis	Daniel Woodward		Benj. Spaulding 68
17 J. C. Baldwin	Hiram Moore	"	"	
18 James Whipple	Moses White	Ephraim Walker jr	"	
19	John M. Bennett	"	Zeb Twitchell	Benoni Tuttle 78
20 Hyren Henry	C. M. Chamberlain	"	John C. Harkell	Alvin Simonds 1800
21 Stephen Smith	"	"	Asa B. Foster	Gilm'n H. Shed 1849
22		Daniel Read	"	Thomas Cooper
23 Dyer Story	Daniel Reed	Hiram Harlow	"	Joab Hoisington 73
24 Julius Converse	"	"	Thomas E. Powers	

SUPREME COURT JUDGES FROM 1778 TO 1850.

'78	M. Robinson 1*	John Shepardson 2	John Fassett jr 3	Thomas Chandler 4	John Throop 5				
79	"	1	" 2	" 3	Paul Spooner 5	" 4			
80	"	1 Increase Mosely 4	" "	" 3	" 2	" 5			
81	"	2 Elisha Payne 1	" "	Bez. Woodward 3	Joseph Caldwell 4	" 5			
82	"	1 Jonas Fay 3	John Fassett 4	Paul Spooner 3	Peter Olcott 2	" 5			
83	"	1 Thomas Porter 1	" 3	" 2	" 4				
84	Nath'l Niles 3	" 4	" 2	" 1	" 5				
85	" 3	" 5	" 4	Moses Robinson 2	" 1				
86	" 3	Nath'l Chipman 4	Luke Knowlton 5	" 2	" 1				
87	" 2		"	" 3	" 1				
88		Step'n R. Bradley 3		" 2	" 1				
89 and 90		N. Chipman 1	Noah Smith 2	Samuel Knight 3					
91, 92 & 93		Elijah Paine 2		" 1	Isaac Tichenor 3				
94 and 95		Lott Hall 2		E. Woodbridge 3	" 1				
96		"	N. Chipman 1	" 3					
97		" 3		" 2	Israel Smith 1				
98, 99 and 1800		" 2		" 1	Noah Smith 3				
1801 and 2		Jona. Robinson 1	Royal Tyler 2	Stephen Jacob 3					
3, 4, 5 and 6		" 1	" 2		Theo's Harrington 3				
7 and 8		Jonas Galusha 3	" 1		" 2				
9, 10, 11, and 12		David Fay 3	" 1		" 2				
13 and 14		N. Chipman 1	Daniel Farrand 2		J. H. Hubbard 3				
15		Asa Aldis 1	Richard Skinner 2		James Fisk 3				
16		Wm. A. Palmer 3	" 1		" 2				
17, 18, 19, and 20		Dudley Chase 1	Joel Doolittle 2	William Brayton 3					
21			C. P. Van Ness 1	"	Joel Doolittle 2				
22			"	C. K. Williams 1	" 2				
23		R. Skinner 1		" 3	Asa Aiken 2				
24		"	J. Doolittle 2	"	" 3				
25 and 26		" 1	Samuel Prentiss 2	T. Hutchinson 3	Stephen Royce jr 4				
27		" 1	" 2	"	Bates Turner 3	" 4			
28		" 1	" 2	" 3	" 4	Ephr'm Paddock 5			
29		C. K. Williams 3	" 1	" 2	S. Royce jr 4	" 5			
30		"	J. C. Thompson 5	" 1	"	" 3	" 4		
31 and 32		"	Nicholas Baylies 4	" 1	"	Saml. S. Phelps 3	" 5		
33 and 34		"	Jacob Collamer 1	John Mattocks 5	" 2	"	" 3		
35, 36, and 37		"	" 1	Isaac F. Redfield 5	" 2	" 4			
38 and 39		"	" 1	" 3	" 4	Milo L. Bennett 2	" 5		
40, 41,		"	" 1	" 3	Stephen Royce 2	"	" 5		
42		"	William Hebard 5	" 3	" 2	"	" 4		
43		"	Daniel Kellogg 5	" 3	" 2	"	" 4		
44		"	Wm. Hebard 5	" 3	" 2	"	" 4		
45		"	D. Kellogg 5	" 3	" 2	"	" 4		
46, 47	Hil'nd Hall 5	Charles Davis 6	" 4	" 3	" 2	" 1	" 3		
48 & 49	" 5	Luke P. Poland 6	" 3	" 2	"	" 1	" 3		
50			" 3	" 2	"	" 1			

By a law passed in 1849, and which took effect in 1850, the number of Supreme Court Judges were reduced to three, and four Circuit Judges to be elected, one for each of the Circuits to act as Chief Justices of the County Courts of their respective Circuits, and in pursuance of that law, the following Judges were appointed at the last session of the Legislature. In the first Circuit, Bennington, Rutland and Addison Counties, Robert Pierpoint was chosen. In the second circuit, Windham, Windsor and Orange, Jacob Collamer was appointed. In the third circuit, Chittenden, Franklin, Lamoille, and Grand Isle, Milo L. Bennett was elected, In the fourth circuit, Washington, Caledonia, Orleans and Essex, Luke P. Poland was chosen.

By the above table it appears that Stephen Royce, jr., and Stephen Royce, the same person, has received 24 elections of Judge. Charles K. Williams 19. Isaac F. Redfield 16. Royal Tyler 12. Milo L. Bennett 12. Theophilus Harrington and Moses Robinson 10 each. Paul Spooner Titus Hutchinson and Jacob Collamer, 9 each. John Fassett, jr., and Richard Skinner, 8 each. Daniel Kellogg, Lott Hall, Samuel S. Phelps, Enoch Woodbridge, and Joel Doolittle, 7 each. Nathaniel Chipman, and Jonathan Robinson, 6 each. Noah Smith, Isaac Tichenor, William Brayton, Samuel Prentiss, and Samuel Knight, 5 each. Hiland Hall, Nathaniel Niles, David Fay and Dudley Chase, 4 each. John Throop, Peter Olcott, Thomas Porter, Elijah Paine and Ephraim Paddock, 3 each, and the remainder, a less number, making 60 Supreme Judges in 72 years past.

---oo---

SENATORS TO CONGRESS FROM VERMONT.

Moses Robinson	1791 to 1796	Benjamin Swift	1833 to 1839	James Fisk	1817 to 1819
Isaac Tichenor	1796 to 1797	Samuel S. Phelps	1839 to 1851	Wm. A. Palmer	1819 to 1825
Nathaniel Chipman	1797 to 1803	Solomon Foot	1851 ——	Dudley Chase	1825 to 1831
Israel Smith	1803 to 1807	Stephen R. Bradley	1791 to 1794	Samuel Prentiss	1831 to 1842
Jona. Robinson	1807 to 1814	Elijah Paine	1794 to 1801	Samuel C. Crafts	1842 to 1843
Isaac Tichenor	1814 to 1821	Stephen R. Bradley	1801 to 1813	William Upham	1843 ——
Horatio Seymour	1821 to 1833	Dudley Chase	1813 to 1817		

*The figures 1, 2, 3, 4, 5, and 6, denote the manner in which they were elected.

COUNTY OFFICERS FROM 1778 TO 1850.

BEN. CO. MAR. 1778	JUNE 1778.	OCT. 1778.	1779	1780
1 Jeremiah Clark	"			
2 Samuel Robinson	"			
2 Martin Powell	John Fassett			
2 John Fassett jr.	"			
2 Thomas Jewett	Gideon Olin			
3 *				
4	Benjamin Fay			
5				
6		John Fassett	"	"
6		Martin Powell		
7		Roswell Hopkins	"	"
7		James Murdock	"	"
CUMBERLAND CO.				
Westminstershire				
1 J. Shephardson	"			
2 Stephen Tilden	"			
2 Hubbell Wells	Samuel Fletcher			
2 Hez'h Thompson	"			
2 Nath'l Robinson	Joshua Webb			
RUTLAND SHIRE				
1 Joseph Bowker	Thomas Rowley			
2 Heber Allen	"			
2 Charles Brewster	Theodus Curtis			
2 John Starks	"			
2 Jonathan Fassett	"			
NEWBURY SHIRE.				
1 Jacob Bailey	Deacon Smalley			
2 Jacob Burton	John Burnett			
2 William Heaton	"			
2 Reuben Foster	"			
2 John French	Benjamin Baldwin			

By a law passed in February, 1781, the election of County Officers were given to the people of their respective districts, except the State's Attorneys. The law was very similar to the one now in force, hence arises the difficulty of ascertaining who our County officers were during the continuance of that law, as they were not to be found on the Legislative Journals.

*In the following pages, figure 1 denotes Chief Justices, 2. Assistants, 3, Clerks of the Courts, 4, Sheriffs, 5, State's Attorneys, 6, Judges of Probate, 7, Registers of Probate.

The above are all the Judges of a Special Court that I can find were appointed previous to 1781 Nor have I been able to find by any county records that they had Clerks, Sheriffs or State's Attorneys till 1781. It does, however, appear from other sources that Clerks, Sheriffs, and States Attorneys were appointed previous to the time above stated. Slade's State papers inform us that David Redding who was executed at Bennington, June 11, 1778, was, or had been in the custody of Benjamin Fay, Sheriff of the County of Bennington, (page 239,) By the same authority it appears that Joseph Fay on the 10th of December, 1778, was appointed Clerk of the Supreme Court for Bennington Co., and on the 26th of May, 1779, Stephen R. Bradley was appointed Clerk for Cumberland County, pages 249, 251 and 252 we are informed that Noah Smith was appointed State's Attorney *pro tem* for Cumberland Co., in May, 1779, and in June, 1779, was appointed State's Attorney for Bennington County. Thus it appears that those officers were appointed notwithstanding the court records do not show it.

In February, 1779, a law was passed dividing the State into two counties. Bennington on the west and Cumberland on the east side of the mountain. If it was divided as laid down in the law published in Slade's State papers, (pages 294-5,) the county of Cumberland would look rather waspish, being but 6 miles wide near the center, but as there was then no town in the State by the name of Bradford, it is presumed that Barnard is the town on which the line should be described; as that would be running a very proper course, between the last and next mentioned points.

Since the above was in type, I have received a letter from the Clerk of the Court in Bennington, which says. " I could not find any Record, nor anything else to show who were the Sheriffs of the County before 1786, but I have just had a conversation with Samuel Fay, who resides in the house where the " Council of Safety" held its meetings in this town, and he says that Benjamin Fay, his father, was Sheriff two or three years, and remembers when he hung Redding, and when his father's time had expired Jonas Galusha took the office, and he continued in it till David Robinson was appointed. He is now 79 years old, and has been Deputy Sheriff 18 years and Sheriff 12, making 30 years in the Sheriff department.

HON. SAMUEL SAFFORD.

On page 37 is a short account of the Hon. Samuel Safford. I have since that was printed found that his grandfather, Joseph Safford, came from England and settled first at Plymouth, Mass, and removed to Norwich, Conn., in 1723. Joseph Safford, jr., the father of Samuel, was born at Ipswich, Mass, in 1705. Samuel Safford was born at Norwich, Conn., April 14, 1737, and died at Bennington March 13th, 1813, being very near 76 years of age. On page 38, last line but one, for 1786 read 1781.

COUNTY OFFICERS FROM 1778 TO 1850. CONTINUED.

BENNINGTON, 1781.	1782	1783	1784	1785
1 Samuel Safford	"	"	"	"
2 Gideon Olin	"	"	"	"
2 John Strong	"	Elisha Barber	"	"
2 Elisha Barber	"	Gideon Brownson	"	"
2 David Lee, jr.	"	John White	"	"
3 Noah Smith	Lewis Beach	"	"	"
4 Jonas Galusha	"	"	"	"
5 Noah Smith	"	"	Jonathaan Brace	"
6 Nathaniel Brush	Jonas Fay	"	"	"
6 Martin Powell	"	"	"	"
7 Roswell Hopkins	Jonathan Robinson	"	"	"
7 Enoch Woodbridge.	"	"	"	"
WINDHAM CO.				
1				
2				
2				
2				
2				
3				
4				
5				
6 Micah Townsend	"	"	"	"
6				
7 Micah Townsend	"	"	"	"
7				
RUTLAND CO.				
1 Increase Mosely	"	"	"	"
2 Joseph Bowker	"	Benjamin Whipple	"	"
2 Thomas Porter	William Ward	"	"	"
2 Benjamin Whipple	"	Samuel Mattocks	"	"
3 J. Brace [2 months				
3 Obabiah Noble	"	"	"	"
4 Abraham Ives	"	"	"	"
5 Nathaniel Chipman	"	"	"	Darius Chipman
6 Joseph Bowker	"	"	Elisha Clark	"
7 Joseph Bowker	"	"	Elisha Clark	"
WINDSOR CO.				
1	Joseph Marsh	"	"	"
2	Thomas Murdock	"	"	"
2	Elias Weld	"	"	"
2	Elijah Robinson	"	"	"
2	Abel Curtis	"	Paul Brigham	"
3	Bryant Brown	"	"	"
4				
5				
6		Ebenezer Curtis	"	"
6 Paul Spooner	"	John Throop	"	"
7		Daniel Farran	"	"
7 Paul Spooner	"	John Throop	"	"
ADDISON CO.				
1				
2				John Strong
2				Gamaliel Painter
3				Ira Allen
4				Samuel Chipman jr
ORANGE CO.				Noah Chittenden
1				
2				
2				
2				
2				
3				
4				
5				
6				
6	Isael Smith	"	"	"
7	Jed. P. Buckingham	"	"	"

REV. ELISHA HUTCHINSON,

The first minister of Pomfret, had some singularities about him. He was preaching a sermon in Hartland at a private house, with two rooms, and he stood in the door way. When about half through his discourse, Lieutenant Governor Spooner came in, upon which, he informed his audience that he had got about half through his sermon, but as Governor Spooner has come to hear it, I will begin it again, and looking at a woman near him says, good woman, get out of that chair and let Gov. Spooner have a seat, if you please.

COUNTY OFFICERS FROM 1778 TO 1850. CONTINUED.

1786	1787	1788	1789	1790
BENNINGTON 1786		"	"	
1 Samuel Safford	1 Samuel Safford	"	"	"
2 Gideon Olin	2 Gideon Olin	"	"	"
2 Elisha Barber		"	"	"
2 Gideon Brownson	2 GideonBrownson	"	"	"
2 John White	3 Nathaniel Brush	"	"	"
3 Lewis Beach	4 David Robinson	"	"	"
4 Jonas Galusha				
5 Noah Smith	5 Noah Smith	"	E. Woodbridge	"
6 Jonas Fay	6 Nathaniel Brush	"	"	"
6 Enoch Woodbridge	6 Martin Powell	"	"	"
7	7			
7 Truman Powell	7 Truman Powell	"	"	"
WINDHAM CO.				
1 Samuel Knight	1 Luke Knowlton	"	"	"
2 John Bridgeman	2 John Bridgeman	"	"	"
2 Samuel Fletcher	2 Benjamin Burt	"	"	"
2 Benjamin Burt	3			
2 Hubbell Wells				
3	4 Elkanah Day	Samuel Fletcher	"	"
4 Elkanah Day	5			
5				
6 Micah Townsend	6 Micah Townsend	"	John Bridgeman	"
6 Noah Sabin	6 Noah Sabin	"	"	"
7 Micah Townsend	7 Micah Townsend	"	John W. Blake	"
7	7			
RUTLAND CO.				
1 Increase Moseley	1 Thomas Porter	Samuel Mattocks	Ebenezer Marvin	"
2 Samuel Mattocks	2 Samuel Mattocks	Ebenezer Marvin	Lemuel Chipman	"
2 Ebenezer Marvin	2 William Ward	Lemuel Chipman	Simeon Smith	Samuel Williams
2 Mathew Lyon	3 Obadiah Noble	"	"	"
2 William Ward	4 Jonathan Bell	"	"	"
3 Obadiah Noble	5 Darius Chipman	"	"	"
4 Jonathan Bell	6 Elisha Clark	"	"	"
5 Darius Chipman	6 William Ward	"	"	"
6 Elisha Clark	7 Elisha Clark	"	"	"
6	7 William Ward	"	"	"
7 Elisha Clark				
7				
WINDSOR CO.				
1 Thomas Moredock	1 Joseph Marsh	"	"	"
2 Elias Weld	2 Thomas Murdock	Elias Weld	"	Paul Brigham
2 Elijah Robinson	2 Elias Weld	Elijah Robinson	"	"
2 Paul Brigham	3 Bryant Brown	"	"	Lewis R. Morris
2 Thomas Chandler	4 Paul Brigham	"	"	William Sweetser
3 Bryant Brown	5			
4				
5	6 Elijah Robinson	"	"	"
6 Bryant Brown	6 John Throop	"	"	"
6 John Throop	7 Bryant Brown	"	"	"
7 Bryant Brown	7 Benjamin Swan			
7 John Throop				
ADDISON CO.				
1 John Strong	1 John Strong	"	"	"
2 Ira Allen	2 Gamaliel Painter	"	"	"
2 William Brush	2 Hiland Hall	"	Abel Thompson	"
2 Abel Thompson	3 Roswell Hopkins	"	"	"
2 Samuel Lane	4 Samuel Strong	"	John Chipman	"
3 Roswell Hopkins	5 Seth Storrs	"	"	"
4 Gamaliel Painter	6 John Strong	"	"	" *
5 Seth Storrs	7 John Strong	Seth Storrs	"	"
6 John Strong				
7 John Strong				
ORANGE CO.				
1 Jacob Bailey	"	"	"	"
2 Israel Smith	"	"	"	"
2 Alexander Harvey	"	"	"	"
2 Israel Morey			"	
2 Thomas Johnson		"		
3	3			
4 John G. Bailey	"	"	Fry Bailey	"
5				
6 T. Bartholomew	"	"	"	"
6 Jacob Kent	"	"	"	"
6				"
6			6 Elijah Paine	6 Eben W. Judd
7 J. P. Buckingham	"	"	"	"
7 Nathan Godard	"	Daniel Farrand	"	"

*In October, 1790, Roswell Hopkins was appointed Judge of Probate, but did no official business and in January, 1791, John Strong was again appointed.

COUNTY OFFICERS FROM 1778 TO 1850. CONTINUED.

BENNINGTON 1791.	1792	1793	1794	1795
1 Samuel Safford	"	"	"	"
2 Gideon Olin	"	"	"	"
2 Gideon Brownson	"	"		Jonas Galusha
3			Samuel Robinson	"
3 Nathaniel Brush	"	"	"	"
4 David Robinson	"	"	"	"
5 Noah Smith	Joshua Hathaway	"	"	David Fay
6 Nathaniel Brush	"	"	"	Jonathan Robinson
6 Martin Powell	"	"	Timothy Todd	John Shumway
7				
7 Truman Powell	"	Silas Powell	John Todd	John Shumway jr.
WINDHAM CO.				
1 Luke Knowlton	"	"	Samuel Knight	"
2 John Bridgman	"	"	"	"
2 Benjamin Burt	"	"	"	"
3				
4 Samuel Fletcher	"	"	"	"
5				
6 John Bridgman	"	"	"	"
6 Noah Sabin	"	"	"	"
7 John W. Blake	"	"	"	"
7				
RUTLAND CO.				
1 Ebenezer Marvin	"	"	Samuel Williams	"
2 Lemuel Chipman	"	"	Samuel Mattocks	Abel Cooper
2 Samuel Williams	"	"	Abel Cooper	Ebenezer Wilson
3 Nathan Osgood	"	"	"	"
4 Jonathan Bell	"	"	"	"
5 Darius Chipman	"	"	"	"
6 Elisha Clark	"	"	"	"
6 William Ward	Simeon Smith	William Ward	"	"
7 Elisha Clark	"	"	"	"
7 William Ward	Chauncey Langdon	"	"	John Brown
WINDSOR CO.				
1 Joseph Marsh	"	"	"	"
2 Paul Brigham	"	"	"	"
2 Eljah Robinson	"	"	"	"
3 Lewis R. Morris	"	"	"	"
4 William Sweetser	"	"	"	"
5				
6 Elijah Robinson	"	"	"	"
6 John Throop	"	Paul Brigham	William Perry	"
7 Bryant Brown	"	"	"	"
7 John Throop	"	"	"	Benjamin Swan
ADDISON CO.				
1 John Strong	"	"	"	"
2 Gamaliel Painter	"	"	"	"
2 Abel Thompson	"	"	"	Abel Thompson
3 Roswell Hopkins	"	"	"	Joel Linsley
4 John Chipman	"	"	"	"
5				
6 John Strong	"	"	"	"
7 Seth Storrs	"	"	"	"
ORANGE CO.				
1 Jacob Bailey	Jonathan Arnold	Israel Smith	"	"
2 Israel Smith	"	Alexander Harvey	"	Cornelius Lynde
2 Alex. Harvey	"	Cornelius Lynde	"	Wm. Chamberlain
3				
4 Fry Bailey	"	"	"	"
5				
6 T. Bartholomew	"	"	"	"
6 Jacob Kent	"	"	"	6 James Lucas
6	Israel Converse	"	"	"
6 Eben W. Judd	"	"	"	"
J. P. Buckingham	"	"	"	"
7 Isaac Bailey	"	"	"	"

COUNTY OFFICERS FROM 1778 TO 1850. CONTINUED.

	BENNINGTON 1796.	1797.	1798	1799	1800
1	Samuel Safford	"	"	"	"
2	Gideon Olin	"	Solomon Wright	"	Gideon Olin
2	Jonas Galusha	"	Christopher Roberts	"	Jonas Galusha
3	Samuel Robinson	"	"	"	"
3	Nathaniel Brush	"	"	"	"
4	David Robinson	"	William Cooley	"	David Robinson
5	David Fay	"	Trumon Squire	"	David Fay
6	Jona. Robinson	"	Timothy Follett	"	Jona. Robinson
6	John Shumway	Luther Stone	Truman Squire	"	"
7					
7	Anson Shumway	"	Martin Roberts	"	"
WINDHAM CO					
1	John Bridgman	"	"	"	"
2	Benjamin Burt	"	"	"	"
2	William Bigelow	"	"	"	"
3					
4	Samuel Fletcher	"	"	"	"
5	Royal Tyler	"	"	"	"
6	John Bridgman	"	"	"	"
6	Noah Sabin	"	"	"	"
7	John W. Blake	"	"	"	"
7					
RUTLAND CO.					
1	Samuel Williams	"	"	"	Theo's Harrington
2	Ebenezer Wilson	"	Jonas Safford	Ebenezer Wilson	"
2	Jonas Safford	"	Hiram Horton	Jonas Safford	"
3	Nathan Osgood	"	"	"	"
4	Jonathan Bell	"	"	"	"
5	Abel Spencer	"	"	"	"
6	Elisha Clark	"	"	"	"
6	William Ward	"	Chauncey Langdon	"	William Ward
7	Elisha Clark	"	"	Obadiah Noble jr	Elisha Clark jr
7	C. Langdon	John Brown	"	Selah Gridley	"
WINDSOR CO.					
1	Lewis R. Morris	Stephen Jacob	"	"	"
2	Elijah Robinson	"	"	"	"
2	Jesse Williams	"	"	"	"
3	Benjamin Swan	"	"	"	"
4	Lucius Hubbard	"	William Rice	"	"
5	Amasa Paine	"	"	"	"
6	Elijah Robinson	"	"	"	"
6	William Perry	"	"	"	Paul Brigham
7	Bryant Brown	Isaac Green	William Hunter	"	"
7	Benjamin Swan	"	Titus Hutchinson	"	"
ADDISON CO.					
1	John Strong	"	"	"	"
2	Abel Thompson	"	"	"	"
2	Joel Linsley	"	"	"	"
3	Roswell Hopkins	"	"	"	"
4	John Chipman	"	"	"	"
5	Seth Storrs	Daniel Chipman	"	"	"
6	John Strong	"	"	"	"
7	Seth Storrs	Albon Mann	"	"	"
ORANGE CO.					
1	Israel Smith	Cornelius Lynde	"	Jed. P. Buckingham	"
2	Cornelius Lynde	Beriah Loomis	"	"	"
2	Wm. Chamberlin	Elisha Allis	"	"	"
3					
4	Fry Bailey	Josiah Edson	"	"	"
5	Daniel Farrand	Jed. P. Buckingham	Daniel Farrand	Oramel Hinckley	Charles Bulkley
6	Daniel Farrand	Jed. P. Buckingham	"	"	"
6		Aaron Storrs	"	"	Jonathan Fisk
7	Isaac Bailey	J. Hinckley	"	"	"
7					

COUNTY OFFICERS FROM 1778 TO 1850, CONTINUED.

	1801	1802	1803	1804	1805
BENNINGTON					
1	Samuel Safford	"	"	"	"
2	Gideon Olin	"	Jonas Galusha	"	"
2	Jonas Galusha	"	David Sheldon	"	"
3	Sam'l Robinson 2	"	"	"	"
3	Nathaniel Brush	"	Joel Pratt Co. Clk	"	"
4	David Robinson	"	"	"	"
5	Richard Skinner	"	"	"	"
6	Josiah Wright	"	"	"	"
6	Christofr Roberts	"	"	"	"
7					
7	Martin Roberts	"	"	"	"
WINDHAM CO.					
1	Samuel Knight	LukeKnowlton	Samuel Porter	"	"
2	Benjamin Burt	"	James Roberts	"	"
2	Jason Duncan	"	Ebenezer Allen	Elijah Knight	"
3	Lemuel Whitney	"	"	"	"
4	Samuel Fletcher	"	"	"	"
5	Daniel Farrand	"	"	Wm. C. Bradley	"
6	John Bridgeman	"	Ebenezer Miller	Samuel Porter	"
6	Noah Sabin	"	"	"	"
7	John W. Blake	"	Martin Field	Lemuel Whitney	"
7					
RUTLAND CO.					
1	Theo. Harrington	"	James Witherill	"	"
2	Ebenezer Wilson	"	"	"	Nathan B. Graham
2	James Witherell	"	Nathan B. Graham	"	Pliny Smith
3	Nathan Osgood	"	"	"	"
4	Jonathan Bell	Arunah W. Hyde	"	Robert Temple	"
5	Abel Spencer	"	Darius Chipman	"	"
6	Elisha Clark	"	James Harrington	"	Joseph Randall
6	William Ward	"	"	"	"
7	Elisha Clark jr,	"	"	"	"
7	John Stanley	"	William Ward jr.	Nathan Osgood	'
WINDSOR CO.					
1	Paul Brigham	Elijah Robinson	Elias Keyes	"	"
2	Asaph Fletcher	"	"	"	Aaron Leland
2	Jesse Williams	"	Aaron Leland	"	William Hunter
3	Benjamin Swan	"	"	"	"
4	William Rice	William Strong	"	"	"
5	Amasa Paine	Daniel Buck	Titus Hutchinson	"	"
6	William Hunter	"	"	"	"
6	Oliver Gallup	"	Jesse Williams	"	"
7	Luther Mills	"	"	"	"
7	Titus Hutchinson	"	"	"	"
ADDISON CO.					
1	Joel Linsley	"	"	"	"
2	Abraham Dibble	"	"	"	"
2	Henry Olin	"	"	"	Henry Olin
3	Roswell Hopkins	"	Darius Mathews	"	Samuel Strong
4	William Slade	"	"	"	"
5	Daniel Chipman	"	"	"	"
6	John Strong	Darius Mathews	"	"	Loyal Case
7	Albon Mann	"	Chester Wright	"	"
ORANGE CO.					
1	J. P. Buckingham	"	"	"	"
2	Beriah Loomis	"	"	"	"
2	Elisha Allis	James Fisk	Moulton Morey	"	"
3	Isaac Bailey	"	"	"	"
4	Josiah Edson	"	Micah Barron	"	"
5	Charels Buikley	"	Dudley Chase	"	"
6	J. P Buckingham	"	"	"	"
6	Jonathan Fisk	"	"	"	"
7	J. Hinckley	"	"	"	"
7					

COUNTY OFFICERS FROM 1778 TO 1850. CONTINUED.

BENNINGTON 1806	1807	1808	1809	1810
1 Samuel Safford	Gideon Olin	"	"	"
2 Jonas Galusha	David Sheldon	"	"	Josiah Wright
2 David Sheldon	Josiah Wright	"	"	Josiah Rising
3 Saml. Robinson 2	"	"	"	"
3 Joel Pratt	"	"	"	"
4 David Robinson	"	"	"	"
5 Richard Skinner	"	"	"	"
6 Josiah Wright	"	"	"	"
6 Richard Skinner	"	"	"	"
7				
7 Ezra Isham	"	"	Calvin Sheldon	"
WINDHAM CO.				
1 James Roberts	"	"	"	"
2 Jason Duncan	Alex'r Campbell	Jason Duncan	Oliver Chapin	John Aiken
2 Alex'r Campbell	Oliver Chapin	James Aiken	John Aiken	Jairus Hall
3 Lemuel Whitney	"	"	"	"
4 Mark Richards	"	"	"	"
5 Wm. C. Bradley	"	"	"	"
6 Gilbert Dennison	"	"	"	"
6 Noah Sabin	"	"	Elijah Knight	"
7 Saml. Shepardson	Samuel Elliott	"	John Phelps	"
7				
RUTLAND CO.				
1 Isaac Clark	"	"	"	"
2 Caleb Hendee jr	Pliny Smith	"	"	"
2 James Harrington	"	Amos Thompson	"	"
3 Robert Temple	"	"	"	"
4 Arunah W. Hyde	"	"	Eleazer Flagg	"
5 N. B. Graham	"	"	"	Rollin C. Mallory
6 Joseph Randall	"	"	Caleb Hendee jr	"
6 William Ward	"	"	"	"
7 Nathan Osgood	"	"	"	William D. Smith
7 William Ward jr	"	"	"	"
WINDSOR CO.				
1 Elias Keyes	"	"	"	"
2 Aaron Leland	"	"	"	"
2 William Hunter	"	"	"	"
3 Benjamin Swan	"	"	"	"
4 William Strong	"	"	"	Paschal P. Enos
5 Titus Hutchinson	"	"	"	"
6 William Hunter	"	"	"	"
6 Jesse Williams	"	"	"	"
7 Luther Mills	"	"	"	"
7 Alex Hutchinson	"	"	"	"
ADDISON CO.				
1 Joel Linsley	Henry Olin	Joel Linsley	"	Henry Olin
2 Henry Olin	Samuel Strong	Henry Olin	"	Charles Rich
2 Samuel Strong	Charles Rich	"	"	Mathew Phelps jr
3 Darius Mathews	"	"	"	"
3		Martin Post	"	John S. Larrabee
4 William Slade	"	"	"	"
5 Loyal Case	"	David Edmond	"	Horatio Seymour
6 Darius Mathews	"	"	"	"
7 Chester Wright	John Simmons	"	"	"
ORANGE CO.				
1 Moulton Morey	"	"	James Fish	Elisha Hotchkiss
2 Beriah Loomis	"	"	"	"
2 ames Tarbox	"	"	"	"
3 Isaac Bailey	"	"	"	"
4 Micah Barron	"	"	"	"
5 Dudley Chase	Daniel Peaslee	"	"	"
6 Elisha Thayer	"	"	"	"
6 Jonathan Fisk	"	"	"	"
7 William Niles	"	"	"	"
7				

COUNTY OFFICERS FROM 1778 TO 1850. CONTINUED. 81

	1811	1812	1813	1814	1815
BENNINGTON					
1	Josiah Wright	"	"	Solomon Wright	Josiah Wright
2	Josiah Graves	"	Edmond Graves	Josiah Graves	"
2	Edmond Graves	"	Grove Moore	"	Edmond Graves
3	S. Robinson 2d	"	"	"	"
3	Joel Pratt	"	"	"	"
4	Samuel Fay	"	"	"	"
5	Richard Skinner	"	Anson J. Sperry	"	Calvin Sheldon
6	Josiah Wright	"	"	Solomon Wright	Jonathan Robinson
6	Richard Skinner	"	Grove Moore	"	John Underhill
7					
7	Calvin Sheldon	"	Nathan Burton	Henry B. Moore	Calvin Sheldon
WINDHAM CO.					
1	James Roberts	"	"	Phinehas White	Elijah Knight
2	John Aiken	"	Jairus Hall	"	John Aiken
2	Jairus Hall	"	Luke Knowlton	"	"
3	Lemuel Whitney	"	"	"	"
4	Gilbert Denison	"	Jonathan Barron	"	Aaron Wales
5	Wm. C. Bradley	Martin Field	Phinehas White	Samuel Elliott	Martin Field
6	James Roberts	"	Darius Bullock	"	Gilbert Denison
6	Elijah Knight	"	"	Phinehas White	Elijah Knight
7	John Phelps	"	Samuel Elliott	"	Royal Tyler
7					
RUTLAND CO.					
1	Pliny Smith	"	"	"	"
2	Amos Thompson	"	"	"	"
2	John H. Andrus	Thos. Hammond	John H. Andrus	Chauncey Smith	Thos. Hammond
3	Robert Temple	"	"	"	"
4	Eleazer Flagg	Ralph Paige	Estus Barker	Thomas Hooker	Estus Barker
5	R. C. Mallary	"	CharlesK.Williams	"	Rollin C. Mallory
6	Wm. Harrington	"	"	Obadiah Noble	"
6	William Ward	"	Erastus Higley	"	"
7	William D.Smith	"	"	William Page	"
7	William Ward jr	"	Chauncey Langdon	Selah H. Merrill	"
WINDSOR CO.					
1	Elias Keyes	"	"	Ebenezer Brown	Elias Keyes
2	Aaron Leland	"	"	"	"
2	William Hunter	"	"	"	"
3	Benjamin Swan	"	"	"	"
4	Paschal P. Enos	"	"	Amos Heald	Solomon W. Burke
5	Titus Hutchinson	"	Horace Everett	"	"
6	William Hunter	"	"	"	"
6	Jesse Williams	"	"	"	Benjamin Clapp
7	Luther Mills	"	"	"	"
7	Alex Hutchinson	"	"	Norman Williams	Alex. Hutchinson
ADDISON CO.					
1	Henry Olin	"	"	"	"
2	Charles Rich	"	Samuel Strong	"	"
2	Mathew Phelps jr	Samuel Shepherd	Ezra Hoyt	"	"
3	Darius Mathews	"	"	"	"
3	John S. Larrabee	"	"	Samuel Swift	"
4	Jonathan Hoyt jr	John Willard	Samuel Mattocks	"	Jonathan Hoyt jr
5	Horatio Seymour	"	David Edmond	"	Horatio Seymour
6	Darius Mathews	"	"	"	"
7	John Simmons	"	"	"	"
ORANGE CO.					
1	Elisha Hotchkiss	Daniel Peaslee	J. P. Buckingham	"	"
2	Beriah Loomis	Josiah Dana	Beriah Loomis	"	"
2	James Tarbox	John H. Cotton	"	"	"
3	Elisha Hyde	H E G M'Laughlin	"	"	"
4	Daniel Peaslee	Joseph Edson	"	Harry Hale	Joseph Edson
5	Dudley Chase	Elisha Hotchkiss	"	Thomas Jones	Horace Bassett
6	Elisha Thayer	"	"	"	"
6	Jonathan Fisk	"	"	"	"
7	William Niles	"	"	"	"
7					

COUNTY OFFICERS FROM 1778 TO 1850. CONTINUED.

	1816	1817	1818	1819	1820
BENNINGTON			"	"	"
1 Josiah Wright		Nathan Burton			
2 Edmond Graves		John H. Olin			
2 Josiah Graves		Edmond Graves	Stephen Robinson	"	"
3 O. C. Merrill					
3 Joel Pratt		S. & C. Clerk "	"	"	"
4 Samuel Fay		"	"		"
5 Calvin Sheldon		"	"	Richard Skinner	Calvin Sheldon
6 Jona'n Robinson		"	"	David Fay	"
6 John Underhill		"	John S. Pettibone	"	"
7					
7 Calvin Sheldon		Daniel Wellman	"	"	Jabez Pratt
WINDHAM CO.					
1 Elijah Knight		Phinehas White	"	"	John Roberts
2 John Aiken		Gilbert Denison	"	"	Jairus Hall
2 Luke Knowlton		John Roberts	"	"	Eben'r Huntington
3 Lemuel Whitney		"	"	"	"
3				James Elliott	
4 Aaron Wales		"	"	Theop's Crawford	Jonathan Barron
5 Martin Field		"	"	"	"
6 Gilbert Denison		Lemuel Whitney	"	"	"
6 Elijah Knight		"	"	Daniel Kellogg	"
7 Royal Tyler		"	"	"	"
7					
RUTLAND CO.					
1 Pliny Smith		"	"	"	Amos Thompson
2 Amos Thompson		"	"	"	Thomas Hammond
2 Thos. Hammond		"	"	"	Henry Hodges
3 Robert Temple		"	"	Robert Pierpoint	"
4 Estus Barker		William Fay	Estus Barker	Jonathan Dyke jr	"
5 Jonas Clark		"	"	"	"
6 Obadiah Noble jr		"	"	"	"
6 Erastus Higley		"	"	"	"
7 William Page		"	"	"	"
7 Selah H. Merrill		"	"	"	"
WINDSOR CO.					"
1 Elias Keyes		William Strong	Elihu Luce	"	"
2 Aaron Leland		Elihu Luce	Aaron Leland	"	John Bridge
2 William Strong		Amos Heald	Daniel Dana	"	
3 Benjamin Swan		"	"	"	Asaph Fletcher jr
4 Solomon W. Burk		"	"	"	Jacob Collamer
5 Horace Everett		"	Asa Aiken	"	"
6 Uriel C. Hatch		"	"	"	Henry C. Denison
6 Benjamin Clapp		"	"	"	
7 Zenas Clark		Reuben Washburn	"	"	Norman Williams
7 Alex. Hutchinson		"	Jacob Collamer	"	
ADDISON CO.					
1 Henry Olin		"	"	"	"
2 William Slade jr		"	"	"	"
2 Ezra Hoyt		"	Stephen Haight jr	"	"
3 Darius Mathews		"	"	William Slade jr	"
3 Samuel Swift		"	"	"	"
4 Jonathan Hoyt		"	"	Abel Tomlinson	"
5 Horatio Seymour		"	"	David Edmond	"
6 Darius Mathews		"	"	Samuel Swift	"
6 John Simmons		"	"	"	"
ORANGE CO.					
1 Josiah Dana		"	"	"	William Spencer
2 Beriah Loomis		"	John H. Cotton	"	Timothy Baylies
2 John H. Cotton		"	Joseph Reed	"	Jed. H. Harris
3 H. E. G. M'Laughlin		"	"	"	"
4 Joseph Edson		"	"	"	"
5 Horace Bassett		"	"	Daniel A. A. Buck	"
6 Elisha Thayer		"	"	"	"
6 Jonathan Fisk		"	Frederick Griswold	"	"
7 William Niles		"	"		
7					

COUNTY OFFICERS FROM 1778 TO 1850. CONTINUED.

	1821	1822	1823	1824	1825
BENNINGTON					
1	Nathan Burton	"	"	Sylvanus Danforth	No. 1 ends here
2	John H. Olin	"	"	"	Sylvanus Danforth
2	Samuel Wright	"	"	Myron Clark	"
3	Joel Pratt	"	"	"	"
4	Samuel Fay	"	Josiah Burton	"	"
5	Milo L. Bennett	"	O. C. Merrill	"	Phineas Smith
6	William Henry	Orsamas C. Merrill	William Henry	Nathan H. Bottum	John H. Olin
6	John S. Pettibone	"	"	Milo L. Bennett	"
7					
7	Jabez Pratt	"	"	John Aiken	"
WINDHAM CO.					
1	John Roberts	"	"	"	
2	Jairus Hall	"	James L. Stark	"	John Roberts
2	Ebe'r Huntington	"	Tim'y H. Whitney	Jona. Robinson	James L. Stark
3	L.W. S. J. E.C.C.	" "	" "	" "	J. E., S. & C. Cl'k
4	Jonathan Barron	Paul Chase jr	"	Paul Chase	"
5	Martin Field	Samuel Elliott	"	"	Alex. S. Campbell
6	Lemuel Whitney		"	"	"
6	Charles Phelps	"	Dana Miller	Charles Phelps	Horace Baxter
7	Royal Tyler	James Elliott	"	"	"
7					
RUTLAND CO.					
1	Amos Thompson	"	"	Moses Strong	
2	Henry Hodges	"	"	"	Moses Strong
2	Joseph Warner	"	"	John P. Colburn	"
3	Robert Pierpoint	"	"	"	"
4	Jonathan Dyke jr	"	"	"	"
5	Jonas Clark	"	"	"	"
6	Obadiah Noble jr	"	"	"	"
6	Samuel Moulton	Erastus Higley	John Stanley	"	"
7	William Page	"	"	"	Rodney C. Royce
7	Selah H. Merrill	"	Almon Warner	"	"
WINDSOR CO.					
1	Elihu Luce	Jona. H. Hubbard	Aaron Loveland	Abner Forbes	
2	Aaron Leland	Abner Forbes	"	John Bridge	Abner Forbes
2	John Bridge	"	"	Thomas Emerson	"
3	Benjamin Swan	"	"	"	"
4	Asaph Fletcher jr	"	"	"	"
5	Jacob Collamer	"	"	Isaac N. Cushman	"
6	Uriel C. Hatch	Jonathan Whipple	"	"	"
6	Henry C. Denison	"	"	"	"
7	Reuben Washburn	Nomlas Cobb	"	"	"
7	Norman Williams	"	Jasper Hazen	"	"
ADDISON CO.					
1	Henry Olin	"	"	Dorastus Wooster	
2	William Slade jr	Stephen Haight	Elisha Bascom	John S. Larrabee	Dorastus Wooster
2	Stephen Haight jr	Elisha Bascom	Ezra Hoyt	Daniel Collins	Eben W. Judd
3	W. S., S S.S.CC.	" "	" "	S. S., S. & C. Cl'k	"
4	Abel Tomlinson	"	"	Stephen Haight	"
5	David Edmond	"	"	E. D. Woodbridge	"
6	Samuel Swift	"	"	"	"
6					
7	John Simmons	"	"	Ezra Hoyt	"
7				Noah Hawley	"
ORANGE CO.					
1	William Spencer	"	"	"	
2	Timothy Baylies	Jedediah H. Harris	Timothy Baylies	Stuart Brown	William Spencer
2	Jed'h H. Harris	Stuart Brown	"	Daniel Cobb	"
3	HEGM'Laughlin	"	"	"	"
4	Joseph Edson	"	Abel Carter	"	"
5	D. A. A. Buck	William Nutting	"	"	"
6	Elisha Thayer	"	"	William Spencer	"
6	Fredr'k Griswold	"	"	"	"
7	William Niles	"	Simeon Short	"	"
7					

COUNTY OFFICERS FROM 1778 TO 1850, CONTINUED.

BENNINGTON 1826	1827	1828	1829	1830
2 S. Danforth	"	Nathan Burton	"	"
2 Myron Clark	Stephen Robinson	Jona. E. Robinson	Nathan H. Botrum	"
3 Joel Pratt	"	Hiland Hall	Henry Robinson	"
4 Samuel Canfield	"	"	"	"
5 Phineas Smith	"	"	Hiland Hall	"
6 Jonathan Draper	"	Sylvanus Danforth	"	"
6 Milo L. Bennett	"	"	Leonard Sargeant	"
7				
7 John Aiken	"	"	Henry Robinson	"
WINDHAM CO.				
2 John Roberts	"	"	"	"
2 James L. Stark	"	"	"	"
3 James Elliott	"	"	"	"
4 Paul Chase	"	"	"	Henry Smith
5 Alex S. Campbell	Daniel Kellogg	A. S. Campbell	"	"
6 Lemuel Whitney	"	"	Samuel Elliott	"
6 Horace Baxter	Asa Keyes	Horace Baxter	"	Peter R. Taft
7 James Elliott	"	"	"	"
7				
RUTLAND CO.				
2 Henry Hodges	"	"	"	"
2 John P. Colburn	"	"	"	"
3 Robert Pierpoint	"	"	"	"
4 Jonathan Dyke jr	"	"	"	"
5 Jonas Clark	"	"	Selah H. Merrill	"
6 Obadiah Noble jr	"	"	Obadiah Noble	"
6 John Stanley	"	"	John Meacham	Almon Warner
7 Rodney C. Royce	"	"	"	"
7 Almon Warner	"	"	Selah H. Merrill	"
WINDSOR CO.				
2 Abner Forbes	"	"	Samuel W. Porter	"
2 Thomas Emerson	"	Samuel W. Porter	William Steele	"
3 Benjamin Swan	"	"	"	"
4 Asaph Fletcher jr	"	"	"	Lysander Raymond
5 Isaac N. Cushman	Wyllis Lyman	"	"	"
6 Jona. Whipple	"	"	"	Jabez Proctor
6 Isaiah Raymond	"	"	"	"
7 Nomlas Cobb	"	"	"	"
7 Jasper Hazen	Lyndon A. Marsh	"	"	"
ADDISON CO.				
2 Dorastus Wooster	"	"	"	"
2 Eben W. Judd	"	"	Silas H. Jenison	"
3 Samuel Swift	"	"	"	"
4 Stephen Haight	"	Seymour Sellick	"	"
5 E. D. Woodbridge	George Chipman	"	"	William Slade
6 Samuel Swift	"	"	"	"
6 Ezra Hoyt	"	"	"	Noah Hawley
7 John Simmons	"	"	William G. Hooker	J. Winslow, jr.
7 Noah Hawley	"	"	"	John Parker
ORANGE CO.				
2 William Spencer	"	"	"	"
2 Daniel Cobb	"	"	"	"
3 H. E. G. M'Laughlin	"	"	"	"
4 Abel Carter	"	"	"	William Barron
5 William Nutting	"	"	"	Daniel A. A. Buck
6 William Spencer	"	"	"	"
6 Fred. Griswold	"	"	"	"
7 Simeon Short	"	"	"	"
7				

COUNTY OFFICERS FROM 1778 TO 1850. CONTINUED.

	1831	1832	1833	1834	1835
BENNINGTON.					
1	Nathan Burton	"	"	"	"
2	Luman Norton	Nathan H. Bottum	"	Luman Norton	"
3	Henry Robinson	"	"	"	"
4	Samuel Canfield	"	"	"	"
5	Hiland Hall	"	Milo L. Bennett	Leonard Sargeant	"
6	Sylvanus Danforth	"	"	Jesse Blackmer	Aaron Robinson
6	Myron Clark	"	"	"	John S. Pettibone
7					
7	Henry Robinson	"	Reub. H. Blackmer	"	Ahiman L. Miner
WINDHAM CO.					
2	John Roberts	"	Samuel Clark	Charles Phelps	James L. Stark
2	James L. Stark	Charles Phelps	"	James L. Stark	Peter R. Taft
3	James Elliott	"	"	"	"
4	Henry Smith	"	"	"	"
5	Roswell M. Field	Alex'r S. Campbell	Roswell M. Field	"	"
6	Marshall Miller	"	John Roberts	Asa Knight	"
6	Peter R. Taft	"	"	Alex'r S. Campbell	"
7	James Elliott	"	"	Asa Keyes	"
7					
RUTLAND CO.					
2	Henry Hodges	"	Nathan T. Sprague	Wm. C. Kittredge	"
2	John P. Colburn	Wm. C. Kittredge	"	Nathan T. Sprague	"
3	Robert Pierpoint	"	"	"	"
4	Jacob Edgerton jr	"	John A. Conant	"	Ira Parsons
5	Selah H. Merrill	"	"	"	Reuben R. Thrall
6	Robert Pierpoint	Ambrose L. Brown	"	"	William Marsh
6	Almon Warner	"	"	"	"
7	Rodney C. Royce	Fred. W. Hopkins	"	"	"
7	Selah H. Merrill	"	"	"	"
WINDSOR CO.					
2	Samuel W. Porter	"	"	"	"
2	Royal M. Ransom	Saml. C. Loveland	"	Ephraim D. Briggs	"
3	Benjamin Swan	"	"	"	"
4	Lysan'r Raymond	"	"	Daniel Bowen	"
5	Carlos Coolidge	"	"	"	"
6	Jabez Proctor	"	"	Nomlas Cobb	Thos. F. Hammond
6	Isaiah Raymond	"	"	"	"
7	Reuben Washburn	"	"	"	Salmon F. Dutton
7	Lyndon A. Marsh	Edwin Hutchinson	"	Norman Williams	"
ADDISON CO.					
2	Silas H. Jenison	"	"	"	Samuel H. Holley
2	William Myrick	"	Samuel H. Holley	"	Calvin Solace
3	Samuel Swift	"	"	"	"
4	Marshall S. Doty	"	Azariah Rood	"	William B. Martin
5	Eben'r N. Briggs	"	"	"	"
6	Samuel Swift	"	"	"	"
6	Noah Hawley	Jesse Grandey	"	Adin Hall	"
7	J. Winslow jr	Samuel Swift	"	Edward D. Barber	"
7	John Parker	"	"	"	"
ORANGE CO.					
2	Daniel Cobb	"	Lyman Fitch	Daniel Cobb	Lyman Fitch
2	Daniel Jones	"	Luther Carpenter	Thomas Jones	Jacob K. Parish
3	H.E.G. M'Laughlin	"	Harry Hale	"	"
4	Lyman Fitch	"	I. H. Smith	A. B. W. Tenney	Luther S. Burnham
5	D. A. A. Buck	William Hebard	Daniel A. A. Buck	William Hebard	Edmond Weston
6	William Spencer	"	"	"	"
6	Fred'k Griswold	Calvin Blodgett	Jacob K. Parish	Calvin Blodgett	"
7	Simeon Short	"	"	"	"
7					

COUNTY OFFICERS FROM 1778 TO 1850. CONTINUED.

	1836	1837	1838	1839	1840
BENNINGTON.					
2	Darius Moore	Luman Norton	Darius Moore	Samuel Wright	Luman Norton
3	Luman Norton	Darius Moore	Green Blackmer	Alexander Bliss	G. B. Southworth
5	Henry Robinson	"	"	"	SamuelHBlackmer
4	John Norton	Gurdin H. Smith	"	Richmond Fisk	Gurdin H. Smith
5	Leonard Sargeant	SamuelHBlackmer	"	Harmon Canfield	"
6	Aaron Robinson	Artemas Mattison	"	"	"
6	MartinC.Deming	"	Loring Dean	"	"
7					
7	Harmon Canfield	"	Ahiman L. Miner	"	"
WINDHAM CO.					
2	Peter R. Tatt	"	Henry Wheelock	"	"
2	Henry Wheelock	"	William R. Shafter	"	"
3	James Elliott	Marshall Miller	"	"	"
4	Gates Perry jr	"	"	"	"
5	A. S. Campbell	James Elliott	"	Alex. S. Campbell	"
6	Asa Knight	Dana Hyde	"	Henry Smith	Marshall Miller
6	David L.Putnam	"	Ellery Albee	"	"
7	Asa Keyes	John Phelps	Samuel Elliott	Asa Keyes	Lemuel Whitney
7					
RUTLAND CO.					
2	W. C. Kittredge	"	Zimri Howe	"	"
2	N. T. Sprague	"	"	Obadiah Noble	"
3	Robert Pierpoint	"	"	Fred'k W. Hopkins	"
4	Ira Parsons	Asa Parsons	Ira Parsons	"	"
5	Solomon Foot	"	"	"	"
6	William Hall	"	Ambrose L. Brown	William Hall	"
6	Almon Warner	"	"	"	"
7	Henry B,Towslee	"	Fred'k W. Hopkins	Henry Hall	"
7	S. H. Merrill	Benj. F. Langdon	"	"	"
WINDSOR CO.					
2	Sam'l W, Porter	"	David Pierce	"	"
2	David Pierce	"	Reuben Washburn	"	"
3	Benjamin Swan	"	"	Norman Williams	"
4	Daniel Bowen	John Pettis	"	Joel Lull jr	"
5	O. P. Chandler	"	Edwin Hutchinson	"	Henry Closson
6	T. F. Hammond	"	"	"	"
6	John S. Marcy	"	"	James Udall	Thomas P, Russell
7	Salmon F.Dutton	"	"	"	"
7	Oel Billings	"	"	"	"
ADDISON CO.					
2	Sam'l H. Holley	"	"	"	"
2	Calvin Solace	"	Davis Rich	"	"
3	Samuel Swift	"	"	"	"
4	Azariah Rood	Ethan Smith	"	William B, Martin	Adnah Smith
5	Eben'r N. Briggs	"	"	Ozias Seymour	"
6	Samuel Swift	"	"	"	"
6	Harvey Munsill	"	"	"	"
7	Ed'rd D, Barber	"	"	"	"
7	John Pierpoint	"	"	"	"
ORANGE CO.					
2	Thomas Jones	Daniel Cobb	Simeon Short	Daniel Cobb	Jacob K. Parish
2	Calvin Blodgett	Lyman Fitch	Jacob K. Parish	Joshua Dickinson	John W. Smith
3	Harry Hale	J. W. D. Parker	John W. Smith		Perley C. Jones
4	Lement Bacon	Tappan Stevens	Lement Bacon	Asa Storey	William Barron
5	William Hebard	Edmond Weston	Abel Underwood	Elijah Farr	Abel Underwood
6	William Spencer	"	"	"	Simeon Short
6	John W. Smith	Calvin Blodgett	William Hebard	Calvin Blodgett	William Hebard
7	Simeon Short	J. W. D. Parker	"	"	Joseph Berry
7					

COUNTY OFFICERS FROM 1778 TO 1850. CONTINUED.

BENNINGTON.	1841	1842	1843	1844	1845
2	G. B. Southworth	"		"	Benj. F. Morgan
2	Benjamin F. Olin	"	John H. Sanderson	"	Major Hawley
3	S. H. Blackmer	"		"	"
4	Gurdin H Smith	J.V.D. S. M'Eowen	"	"	Jasper Viall
5	Harmon Canfield	"	Ahiman L. Miner	"	A. P. Lyman
6	O. C. Merrill	"	"	"	Hiram Barton
6	Loring Dean	Leonard Sargeant	"	"	Nathan Burton
7					
7	Ahiman L. Miner	"	Harvey K. Fowler	"	Elias B. Burton
WINDHAM CO.					
2	Henry Wheelock	William R, Shafter	John Smith	Samuel Elliott	"
2	William R.Shafter	John Smith	Emery Wheelock	"	"
3	Marshall Miller	"	"	"	"
4	Gates Perry jr	Russell Hyde	"	"	Timothy H. Hall
5	Royal Tyler	"	John Kimball	"	"
6	Marshall Miller	"	Henry Smith	Lemuel Whitney	"
6	Ellery Albee	"	"	"	"
7	Lemuel Whitney	"	Asa Keyes	Royal Tyler	"
7					
RUTLAND CO.					
2	Zimri Howe	"	"	Ezra June	"
2	Obadiah Noble	"	Ezra June	Ambrose L. Brown	"
3	F. W. Hopkins	"	"	"	"
4	Jacob Edgerton	"	"	"	"
5	Solomon Foot	Wm. C. Kittredge	"	"	Edgar L. Ormsbee
6	William Hall	"	"	"	"
6	Almon Warner	"	"	"	"
7	Henry Hall	"	"	"	
7	B. F. Langdon	"	"	"	J. A. Warner
WINDSOR CO.					
2	David Pierce	"	"	"	Walter Palmer
2	Reuben Washburn	"	"	"	Thomas T. Barrett
3	Norman Williams	"	"	"	"
4	Joel Lull jr	Zenas F. Hyde	"	David Bosworth	Gilman Henry
5	Henry Closson	Sewall Fullum	"	Julius Converse	"
6	T. F. Hammond	"	"	"	"
6	Thos. P. Russell	"	George E. Wales	"	"
7	Salmon F. Dutton	"	"	"	"
7	Oel Billings	"	"	"	Lyndon A. Marsh
ADDISON CO.					
2	Samuel H. Holley	Calvin Solace	"	Dorastus Wooster	"
2	Davis Rich	Ford'ce Huntington	"	J. Grandey & V. L.	Ville Lawrence
3	Samuel Swift	"	"	"	"
4	Adnah Smith	Gaius A. Collamer	"	David S. Church	"
5	Ozias Seymour	"	"	"	George W. Grandey
6	Silas H. Jenison	"	"	"	"
6	Harvey Munsill	"	"	"	"
7	Jed. S. Bushnell	"	"	"	"
7	John Pierpoint	"	"	"	"
ORANGE CO.					
2	Martin Flint	"	"	Tappan Stevens	Frederick Smith
2	Joshua Dickinson	Daniel Cobb	Tappan Stevens	Frederick Smith	John McLane
3	Robbins Dinsmore	Perley C. Jones	"	"	Calvin Blodgett
4	Asa Story	Jacob Kent jr	"	Hoel Sayre	"
5	Elijah Farr	Edmond Weston	Jefferson P. Kidder	"	"
6	J. W. D. Parker	"	"	"	"
6	William Hebard	John Colby	Levi B. Vilas	John Colby	Edmond Weston
7	Stephen Thomas	"	"	"	"
7					

COUNTY OFFICERS FROM 1778 TO 1850. CONTINUED.

	1846	1847	1848	1849	1850
BENNINGTON		"	"		"
2	Benj. F. Morgan	"	"	Perez Harwood jr	"
2	Major Hawley	"	"	Cyrus Farwell	"
3	Saml. H. Blackmer	"	"		"
4	Jasper Viall	"	"		"
5	A. P. Lyman	W. S Southworth	"	James S. Merrill	"
6	O. C Merrill	John H. Olin	B. E. Brownell	Harmon Canfield	"
6	Ahiman L. Miner	"	"	Elias B. Burton	Elijah Barber
7					Leonard Sargeant
7	Elias B. Burton	"	"	Harvey K. Fowler	"
WINDHAM CO.					
2	Emery Wheelock	James H. Phelps	Thomas Miller	David Arnold	"
2	James H. Phelps	Thomas Miller	David Arnold	Henry Clark	"
3	Marshall Miller	"	"	"	"
4	Timothy H. Hall	Marshall Newton	Timothy H. Hall	Chandler Pratt	"
5	Richard W. Smith	Edward Kirkland	"	George B. Kellogg	"
6	Royal Tyler	"	"	"	"
6	Ellery Albee	David Chandler	"	Abishai Stoddard	"
7	B. D. Harris	Fred'k Holbrook	"	"	"
7					
RUTLAND CO.					
2	Ezra June	Gordon Newell	"	Isaac T. Wright	Elisha Allen
2	Ambrose L Brown	Isaac T. Wright	Elisha Allen	"	Samuel H. Kellogg
3	F. W. Hopkins	"	"	"	"
4	Jacob Edgerton jr	"	"	"	"
5	Edgar L Ormsbee	Wm. C. Kittredge	"	Ezra June	"
6	William Hall	"	Harvey Button	"	"
6	Almon Warner	"	"	"	"
7	Henry Hall	"	"	"	"
7	J. A. Warner	Almon Warner	"	"	"
WINDSOR CO.					
2	Walter Palmer	"	"	Hampden Cutts	"
2	Thos. T. Barrett	"	"	Calvin French	"
3	Norman Williams	"	"	"	"
4	Gilman Henry	"	"	"	Lorenzo Richmond
5	Julius Converse	Sewall Fullum	"	Luther Adams	"
6	T. F. Hammond	"	"	Salmon F. Dutton	"
6	Geo. E. Wales	"	Joseph B. Danforth	"	John Porter
7	Salmon F. Dutton	"	"	Clark H. Chapman	Henry Closson
7	Lyndon A. Marsh	"	"	"	"
ADDISON CO.					
2	Ville Lawrence	George Chipman	"	Calvin G. Tilden	Nathan L. Keese
2	George Chipman	Elias Bottum	"	Nathan L. Keese	Calvin G. Tilden
3	Samuel Swift	George S. Swift	"	"	"
4	David S. Church	"	"	"	"
5	Geo. W. Grandey	"	John Prout	"	"
6	Silas H Jenison	Horatio Seymour	"	"	"
6	Harvey Munsill	"	"	"	"
7	Jed. S. Bushnell	"	"	"	"
7	John Pierpont	"	"	"	"
ORANGE CO.					
2	Frederick Smith	Ariel Burnham	"	Elisha Tracy	Ira Kidder
2	John M'Lane	George P. Baldwin	"	A. H. Gilmore	Gouldsb'n Taplin jr
3	Calvin Blodgett	"	"	"	Joseph Berry
4	George Sleeper	"	Oramel H. Watson	L. D. Whitcomb	Oramel H. Watson
5	J. P. Kidder	Philander Perrin	J. P. Kidder	Burnham Martin	Asa M. Dickey
6	Stephen Thomas	"	"	Arad Stebbins	Royal Hatch
6	Edmond Weston	Levi B. Vilas	"	B. W. Bartholomew	Philander Perrin
7	J. W. Batchelder	"	Daniel B. James	Simeon Short	Charles B Leslie
7					

COUNTY OFFICERS FROM 1778 TO 1850. CONTINUED.

CHITTENDEN 1787	1788	1789	1790	1791
1 John Fassett	"	"	"	"
2 John White	"	"	"	"
2 Samuel Lane	"	John McNeil	"	"
3 J. Knickerbocker	"	Martin Chittenden	"	"
4 Noah Chittenden	"	"	Stephen Pearl	"
5 Samuel Hitchcock	"	"	"	Wm.C. Harrington
6 John McNeil	"	"	Mathew Cole	"
6			Jonathan Hoit	"
6			Timothy Pearl	"
7 Isaac McNeil	"	"	"	"

CHITTENDEN 1792	1793	1794	1795	
1 John Fassett	"	Ebenezer Marvin	"	
2 John White	John McNeil	John White	"	
2 John McNeil	Martin Chittenden	"	"	
3 M. Chittenden	Solomon Miller	"	"	
4 Stephen Pearl	"	"	"	
5 W.C Harrington	"	"	"	
6 Mathew Cole	"	"	"	
6 Jonathan Hoit	"	"	"	
6 Timothy Pearl	"	"	"	
6		Ebenezer Crafts	"	
7 Isaac McNeil	"	"	"	

CHITTENDEN 1796	1797	1798	1799	1800
1 M. Chittenden	"	"	"	"
2 Josh. Staunton jr	"	Elias Buel	John Law	"
2 John Law	"	Lemuel Bottum	"	"
3 Solomon Miller	"	S. & C. " Clerk	"	"
4 Timothy Pearl	James Sawyer	"	"	"
5 Elnathan Keyes	"	Wm. C.Harrington	"	"
6 Solomon Miller	"	"	"	"
7 Isaac McNeil	"	"	"	"

CALEDONIA CO.				
1 Wm.Chamberlain	"	"	"	"
2 Benjamin Sias	"	"	"	"
2 David Wing jr	"	"	"	David Wing jr
3 David Dunbar	"	"	"	John W. Chandler
4 John Rankin	"	"	"	David Elkin
5	William Mattocks	"	"	"
6	John W. Chandler	"	"	S. Chamberlin
6 James Lucas	"	"	Daniel Dana	"
7				
7 Lemuel Dana	"	"	Reuben Blanchard	David Dunbar

FRANKLIN CO.				
1 Ebenezer Marvin	"	"	"	"
2 John White	"	Samuel Barnard	Isaac Smith	Elnathan Keyes
2 Samuel Barnard	"	Silas Hathaway	Elnathan Keyes	Jonathan Janes
3	Seth Pomeroy S.C.	" for both	"	"
3	Samuel Willard			
4 Prince B. Hall	"	"	"	"
5 Levi House	"	"	"	"
6 Jonathan Hoit	"	"	"	"
6	Nathan Hutchins jr	"	"	"
7 Jonathan Hoit jr	"	"	"	"
7				

ORLEANS CO.
1 Timothy Hinman
2 Sam. C. Crafts
2 Jesse Olds
3 Timothy Stanley
4 Joseph Scott
5 Joseph Bradley
6 Ebenezer Crafts
7

DUBARTUS WILLARD,

Known more familiarly by the name of Bartie Willard, in an early day resided at Essex, and was a wheelright by trade. He was also a satirical poet, and prided himself on taking some one off in a short way. He was the first Representative of Essex, chosen in 1786, but not afterwards. The next day after he was chosen, he went to pay his respects to Gov. Chittenden, and the Governor had been informed who was chosen from Essex, but thinking to give Bartie a small shot—knowing it would be returned with interest, he asked him who they chose in his town for Representative? Bartie answered, for the want of better stock they took me. "Well," said the Governor. "It's a misfortune that we have got to be so poor in some of our towns about here, as not to be able to get iron, and have to use wood for wedges." "That's a

	1801	1802	1803	1804	1805
CHITTENDEN					
1 Martin Chittenden		"	Joshua Staunton	"	"
2 Elias Buel		John Law	Ezra Butler	"	"
2 Lemuel Bottom		"	"	Noah Chittenden	"
3 Solomon Miller		"	"	"	"
4 James Sawyer		"	Daniel Staniford	"	"
5 W.C. Harrington		"	"	"	"
6 Solomon Miller		"	"	"	"
7 Solomon Miller		"	"	"	"
CALEDONIA CO.					
1 Wm. Chamberlin		"	David Wing jr	"	"
2 David Wing jr		"	John W. Chandler	"	"
2 John W. Chandler		"	Joseph Moffitt	"	"
3 David Dunbar		"	Elkanah Phelps	"	"
4 David Elkins		"	"	"	"
5 William Mattocks		"	Wm. A Griswold	"	"
6 S. Chamberlain		"	"	Reuben Blanchard	"
7 David Dunbar		"	"	Wm. A. Griswold	John W. Chandler
FRANKLIN CO.					
1 Ebenezer Marvin		"	Jonathan Janes	"	"
2 Jonathan Janes		"	Zera Willoughby	"	"
2 Zera Willoughby		"	Amos Fassett	Frederick Bliss	"
3 Seth Pomeroy		"	"	"	John White jr
4 Prince B. Hall		"	"	Thomas Russell	"
5 Levi House		"	"	Asa Aldis	"
6 Jonathan Hoit		"	"	"	"
6 Nath. Hutchins jr		"	"	"	"
7 Jonathan Hoit jr		"	"	"	Horace Janes
7					
ORLEANS CO.					
1 Timothy Hinman		"	"	"	"
2 Samuel C. Crafts		"	"	"	"
2 Jesse Olds		Timothy Stanley	"	"	"
3 Timothy Stanley		"	John Ellsworth	"	"
4 Joseph Scott		"	"	"	"
5 Joseph Bradley		William Baxter	"	"	"
6 Ebenezer Crafts		"	"	"	"
7					
ESSEX CO.					
1 Daniel Dana		"	"	"	"
2 Samuel Phelps		"	Mills De Forest	"	"
2 Mills De Forest		"	Samuel Weatherby	"	"
3		Haines French	"	"	"
4 Joseph Wait		"	"	"	"
5 Elijah Foot		"	Levi Barnard	"	"
6 Daniel Dana		"	"	"	"
7					

GRAND ISLE CO.
1 Asa Lyon
2 Nath. Hutchins jr
2 Alexander Scott
3 Alpheus Hall
4 Amos Morrill
5 Philo Berry
6 Nath. Hutchins jr
7 Jedediah P. Ladd*

*My correspondent informs me that those eight persons named in the following pages have been Register of Probate, but does not inform me how long or when each ones term began or expired, I have therefore divided the time between them as near even as I could without dividing years.

fact, but misfortunes never come single," said Bartie, "it is a greater misfortune that the State is so poor as not to be able to procure a good decent made beetle, but be compelled to use an old basswood maul to drive them with?"

While at the Legislature, he was found by some of his brother members taking his rations at the bar before he had paid the wash room a visit. They insisted that he should either treat the company or deal out some poetry. Bartie concluded that as money was more scarce with him than poetry, he would pay the latter, and did as follows:

"Our forefathers were like the goats,
First wash'd their eyes, and then their throats;
But we their sons have grown more wise,
First, wash our throats, and then our eyes."

COUNTY OFFICERS FROM 1778 TO 1850. CONTINUED.

CHITTENDEN 1806	1807	1808	1809	1810
1 Ezra Butler	"	"	"	"
2 Noah Chittenden	"	"	"	"
2 James A..Potter	"	"	Hezekiah Barnes	"
3 Solomon Miller	"	William Barney	"	"
4 Daniel Staniford	"	Heman Allen	"	Heman Lowry
5 W C. Harrington	"	"	"	"
6 Solomon Miller	"	"	Joel Brownson	"
7 Milo Cook	"	"	John Brownson	"
CALEDONIA CO.				
1 Reuben Blanchard	"	Cyrus Ware	"	"
2 Joseph Moffett	John Cameron	"	"	"
2 John Cameron	Isaiah Fisk	"	"	"
3 Elkanah Phelps	Wm. A. Palmer	"	"	"
4 David Elkins	Joseph Armington	Israel P. Dana	"	"
5 Wm.A. Griswold	"	"	"	"
6 J. W. Chandler	Wm. A. Palmer	John W. Chandler	"	Gershom Palmer
7 Reuben Blanchard	"	"	"	George Rich
FRANKLIN CO.				
1 Jonathan Janes	"	Ebenezer Marvin	J, D. Farnsworth	"
2 Frederick Bliss	"	"	"	"
2 Amos Fassett	J. D. Farnsworth	"	Amos Fassett	Joseph Beaman jr
3 John White jr	Seth Wetmore	"	Jonathan Janes	"
4 Thomas Russell	Oliver Day	"	Seth Wetmore	"
5 Ebenezer Marvin,jr	"	"	"	"
6 Jonathan Janes	"	"	"	"
7 Horace Janes	"	"	"	Francis Davis
ORLEANS CO.				
1 Timothy Hinman	"	"	"	Samuel C. Crafts
2 Samuel C. Crafts	"	"	"	Timothy Stanley
2 Timothy Stanley	"	"	"	George Nye
3 John Ellsworth	"	"	"	"
4 Joseph Scott	"	"	"	"
5 William Baxter	"	"	"	"
6 Ebenezer Crafts	"	Royal Corbin	"	"
7				
ESSEX CO.				
1 Daniel Dana	"	Micajah Ingham	Daniel Dana	Micajah Ingham
2 Mills De Forest	Noah Sabin	"	Micajah Ingham	Charles Cutler
2 Saml. Weatherbee	Micajah Ingham	Samuel Clark	Samuel Weatherbee	Samuel Gates
3 Haines French	"	"	"	"
4 William Hewes	"	"	"	"
5 Seth Cushman	"	"	"	"
6 Daniel Dana	"	"	"	Joseph Wait
7				
GRAND ISLE CO.				
1 Asa Lyon	Benjamin Adams	Asa Lyon	Benjamin Adams	"
2 Nathan Hutchins	Stephen Kinsley	Nathan Hutchins	Abner Keeler	"
2 Alexander Scott	James W. Wood	Lewis Sowles	"	"
3 Alpheus Hall	Jedediah Hyde jr	Alpheus Hall	Jedediah Hyde jr	"
4 Amos Merrill	Melvin Barnes	"	"	"
5 Philo Berry	Solomon Morgan	Eleazer Miller	"	Asa Robinson
6 Nathan Hutchins jr	Thomas Cochran	Nathan Hutchins jr	"	"
7 Jedediah P. Ladd	"	"	"	"

Bartie was driving a team with a load of hay, and upset the load, and he came into a ditch so situated that he could move some, but could not extricate himself. A man, who had a short time previous sworn out of jail on a debt Bartie held against him, came along and found there was trouble, went to work and removed the load, and out came Bartie from under it. Now Bartie, what would you have done if I had not come along and helped you out. I would do as you did, stayed there twenty days and swore out.

JUDGE HUTCHINSON AND JUDGE PADDOCK.

During the time the above named gentlemen were Judges of the Supreme Court, then consisting of five Judges, they were travelling down Onion river in the stage. A few days before, a severe

[Continued on 95th page.]

92   COUNTY OFFICERS FROM 1778 TO 1850. CONTINUED.

	1811	1812	1813	1814	1815
CHITTENDEN					
1	Heman Allen	"	"	"	Zadock Wheeler
2	Joel Brownson	"	"	Zadock Wheeler	Joel Brownson
2	John Jackson	"	"	"	Truman Chittenden
3	Daniel Staniford	"	David Russell	"	"
3	John Johnson	"	"	"	"
4	Heman Lowry	"	"	Jacob Davis	Heman Lowry
5	W. C. Harrington	Lewis Johnson	George Robinson	"	Sanford Gadcomb
6	Noah Chittenden	Truman Chittenden	"	Solomon Miller	Truman Chittenden
7	Thom. Chittenden	Milo Cook	Solomon S. Miller	"	Chauncey Brownell
CALEDONIA CO.					
1	John Cameron	"	"	Wm. Chamberlain	Isaiah Fisk
2	Isaiah Fisk	"	John W. Chandler	"	"
2	William Cahoon	"	Luther Jewett	William Cahoon	"
3	Wm. A. Palmer	"	"	"	Curtis Stanley
4	Israel P. Dana	"	Adam Duncan	"	Jude Kimball
5	Wm. A. Griswold	"	William Mattocks	"	Wm. A. Griswold
6	Wm. A. Palmer	"	"	"	"
7	Wm. A. Griswold	"	"	"	"
FRANKLIN CO.					
1	J. D. Farnsworth	"	"	"	William Brayton
2	Frederick Bliss	"	Zerah Willoughby	"	Frederick Bliss
2	Joseph Beaman jr	Martin D. Follett	Chauncey Fitch	"	"
3	Jonathan Janes	"	"	"	"
3				Abijah Stone C.C'k	Abner Morton
4	Solo'n Walbridge	"	Joseph H. Munson	"	Benjamin Fay
5	Eben'r Marvin jr	"	Ebenezer Marvin	"	Ebenezer Marvin jr
6	Jonathan Janes	"	Frederick Bliss	Abner Morton	Seth Wetmore
7	Francis Davis	"	"	Seth Wetmore	Elnathan W. Keyes
ORLEANS CO.					
1	Samuel C. Crafts	"	"	"	"
2	Timothy Stanley	"	"	George Nye	Timothy Stanley
2	George Nye	"	"	Nathan'l P. Sawyer	Samuel Cook
3	John Ellsworth	"	"	"	"
4	Joseph Scott	"	"	Ellis Cobb	Harvey Scott
5	William Baxter	"	"	"	David M. Camp
6	Royal Corbin	"	"	"	Joseph Scott
7					
ESSEX CO.					
1	Micajah Ingham	David Hopkinson	Daniel Dana	"	David Hopkinson
2	Samuel Gates	"	Ebenezer Clark	"	Oliver Ingham
2	Azarias Williams	"	Mills De Forest	"	Moody Rich
3	Haines French	"	"	"	"
4	Oliver Ingham	David Hibbard jr	"	"	John Dean
5	Joseph Berry	"	Elijah Foot	"	Joseph Berry
6	Charles Cutler	"	Daniel Dana	"	Isaac Cushman
7					
GRAND ISLE CO.					
1	Benjamin Adams	"	Asa Lyon	Philyer Loop	Benjamin Adams
2	James W. Wood	Abner Keeler	Caleb Hill	Alpheus Hall	"
2	Lewis Sowles	"	Philyer Loop	Jedediah Ladd	Ephraim Mott
3	Jedediah Hyde jr	"	"	"	"
4	Jedediah P. Ladd	Ephraim Mott	Calvin Fletcher	"	"
5	Asa Robinson	"	James Davis	Truman A. Barber	"
6	Nathan Hutchins	"	"	"	"
7	Thomas Cochran	"	"	"	"
JEFFERSON CO.				WASHINGTON CO.	
1	Ezra Butler	"	Charles Bulkley	Denison Smith	Ezra Butler
2	Salvin Collins	"	Seth Putnam	Stephen Pitkin	"
2	Bradford Kinne	"	"	Stephen Pierce	Warren Ellis
3	George Rich	"	Joseph Wing	"	George Rich
4	John Peck	"	Chapin Keith	Geo. Worthington	Chapin Keith
5	Timothy Merrill	"	Nicholas Baylies	"	Timothy Merrill
6	David Harrington	Chapin Keith	Abel Knapp	"	Salvin Collins
7	Joshua Y. Vail	"	"	Jeduthan Loomis	George Rich

COUNTY OFFICERS FROM 1778 TO 1850. CONTINUED.

	1816	1817	1818	1819	1820
CHITTENDEN					
1 Zadock Wheeler		"	"	"	Joel Brownson
2 Joel Brownson		"	"	"	Truman Chittenden
2 T. Chittenden		"	"	"	Burgess Hall
3 David Russell		"	"	"	"
3 John Johnson		Nathan B. Haswell	Phinehas Lyman	"	Nathan B. Haswell
4 Heman Lowry		"	"	"	"
5 S. Gadcomb		"	"	"	Timothy Follett
6 T. Chittenden		Jabez Penniman	"	"	"
7 C. Brownell		Lyman Cummings	"	Alvan Foote	"
CALEDONIA CO.					
1 Isaiah Fisk		"	"	"	"
2 J. W. Chandler		John Rankin	"	John W. Dana	"
2 William Cahoon		"	"	"	Pres West
3 Curtis Stanley		Benj. F. Deming	"	"	"
4 Jude Kimball		Nathan Fuller	"	"	"
5 W. A Griswold		"	"	"	Isaac Fletcher
6 Wm. A. Palmer		John W. Chandler	"	"	"
7 W. A. Griswold		Reuben Blanchard	"	"	Archelaus Sias
FRANKLIN CO.					
1 J. D. Farnsworth		"	"	"	"
2 Frederick Bliss		"	Zerah Willoughby	"	"
2 Peter Fay		"	Peter Sax	Amasa T. Brown	"
3 Horace Janes		"	"	"	"
4 Benjamin Fay		Shiverick Holmes	"	"	"
5 Stephen Royce jr		"	I. P. Richardson	"	"
6 Seth Wetmore		"	"	"	"
7 Francis Davis		Luther Brigham	"	"	Jonathan Janes
ORLEANS CO.					
1 William Howe		"	"	"	"
2 Timothy Stanley		"	"	"	"
2 Samuel Cook		"	"	"	"
3 Ira H. Allen		"	"	"	"
4 Harvey Scott		"	"	"	"
5 Joshua Sawyer		"	"	"	"
6 Joseph Scott		"	"	"	"
7					
ESSEX CO.					
1 Oliver Ingham		"	"	"	"
2 Samuel Gates		"	"	Benjamin Hunkins	"
2 Jesse Hugh		Moody Rich	"	Royal Cutler	Azariah Webb
3			William Gates	"	"
4 Rich Stevens		Henry Hall	Rich Stevens	"	John Dean
5 Joseph Berry		"	"	Bailey Denison	Seth Cushman
6 Isaac Cushman		"	"	"	"
7					
GRAND ISLE CO.					
1 Benjamin Adams		"	"	"	"
2 Alpheas Hall		Joel Allen	"	"	"
2 Lewis Sowles		"	"	"	"
3 Jedediah Hyde jr		"	"	"	"
4 Calvin Fletcher		"	"	"	"
5 Tru'n A. Barber		"	Amos Blodgett	"	"
6 Nathan Hutchins		"	"	"	"
7 Thos. Cochran		Chauncey Burgess	"	"	"
WASHINGTON CO.					
1 Ezra Butler		"	John Peck	Ezra Butler	"
2 Stephen Pitkin		"	"	"	Josiah B. Strong
2 Warren Ellis		"	Joseph Howes	"	"
3 George Rich		"	" J. Y. Vail	Joshua Y. Vail	"
4 Chapin Keith		"	"	John Peck	"
5 Timothy Merrill		"	"	"	"
6 Salvin Collins		"	"	"	Jeduthan Loomis
7 George Rich		"	"	"	Roswell H. Knapp

COUNTY OFFICERS FROM 1778 TO 1850. CONTINUED.

	1821	1822	1823	1824	1825
CHITTENDEN					
1	Joel Brownson	Ezra Meach	"	Timothy Follett	No. 1 ended.
2	T. Chittenden	"	Burgess Hall	"	Timothy Follett
2	Burgess Hall	"	Mitchell Hinsdell	"	Nathaniel Newell
3	David Russell	"	"	"	"
3	N. B. Haswell	"	"	"	N. B. Haswell both
4	Heman Lowry	"	"	"	"
5	Timothy Follett	"	Benjamin F. Bailey	"	"
6	M. Chittenden	"	George Robinson	"	Truman Chittenden
7	Isaac T. Hyde	David French	Nathan B. Haswell	"	David French
CALEDONIA CO.					
1	Isaiah Fisk	"	Samuel Sias	"	
2	Pres West	Samuel Sias	Timothy P. Fuller	Augustine Clark	Samuel Sias
2	Samuel Sias	Joseph Morrill 2d	Joseph Morrill	Samuel A. Willard	"
3	Benj. F. Deming	"	"	"	"
4	Nathan Fuller	"	"	"	"
5	Isaac Fletcher	"	"	"	"
6	Benj F. Deming	"	"	"	"
7	George B. Shaw	"	George C. Cahoon	"	"
FRANKLIN CO.					
1	J. D Farnsworth	"	"	Zerah Willoughby	
2	Amasa T. Brown	Zerah Willoughby	"	Thomas Waterman	"
2	Thos. Waterman	"	"	Joel Barber jr	"
3	Horace Janes	"	"	"	"
4	Joseph Weeks	"	"	"	"
5	I. P. Richardson	"	Joshua K. Smedley	"	"
6	Seth Wetmore	"	"	"	"
7	Jonathan Janes	"	"	Charles Wetmore	"
ORLEANS CO.					
1	William Howe	"	"	"	
2	Timothy Stanley	"	"	Nath'l P. Sawyer	Samuel C. Crafts
2	Nath'l P. Sawyer	"	"	John Ide	Wilham Baxter
3	Ira H. Allen	"	"	"	"
4	Harvey Scott	"	"	"	"
5	Joshua Sawyer	"	"	Augustus Young	
6	Ira H. Allen	"	George Nye	"	Salmon Nye
7					
ESSEX CO					
1	Benjamin Hunkins	Joseph Berry	William Gates	"	
2	Richardson Graves	Moody Rich	Dyer Hibbard	Richardson Graves	Noyes Denison
2	Daniel Edgery	William Gates	Richardson Graves	Noyes Denison	John Dewey
3	William Gates	"	"	"	"
4	Dyer Hibbard	Elijah Hill	Richard Stevens	Azariah Webb jr	"
5	Joseph Berry	Seth Cushman	Joseph Berry	"	Seth Cushman
6	Isaac Cushman	"	William Gates	"	"
7					
GRAND ISLE CO.					
1	Benjamin Adams	"	Lewis Sowles	"	
2	Lewis Sowles	"	Charles Carron	"	Lewis Sowles
2	Joel Allen	"	Samuel Adams	Melvin Barnes	Melvin Barnes jr
3	Jedediah Hyde jr	"	"	Joel Allen	"
4	Calvin Fletcher	"	"	"	"
5	Charles H. Perrigo	Amos Blodgett	"	Truman A. Barber	Benj. H. Smalley
6	Nathan Hutchins	"	"	"	"
7	Chauncey Burgess	"	Augustus Knight	"	"
WASHINGTON CO.					
1	Ezra Butler	"	"	"	
2	Josiah B. Strong	"	Stephen Pitkin	"	Ezra Butler
2	Joseph Howes	"	"	"	Warren Ellis
3	Joshua Y. Vail	"	"	"	"
4	John Peck	"	"	"	Rawsel R. Keith
5	Timothy Merrill	Denison Smith	"	"	Nicholas Baylies
6	Jeduthan Loomis	"	"	"	"
7	Roswell H. Knapp	"	"	"	Dan'l P. Thompson

COUNTY OFFICERS FROM 1778 TO 1850, CONTINUED. 95

	1826	1827	1828	1829	1830
CHITTENDEN					
2	Timothy Follett	"	Alvan Foote	"	Eli Brownson
2	Nathaniel Newell	"	"	Eli Brownson	J. Van Sicklin jr
3	Nathan B. Haswell	"	"	"	"
4	Heman Lowry	"	Moses Bliss	"	"
5	Benj. F. Bailey	Charles Adams	"	"	"
6	T. Chittenden	"	"	William P. Briggs	Truman Chittenden
7	David French	Chauncey Brownell	"	Luman Foote	George B. Manser
CALEDONIA CO.					
2	Wm. A. Palmer	"	Samuel Sias	"	"
2	Tim'y P. Fuller	"	"	"	"
3	Benj. F. Deming	"	"	"	"
4	Nathan Fuller	"	Silas Houghton	"	"
5	Isaac Fletcher	"	Charles Davis	"	"
6	Benj. F. Deming	"	"	"	"
7	Saml B. Mattocks	"	"	"	"
FRANKLIN CO.					
2	Joel Barber jr.	"	Joel Barber	Joel Barber jr.	"
2	Samuel Wead	"	"	George Greene	Joseph Smith
3	Horace Janes	"	"	"	"
4	Joseph Weeks	"	Timothy Foster	"	"
5	John Smith	"	"	"	"
6	Seth Wetmore	"	"	"	William Bridges
7	Ebenezer Barlow	William Bridges	"	"	John Gates
ORLEANS CO.					
2	Samuel C. Crafts	"	Nathaniel P. Sawyer	"	"
2	William Baxter	William Howe	Jasper Robinson	"	David M. Camp
3	Ira H. Allen	"	"	"	"
4	Thomas Jameson	"	"	"	"
5	Augustus Young	"	E. H. Starkweather	"	George C. West
6	Salmon Nye	"	John Kimball	"	Augustus Young
7					
ESSEX CO.					
2	D. Hopkinson jr	Oliver Ingham	William Gates	David Hopkinson jr	Richardson Graves
2	John Dewey	Moody Rich.	Noyes Denison	Nathaniel Beach	Simon Howe jr
3	William Gates	"	"	"	"
4	Rich Stevens	Azariah Webb jr	"	Henry Hall	Chapin K. Brooks
5	Seth Cushman	"	David Hibbard jr	"	"
6	Royal Cutler	William Gates	Royal Cutler	"	"
7					
GRAND ISLE CO.					
2	Lewis Sowles	"	"	"	John M. Sowles
2	Melvin Barnes jr	"	"	Melvin Barnes	Samuel Adams
3	Joel Allen	"	"	"	"
4	Calvin Fletcher	John M. Sowles	"	"	Franklin Robinson
5	Hector Adams	"	"	Frederick Hazen	"
6	Nathan Hutchins	"	Joel Allen	"	"
7	Augustus Knight	"	Gary Whitney	"	"
WASHINGTON CO.					
2	Joseph Howes	Dan Carpenter	"	"	"
2	Warren Ellis	Shubael Wheeler	"	"	"
3	Joshua Y. Vail	"	"	"	"
4	Rawsel R. Keith	"	"	"	"
5	Denison Smith	"	"	William Upham	Azel Spaulding
6	Jeduthan Loomis	"	"	"	Joseph Reed
7	D. P. Thompson	"	"	"	"

freshet had carried away many of the bridges. At Middlesex the coach and horses forded the river and the passengers passed over in a small boat, which made three or four loads. After Judge Paddock had got into the boat, the boatman gave Judge Hutchinson an invitation to get in. He remarked that he should not cross over the river in a boat with Judge Paddock, and another got in, and all crossed safe. After the stage was reloaded and started, Judge Hutchinson asked one of the

COUNTY OFFICERS FROM 1778 TO 1850. CONTINUED.

CHITTENDEN	1831	1832	1833	1834	1835
2 Eli Brownson		John Van Sicklin	"	"	Joseph Marsh
2 J Van Sicklin jr		Thomas Chittenden	"	"	Eli Brownson
3 Nath. B. Haswell		"	"	"	"
4 Roswell Butler		George A. Allen	"	"	Heman Lowry
5 A. G. Whittemore		"	"	"	"
6 T. Chittenden		William P. Briggs	"	"	Truman Chittenden
7 Geo. B. Manser		David French	"	"	George B. Manser
CALEDONIA CO.					
2 Samuel Sias		"	Jacob Blanchard	Timothy P. Fuller	
2 Timothy P. Fuller		Jacob Blanchard	Sylva's Hemenway	"	Benjamin Conner
3 Benj. F. Deming		"	Amos Paul	"	"
4 Silas Houghton		Charles Roberts	"	"	"
5 Charles Davis		"	"	"	George C. Cahoon
6 Benj. F. Deming		"	Samuel Sias	"	"
7 S. B. Mattocks		Amos Paul	"	"	S. B. Mattocks
FRANKLIN CO.					
2 Joel Barber jr		George Green	"	"	"
2 Joseph Smith		"	"	"	Austin Fuller
3 Horace Janes		"	"	Joseph H Brainerd	"
4 Timothy Foster		"	Seymour Eggleston	"	Jeptha Bradley
5 John Smith		"	Henry Adams	"	George W. Foster
6 William Bridges	Stephen S. Brown	"		Joel Barber jr	"
7 John Gates	Aaron S. Beaman	"		J. Allen Barber	"
ORLEANS CO					
2 David M. Camp		"	David P. Noyes	David M. Camp	"
2 Jasper Robinson		"	Isaac Parker	David P. Noyes	"
3 Ira H. Allen		"	"	"	"
4 Thomas Jameson		"	"	"	"
5 George C. West	Isaac F. Redfield	"	"	"	E. H. Starkweather
6 John Kimball		"	"	"	"
7					
ESSEX CO.					
2 Richard'n Graves	Jesse Cooper		B. W. Freeman	Richardson Graves	John Dodge
2 Moses Morrill	Reub'n W. Freeman		Archel's Cummings	Moses Morrill	Samuel Curtis
3 William Gates	"				
4 Henry Hall	Azariah Webb jr		Greenleaf Webb	Chapin K. Brooks	Greenleaf Webb
5 David Hibbard jr	James Steele		Wm. Hayward jr.	James Steele	"
6 William Gates	"		"	"	"
7					
GRAND ISLE CO					
2 John M. Sowles		"	"	"	"
2 Samuel Adams		"	"	"	"
3 Joel Allen		"	"	"	"
4 Frank'n Robinson		"	"	"	Harry Hill
5 Frederick Hazen	Giles Harrington		Hector Adams	"	"
6 Joel Allen		"	"	"	"
7 Gary Whitney		"	"	"	Henry White
WASHINGTON CO.					
2 Dan Cappenter		"	"	"	Roder'k Richardson
2 Warren Ellis	William Martin		"	Israel Goodwin	"
3 Joshua Y. Vail		"	"	"	"
4 Rawsel R. Keith	Milton Brown		Alvan Carter	"	"
5 Azel Spaulding		"	"	"	Paul Dillingham jr
6 Joseph Reed		"	Rawsel R. Keith	"	"
7 D. P. Thompson		"	Lucius B. Peck	"	Jerem'h T. Marston

passengers if he knew why he refused to cross the river with Judge Paddock, and was answered in the negative. "Well," said he, "Mr. D, I will tell you; we are going to Burlington to hold a session of the Court, and if the boat had upset, and both of us drowned, and any thing had befallen one of the other Judges so that he could not attend, no quorum could be had, and the rogues would go unpunished.

COUNTY OFFICERS FROM 1778 TO 1850. CONTINUED.

	1836	1837	1838	1839	1840
CHITTENDEN					
2	Joseph Marsh	William Wood	"	"	Francis Wilson
2	William Wood	Stephen Byington	"	"	Edm'd Wellington
3	NathanB.Haswell	William Noble	"	"	"
4	George A. Allen	"	"	"	"
5	John N. Pomeroy	"	David French	"	George K. Platt
6	Charles Russell	"	"	"	"
7	William Weston	"	"	"	"
CALEDONIA CO.					
2	Benjamin Conner	Marcus O. Fisher	George W.Denison	Marcus O. Fisher	Geo. W. Denison
2	Marcus O. Fisher	Geo. W. Denison	Ezra C.Chamberlin	Epaphras B. Chase	Ezra C Chamberlin
3	Amos Paul	Sam'l B Mattocks	"	"	"
4	John Currier	"	"	"	"
5	GeorgeC. Cahoon	"	Charles Davis	Thomas Bartlett jr	Bliss N. Davis
6	Sam'l B.Mattocks	"	Geo. B. Chandler	Sam'l B. Mattocks	"
7	Theron Howard	Henry Mattocks	Sam'l B. Mattocks	Theron Howard	Ebenezer Eastman
FRANKLIN CO.					
2	George Green	"	Seymour Eggleston	Cornelius Wood	"
2	Austin Fuller	Cornelius Wood	Jesse Carpenter	Augustus Burt	"
3	JosephH.Brainerd	"	"	"	"
4	Jeptha Bradley	"	"	Decius R. Bogue	"
5	GeorgeW Foster	"	Jerome J.Beardsley	Orlando Stevens	"
6	William Bridges	"	"	"	"
7	Romeo H. Hoyt	"	"	"	"
ORLEANS CO.					
2	Portus Baxter	Alvah R. French	"	Charles Hardy	Isaac Parker
2	Alvah R. French	John Kimball	"	Isaac Parker	John Boardman
3	Samuel C. Crafts	"	"	Henry M. Bates	"
4	Jacob Bates	"	"	Sabin Kellum	Merrill Williams
5	Charles Story	"	Samuel Sumner	Jesse Cooper	Samuel Sumner
6	Joseph Wiggins	"	"	George Nye	"
7	George Nye	"	"	Henry M. Bates	"
ESSEX CO.					
2	Azariah Webb jr	Archelus Cummins	David Hibbard jr	Azariah Webb jr	Jesse Cooper
2	Brigham Pike	"	Moses Morrill	"	Spencer Clark
3	William Gates	"	"	"	Lucius R. Webb
4	Greenleaf Webb	"	"	George E. Holmes	Greenleaf Webb
5	Wm. Heywood jr	"	"	"	David Hibbard jr
6	Royal Cutler	Joseph Gleason	"	"	Royal Cutler
7	Wm. Haywood jr	"	"	"	"
GRAND ISLE CO.					
2	William Wait	Samuel Adams	Calvin Fletcher	"	"
2	Samuel Adams	William Wait	"	Joseph M. Mott	"
3	Joel Allen	"	"	"	"
4	Harry B. Mott	"	"	Gary Whitney	"
5	Hector Adams	Frederick Hazen	"	"	"
6	Joel Allen	"	"	"	"
7	Henry White	"	"	"	John M. Sowles
WASHINGTON CO.					
2	William Martin	Rod'k Richardson	Pliny Curtis	Wm. M. Pingrey	John Spaulding
2	Nathan Morse	Pliny Curtis	Wm. M. Pingrey	Horace Hollister	Orson Skinner
3	Joshua Y. Vail	"	"	Stilman Churchill	"
4	Alvan Carter	"	John Starkweather	"	Isaiah Silver
5	PaulDillinghamjr	"	"	Homer W. Heaton	John L. Buck
6	Jason Carpenter	Dan'l P.Thompson	"	"	Geo. Worthington
7	Jeduthan Loomis	Jerem'h T.Marston	"	"	Geo. B. Manser
LAMOILLE CO.					
2	Jonathan Bridge	"	Isaac Pennock	"	David P. Noyes
2	Joseph Waterman	"	Gardner Gates	"	Nathan H. Thomas
3	Philo G. Camp	"	"	"	"
4	Almerin Tinker	"	Riverius Camp	"	Martin Armstrong
5	Orion W. Butler	"	Salmon Wires	"	Harlow P. Smith
6	Daniel Dodge	"	Sam'l A. Willard	"	Daniel Dodge
7	Levi B. Vilas	"	B. W. Poor	"	Samuel A. Willard

COUNTY OFFICERS FROM 1778 TO 1850. CONTINUED.

	1841	1842	1843	1844	1845
CHITTENDEN					
2	Francis Wilson	John Van Sicklin	"	George A. Allen	"
2	Edm'd Wellington	John Allen	"	John H. Tower	"
3	William Noble	"	Henry B. Stacy	"	E. A. Stansbury
4	George A. Allen	Rolla Gleason	"	"	Horace Ferris
5	Geo. K. Platt	Henry Leavenworth	"	I. P. Richardson	"
6	Charles Russell	"	"	"	"
7	William Weston	"	"	"	"
CALEDONIA CO.					
2	E. B. Chase	"	Calvin Morrill	Isaac N. Hall	James Gilchrist
2	Isaac N. Hall	"	James Gilchrist	John P. Ingalls	Calvin Morrill
3	S. B. Mattocks	"	"	"	"
4	James Roberts jr	"	Alexander Harvey	Joseph Preston	Oramel H. Freeman
5	Thos. Bartlett jr	Theron Howard	Bliss N. Davis	Theron Howard	Mordecai Hale
6	S. B Mattocks	"	"	"	Charles Davis
7	Henry W. Palmer	William Mattocks	C. J. Davis	Norman Davis	"
FRANKLIN CO.					
2	Augustus Burt	Luther B. Hunt	Augustus Burt	"	"
2	Cornelius Wood	Joseph Smith	James Davis	"	Jona. H. Hubbard
3	J. H. Brainerd	"	"	"	"
4	Decius R. Bogue	"	John S Foster	"	"
5	Orlando Stevens	Homer E. Hubbell	William C. Wilson	"	Orlando Stevens
6	William Bridges	"	"	"	James Davis
7	Romeo H. Hoyt	James Davis	Joseph H. Brainerd	"	"
ORLEANS CO.					
2	Isaac Parker	"	David M. Camp	Elijah Cleaveland	"
2	John Boardman	Jairus Stebbins	Alvah R. French	Harry Baxter	"
3	Henry M. Bates	"	"	"	"
4	Merrill Williams	Geo. Worthington	"	Elijah G. Strong	"
5	Samuel Sumner	Jesse Cooper	John H. Kimball	"	Nathan S. Hill
6	George Nye	"	"	"	"
7	Henry M. Bates	"	"	"	"
ESSEX CO					
2	John S. Nelson	"	George E. Holmes	Martin French	Reuben C. Benton
2	Owen Brown	"	Martin French	Warner Bingham	William Morrill
3	Lucius R. Webb	Allen Gould	"	"	Isaac L. Cummings
4	Geo. E. Holmes	George W. Gates	"	"	Bench Blodgett
5	Wm. Heywood jr	"	"	"	William T. Barron
6	Azariah Webb jr	"	Moody Rich	"	Wm. Heywood jr
7	Wm. Heywood jr	"	"	"	Isaac Cummings
GRAND ISLE CO.					
2	Calvin Fletcher	"	Samuel Adams	Ira Hill	Wallis Mott
2	Joseph M. Mott	"	Ira Hill	William H. Lyman	"
3	Joel Allen	"	"	"	"
4	Gary Whitney	"	"	Abel Brown	Albert C. Butler
5	Hector Adams	William W. White	Frederick Hazen	Wm. W. White	Frederick Hazen
6	Joel Allen	"	"	Jabez Ladd	Augustus Knight
7	John M. Sowles	"	"	"	"
WASHINGTON CO.					
2	Horace Hollister	Joseph Sawyer	Charles Sampson	Joseph A. Curtis	"
2	Joseph Sawyer	Charles Sampson	Sheffield Hayward jr	Ebenezer Bruce	"
3	Stilman Churchill	"	Daniel P. Thompson	"	Shubael Wheeler
4	Andrew A. Swee.	"	George W. Barker	"	"
5	Homer W. Heator	Oramel H. Smith	"	"	Newell Kinsman
6	D. P. Thompson	Azel Spaulding	"	"	Jerem'h T. Marston
7	Lyman Briggs	"	"	"	"
LAMOILLE CO.					
2	David P. Noyes	John Warner	"	Nathaniel Jones	"
2	Nathan H. Thomas	Calvin Burnett	"	Moses Fisk jr	Moses Fisk
3	Philo G. Camp	"	"	"	"
4	Martin Armstrong	Nath'l P. Keeler	"	Horace Powers	"
5	Harlow P Smith	W. H. H. Bingham	"	Luke P. Poland jr	Luke P. Poland
6	S muel A. Willard	"	Salmon Wires	"	Lucius H. Noyes
7	Charles H Parker	"	H Safford & Lyndej	Wm. W. White	Harlow P. Smith

COUNTY OFFICERS FROM 1778 TO 1850. CONTINUED.

CHITTENDEN	1846	1847	1848	1849	1850
2	Robert White	"	Ira Witters	I. P. Richardson	"
2	U. H. Penniman	"	I. P. Richardson	Truman Galusha	"
3	E. A. Stansbury	"	"	O. B. Bulkley	"
4	Horace Ferris	Luther P. Blodget	Edwin D. Mason	Samuel W. Taylor	"
5	Fred'k G. Hill	"	JeromeJ.Beardsley	Hector Adams	John G. Saxe
6	Charles Russell	Charles Adams	William H. French	Charles Adams	"
7	William Weston	Bradford Rixford	L. E. Chittenden	Bradford Rixford	"
CALEDONIA CO.					
2	Moses Kittredge	Robert Harvey	"	Walter Harvey	Jefferson Cree
2	Lucius Denison	John P. Ingalls	Jefferson Cree	James D. Bell	Alden E. Judevine
3	Sam .B Mattocks	"	"	Gusta's A.Burbank	"
4	O. H. Freeman	Jonas Flint	Hiram Perkins	Sargeant F. Field	Hiram Perkins
5	Mordecai Hale	George C. Cahoon	Bliss N Davis	"	Joseph Potts
6	Charles S. Dana	SamuelB Mattocks	Theron Howard	George B.Chandler	Theron Howard
7	Pliny Moore	G. A. Burbank	Theron Howard	G. A. Burbank	"
FRANKLIN CO.					
2	Arvah Sabin	"	"	"	"
2	J. H. Hubbard	"	William C. Wilson	"	"
3	J. H. Brainerd	"	"	"	"
4	John S. Foster	"	Orson Carpenter	"	"
5	Homer E. Royce	"	John S. Royce	Augustus Burt	"
6	James Davis	"	Jeptha Bradley	James Davis	William Bridges
7	Geo. F.Houghton	"	William Bridges	Geo. F. Houghton	Jeptha Bradley
ORLEANS CO.					
2	Elijah Cleaveland	James A. Paddock	"	Solomon Dwinnell	"
2	Harry Baxter	John Harding	"	Loren W. Clark	"
3	Henry M. Bates	"	"	"	Hubbard Hastings
4	Elijah G. Strong	James Hamilton	Hubbard Hastings	"	Elisha White
5	Nathan S. Hill	Henry F. Prentiss	"	John L. Edwards	Norman Boardman
6	Jacob Bates	"	"	Isaac N. Cushman	"
7	John H. Prentiss	"	"	Henry M. Bates	"
ESSEX CO.					
2	Reuben C.Benton	Horace Hubbard	Samuel G. Babcock	Timothy Fairchild	David Hibbard jr
2	Horace Hubbard	Nathan J. Graves	Heman Nichols	Elias Aldrich	Oramel Crawford
3	Isaac Cummings	John Dodge	Wm.H.Hartshorn	"	"
4	Preston May	Reuben C. Benton	George W. Gates	Greenleaf Webb	"
5	Wm. T. Barron	Wm. H. Hartshorn	Wm. Heywood jr	"	Wm. H Hartshorn
6	Jonah Brooks jr	"	Isaac Cummings	Jonah Brooks	"
7	William Chandler	"	Wm. Heywood jr	William Chandler	"
GRAND ISLE CO					
2	H H. Reynolds	"	Wallace Mott	"	William L. Sowles
2	Lorenzo Hall	"	David Marvin	"	Daniel Wait
3	Joel Allen	Elijah Haynes	"	"	"
4	David G. Dixon	"	Thos. B. Fletcher	"	Charles H. Clark
5	Frederick Hazen	Giles Harrington	"	"	Henry Adams
6	Jabez Ladd	"	Seland Whitney	"	"
7	Augustus Knight	"	"	"	"
WASHINGTON CO.					
2	Daniel Baldwin	"	Rod'k Richardson	Enoch D. Putnam	David W. Hadley
2	Henry Douglass	"	Enoch D. Putnam	Franklin A. Wright	Joseph Hancock
3	Shubael Wheeler	"	"	Jackson A. Vail	Shubael Wheeler
4	Addison Peck	"	Ira McLoud	Joseph W. Howes	Ira McLoud
5	Newell Kinsman	Charles Reed	"	John L. Buck	Stoddard B. Colby
6	Jere. T. Marston	"	Heman Carpenter	"	Jacob Scott
7	Lyman Briggs	"	Ferrand F. Merrill	Timothy R. Merrill	Lyman Briggs
LAMOILLE CO.					
2	V. W. Waterman	"	John West	Henry Stowell	"
2	Alpheus Morse	"	John C. Bryant	John Meigs	"
3	Philo G Camp	"	Harlow P. Smith	"	E. B. Sawyer
4	Jason Crain	"	George W. Bailey	V. W. Waterman	"
5	Wm. W. White	"	Whitman G. Ferrin	W. H.H. Bingham	"
6	Lucius H. Noyes	Harlow P. Smith	ArunahW Caldwell	Andrew Dow	"
7	Harlow P. Smith		William W. White	Cornelius Lynde	W. G Ferrin

MEMBERS OF THE CONSTITUTIONAL CONVENTIONS.

	1791*	1793	1814	1822
ADDISON CO.				
Addison	John Strong	David Whitney	"	Robert Chambers
Bridport	John N. Bennett	Marshall Smith	N. B. Johnson	Phinehas Kitchel
Bristol		Henry M'Laughlin	Noble Munson	Henry Soper
Cornwall	William Slade	Joel Linsley	Darius Mathews	Benjamin Sanford
Ferrisburgh	Abel Thompson	"	Theo. Middleb.ooks	Robert B. Hazzard
Goshen			Grindal Davis	Martin Carlisle
Granville				Joel Rice
Hancock		Daniel Claflin	Esaias Butts	Charles Church
Leicester	John Smith	Benjamin Whitman	Henry Olin	Henry Olin
Lincoln			Joseph Delong	Ebenezer Durfee
Middlebury	Samuel Miller	John Willard	Daniel Chipman	Eb n. W. Judd
Monkton	John Ferguson	Joseph Willoughby	Thomas Smith	Stephen Haight jr
New Haven	Oliver Pier	Elijah Foot	Seth Hoyt	Nathan Barton
Orwell	Ebenezer Wilson	Amos Spafford	J. Q. M'Farland	John Jackson
Panton	Benjamin Holcomb	Thomas Judd	Henry Chamberlain	Jonathan Spencer
Salisbury	Eleazer Claghorn	Stephen Hard	Reuben Saxton	Salathiel Bump
Shoreham	Josiah Pond	Ephraim Doolittle	Charles Rich	Elisha Buscom
Starksboro			David Kellogg	Elisha Ferguson
Vergennes	Alexander Brush	Enoch Woodbridge	David Edmond	Amos W. Burnum
Weybridge		Samuel Jewett	Amos Marsh	Samuel Childs
Whiting	Samuel Beach	Ebenezer Wheelock	David Brown	Ephraim Moulton
BENNINGTON CO.				
Arlington	Timothy Todd	Constant Barney	Nathan Canfield	Cyrus Canfie'd
Bennington		Jonathan Robinson	Samuel Fay	Orsamus C. Merrill
Dorset	John Shumway	William Dunton	Benjamin Deming	Sylvanus Sykes jr
Landgrove				Daniel Tuthill
Manchester	Martin Powell	Isaac Smith	Elijah Littlefield	
Peru			Peter Dudley	Peter Dudley
Pownal	Thomas Jewett	"	Samuel Wright	Stoddart Merchant
Readsboro		Joseph Hartwell	Elijah Bailey	John Walker
Rupert	Israel Smith	Cephas Smith	Josiah Rising	David Sheldon
Sandgate	Reuben Thomas	Nathaniel Jones	Joseph Tuttle	John H Sanderson
Shaftsbury	Gideon Olin	"	Jonas Galusha	Jonas Galusha
Stamford	Andrew Seldon	Oliver Smith		Otis Phillips
Sunderland	Timothy Brownson	Gilbert Bradley	Edmond Graves	Ethan Bradley
Winhall			Job Leonard	Reuben Brooks
Woodford		Caleb Moore	Lebbeus Barney	Joseph C. Hollister
CALEDONIA CO.				
Barnet	Alexander Harvey		John Gilfillan	Adam Duncan
Burke			Abner Coe	Geo. W. Denison
Cabot		Lyman Hitchcock	David Gilman	Jeremiah Babcock
Danville	Abraham Morrill	Benjamin Sias	Wm. A. Griswold	Geo. W. Drew
Groton			Jesse Heath	David Vance
Hardwick			Samuel French	Solomon Aiken
Kirby			Theophilus Grout	Ebenezer Damon
Lyndon		Josiah Arnold	William Cahoon	Isaac Fletcher
Newark			Eleazer Packer	Miles Coe
Peacham	Wm. Chamberlain		Wm. Chamberlain	Josiah Shedd
Ryegate		Josiah Page	John Nelson	Hugh Laughlin
Sheffield			Joseph H. Ingalls	Joseph H. Ingalls
St. Johnsbury	Jonathan Arnold	Josias L. Arnold	Calvin Jewett	Ariel Aldrich
Sutton			Ezra Child	John Beckwith
Walden				James Bell
Waterford			Silas Davison	Jacob Benton
Wheelock			Samuel Fellows	Samuel Fellows jr

JOSEPH BOWKER, ESQ.

In a late publication, in a note from the above name, I find an account. from which I make the following statement: Joseph Bowker came to Rutland at an early period of its settlement and was active and energetic in his opposition to the unjust claims of New York, and was among the first in effecting a general organization of the inhabitants of the Grants in opposition to those claims. This opposition, in an organized form, was first effected by a convention which met at Dorset in January, 1776, at which time an association was formed and entered into " to defend by arms the liberties of these United American States against the fleets and armies of Great Britain."

*This Convention ratified the United States' Constitution before her admission into the Union.

MEMBERS OF THE CONSTITUTIONAL CONVENTIONS. 101

	1828	1836	1843	1850
ADDISON CO.				
Addison	Stephen Spencer	David Whitney	Aaron Merrill	Joseph Hayward
Bridport	Benj. Miner jr	Senaca Austin	David Whitney	Calvin Solace
Bristol	Robert Holley	Henry Soper	Horatio Needham	"
Cornwall	John Sanford	William Hamilton	"	Marcus O. Porter
Ferrisburgh	Theo.Middlebrooks	Daniel Marsh	Noah W. Porter	Nicholas Guindon
Goshen	Nathan Capen	Wm, Carlisle 3d	Justice N. Dartt	Silas D. Gale
Granville	Thomas King	Joel Rice	Jedediah Clerk	Amasa Eaton
Hancock	Charles Church	"	John Hackett	Zerah Barnes
Leicester	Henry Olin			John Bullock
Lincoln	Oliver W. Burnham	John Bush	William Mitchell	Rufus Tabor
Middlebury	Samuel Swift	"	Jed. S. Bushnell	Ozias Seymour
Monkton	Daniel Collins	Luman B. Smith	Roswell Atwood	Alson Collins
New Haven	Benjamin Field	Elias Bottum	Jonathan Hoyt	Elias Bottum
Orwell	Thos.D. Hammond	Jos. H. Chittenden	"	Israel Smith
Panton	Silas Tappan	Friend Adams	Putnam Bishop	Silas Pond
Ripton		Daniel Chipman	"	
Salisbury	Eben. N. Briggs	Prentiss Alden	Sumner Briggs	Cyrus Bump
Shoreham	Elisha Bascom	Kent Wright	Silas H. Jenison	Davis Rich
Starksboro	Myron Bushnell	Ira Bushnell	Pearley Hill	Theron Downey
Vergennes	Philip C. Tucker	Villa Lawrence		Geo. W. Grandey
Waltham	Solomon Hobbs	Lyman E. Husted	George Fisher	Rollin Everts
Weybridge	Asaph Hayward	Milo Stowe	Elijah G. Drake	Edwin Hayward
Whiting	Benj. Needham	Samuel T. Walker	Abel Walker	Whitfield Walker
BENNINGTON CO.				
Arlington	Anson Canfield	Sylvester Deming	Samuel Buck	Martin C. Deming
Bennington	David Robinson	J. Vanderspeigle	Alanson P. Lyman	Thomas M. Daniels
Dorset	Stephen Martindale	Cyrus Armstrong	Chauncey Green	G. B. Holly
Glastenbury		Asa G. Hewes	John H. Mattison	Asa G. Hewes
Landgrove	David Willey	"	James Martin	"
Manchester	Elijah Collins	Leonard Sargeant	Lyman Harrington	Leonard Sargeant
Peru	Josiah Barnard	Samuel Stone	Mark Batchelder	Stephen Dudley
Pownal	Perry Jewett	David Gardner	Sylvenas Danforth	Wm. R. Blanchard
Readsboro	Henry Holbrook	Jacob Hix	"	Isaac Esty
Rupert	Seth Moore	"	"	Nathan Burton
Sandgate	Joseph Tuttle	Samuel Thomas	Theod'e Sanderson	
Searsburgh		John Knapp	Joseph Eames	Joseph Crosier
Shaftsbury	Nathan H. Bottum	"	Samuel Ames	"
Stamford		Stephen C. Millard	Jenckes Phillips	Obed Hall
Sunderland	William Landon	Ethan Bradley	"	Edmond A. Graves
Winhall	Reuben Brooks	Francis Kidder jr	Reuben Brooks	Beriah Wheeler
Woodford	Joseph C. Hollister	Joseph Knapp	"	Alonzo Fox
CALEDONIA CO.				
Barnet	Walter Harvey	William Shearer	Mordecai Hale	Frank'n J. Eastman
Burke	Joel Trull	Rufus Goddings	Ebenezer Darling	Benj. F. Belden
Cabot	John W. Dana	"	Timothy P. Fuller	John R. Putnam
Danville	Wm. A. Palmer	"	Saml. B. Mattocks	Wm. A. Palmer
Groton	David Vance	Thomas Bartlett	Hugh Dunn	Isaac N. Hall
Hardwick	Timothy P. Fuller	"	John R. Skinner	A. E. Judevine
Kirby	Luther Wood	James Church	Timothy Lock	Merritt Newhall
Lyndon	William Cahoon	George C. Cahoon	"	Thomas Bartlett jr
Newark		Alpheus Stoddard	Lauren M. Sleeper	"
Peacham	Jacob Blanchard	John Mattocks	Samuel A. Chandler	James Clark
Ryegate	James Nelson jr	Ebenezer Morrill	Harry Moore	"
Sheffield	Joseph H. Ingalls	James Townsend	Elisha Davis jr	James Roberts
St Johnsbury	Ephraim Paddock	Luther Jewett	Calvin Morrill	Gardner Wheeler
Sutton	Andrew Brown	John Beckwith	"	Geo. W. Roberts
Walden	Daniel Wooster	"	Hiram Perkins	Daniel Wooster
Waterford	Sylv's Hemingway	Robert Taggard	Jona. D. Stoddard	Barron Moulton
Wheelock	Samuel Fellows jr		Edward M. Magoon	Samuel F. Shattuck

And this association was declared to be *independent* and no way under the direction or advice of the Government of New York. A number of conventions were holden upon the same subject, and adopted measures to aid the GREEN MOUNTAIN BOYS in their hard struggle with all their foes. Of all these conventions Mr. Bowker was President, and Capt. Joseph Bowker in the chair, is found

MEMBERS OF THE CONSTITUTIONAL CONVENTIONS.

	1791	1793	1814	1822
CHITTENDEN CO.				
Bolton		Samuel Bell	Samuel Webster	James Whitcomb
Burlington	Samuel Hitchcock	Stephen Keyes	George Robinson	Wm. A. Griswold
Charlotte	John McNeil	John McNeil	Nathaniel Newell	Nathaniel Newell
Colchester	Ira Allen	John Law	Eli Baker jr.	Nathan Bryan
Essex	Timothy Bliss	Timothy Bliss	"	Roswell Butler
Hinesburgh	Elisha Barber	Lemuel Bostwick	Wm. B. Marsh	N. Leavenworth
Huntington	Amos Brownson	"	Elias Buel	James Ambler jr
Jericho	Martin Chittenden	Martin Chittenden	Heman Lowry	Noah Chittenden
Milton	Abel Waters	Amos Mansfield	Moses Davis	Heman Allen
Richmond			William Rhodes	Eli Brownson
Shelburne	Wm. C. Harrington	Wm.C. Harrington	Phinehas Hill	Ezra Meach
St. George			Reuben Lockwood	
Underhill			Caleb Sheldon	William Barney
Westford		Jeremiah Stone	Ebenezer Bowman	Ebenezer Bowman
Williston	Thomas Chittenden	Thomas Chittenden	Jeremiah French	Chauncey Brownell
ESSEX CO.	Presidents in Italics			
Brunswick			John Walls	Daniel Smith
Canaan			Daniel Goss	Oliver Ingham
Concord			Cornelius Judevine	Dyer Hibbard
Granby				Noah Sabin
Guildhall	David Hopkinson	Benoni Cutler	Daniel Dana	Henry Hall
Lemington			Richard Morgan	Edw'd C. Spaulding
Lunenburg	Samuel Gates	Samuel Phelps	Levi Barnard	William Gates
Maidstone	John Rich	Haines French	Moody Rich	Jesse Hugh
FRANKLIN CO.				
Bakersfield			Samuel Sumner	Silas B. Hazeltine
Berkshire			Pearley Hall	Penuel Leavens
Enosburgh			Eliphaz Eaton	
Fairfax	Joseph Beaman	Thomas Russell	Stephen Holmes	Elias Bellows
Fairfield			Joab Smith	Benjamin Wooster
Fletcher			Reuben Armstrong	Zerah Willoughby
Franklin			Samuel Hubbard	William Felton
Georgia	John White	John White	Frederick Bliss	Elijah Dee jr
Highgate			Abel Drury	Ebenezer Starkwell
Montgomery			Seth Goodspeed	Richard Smith jr
Richford			Caleb Royce	Caleb Royce
Sheldon			Zerah Willoughby	Chauncey Fitch
St. Albans	Silas Hathaway	Silas Hathaway	N. M. Kingman	Stephen Royce jr
Swanton		Thomas Butterfield	Shad'k Hathaway jr	James Brown
GRAND ISLE CO.				
Alburgh		Benjamin Marvin	Ephraim Mott	Jirch S. Berry
Grand Isle			Simeon Clark	James Brown
Isle La Mott			Caleb Hill	Charles Carron
North Hero	Enos Wood	Nathan Hutchins	Dan Hazen	Irad Allen
South Hero	Ebenezer Allen	Timothy Pearl	Daniel G. Sawyer	Benajah Phelps
LAMOILLE CO.				
Belvidere				Moody Shattuck
Cambridge	John Fassett	John Fassett	Frederick Hopkins	Enoch Carlton
Eden			Joseph Farrar	Jeduthan Stone
Elmore			Martin Elmore	Martin Elmore
Hydepark			Oliver Noyes	Darius Fitch
Johnson	Jona. M'Connell		Daniel Dodge	Daniel Dodge
Mansfield				Ivory Luce
Morristown			Samuel Cook	David P. Noyes
Sterling				Moses Vilas
Stowe			Asa Raymond	Philo G. Camp
Wolcott			Thomas Taylor	

at the commencement of all their records, He was the first representative from Rutland in the first legislature after the Constitution of 1777 was adopted, and in the forenoon of the first day of the session he was chosen Speaker, and in the afternoon it was found that he was the first elected Councillor by having a larger number of votes than any other person. He was elected to the same office six times afterwards. He was the first Judge of Rutland Shire of the county, or Special

MEMBERS OF THE CONSTITUTIONAL CONVENTIONS.   103

CHITTENDEN CO.	1828	1836	1843	1850
Bolton	John Pinneo	"	Samuel B. Kennedy	John Pinneo
Burlington	Heman Lowry	John N. Pomeroy	Wyllys Lyman	John N. Pomeroy
Charlotte	Nathaniel Newell	Lyman Yale	Everett Rich	Joel S. Bingham
Colchester	Thomas Brownell	James Langshore	Jacob Relie	Hezekiah Bates
Essex	Samuel Bliss	Ezra Slater	Billy B. Butler	Jesse Carpenter
Hinesburgh	Edmund Baldwin	Stephen Byington	Lyman Dorwin	Elmer Beecher
Huntington	James Ambler jr	Selah Ambler	John Snyder	John Work
Jericho	Noah Chittenden	Truman Galusha		Jerome J. Beardsley
Milton	Lemuel B Platt	Daniel H. Onion	Alb. G. Whittemore	Hector Adams
Richmond	Edward Jones	Artemas Flagg	Eli Brownson	E. B. Green
Shelburne	Burgess Hall	Ezra Meach	Henry S. Morse	Garrad Burritt
St. George	Horace Ferris	Reuben Lockwood	"	"
Underhill	Caleb Sheldon	Joseph Wells	Alonson Burroughs	Martin C. Barney
Westford	Ebenezer Bowman	Danforth Wales	John R. Halbert	David S. Hasleton
Williston	Chauncey Brownell	"	Jonas G. Chittenden	Eli Brownson
ESSEX CO.				
Bloomfield	Aden Bartlette	John Stearns	Jeremiah Wright	S. W. Holbrook
Brighton		Elijah Bailey	John Stevens	"
Brunswick	David Hyde	Daniel Schoff jr	Haines Schoff	John D. French
Canaan	Samuel Ingalls		Elias Farnham	William Rich
Concord	Archibald Taggard	Harvey G. Fry	William B. May	Harvey G. Fry
East Haven				Horace B. Coe
Granby	Joel Gleason		Jonathan Mathews	
Guildhall	David Hopkinson jr	John Dewey	Royal Cutler	William Heywod jr
Lemington	Noyes Denison	Stephen Harris	Beach Blodgett	"
Lunenburg	Stephen Howe jr	"	"	Reuben C. Benton
Maidstone	Daniel Rich	Joseph Gleason	Moody Rich	Charles Stevens
Victory				Wm. M. Stearns
FRANKLIN CO.				
Bakersfield	Azariah Corse jr	Thomas Child	William C. Wilson	"
Berkshire	Cromwell Bowen	Penuel Leavens	Jasper Rand	
Enosburgh	Martin D. Follett	Theoph. Mansfield	Horace Eaton	Samuel H. Stevens
Fairfax	Isaac N. Soule	Joseph Beaman	Homer E. Hubbell	Asa S. Gove
Fairfield	Benjamin Wooster	Joseph Soule	Bradley Barlow	
Fletcher	John Kinsley jr.	Ira Hatch	Albert Kinsley	Reuben Armstrong
Franklin	William Felon	Orville Kimpron	John J. Deavitt	Charles Felton
Georgia	Elijah Dee jr	"	Alvah Sabin	"
Highgate	Jesse Carpenter	Robert L Paddock	O. F. Robinson	Benjamin Peake
Montgomery	Daniel Barrows	"	B. W. Fuller	Hiram Rawson
Richford	Alden Sears	"	Arad W. Sears	
Sheldon	Joshua W. Sheldon	James Mason	Lloyd Mason	Alfred Keith
St. Albans	James Davis	Luther B. Hunt	"	"
Swanton	Heman Hopkins	Lewis Janes	Joseph Blake	Isaac B Bowdish
GRAND ISLE CO.				
Alburgh	Thomas Mott	Henry H. Reynolds	Joseph M Mott	William L. Sowles
Grand Isle	Melvin Barns jr	Jabez Ladd	Melvin Barnes	Norman Gordon
Isle La Mott	Charles Carron	Ira Hill	Hiram Hall	D. V. Goodsell
North Hero	Irad Allen	Elijah Haynes	John Martin	Augustus Knight
South Hero	Bird Landon	Calvin Fletcher	Hector Adams	Orange Phelps
LAMOILLE CO.				
Belvidere	John Spencer	Alva Chaffee	A. K. Whittemore	Phinchas Carpenter
Cambridge	James B. Gilmore	Henry Stowell	Nathan Smilie	Giles A. Barber
Eden	Eli Hinds jr	Martin Wheelock	Samuel Plumley jr	"
Elmore	Jonathan Bridge	Peleg Scofield	George W. Bailey	"
Hydepark	Theoph. W. Litch	Russel B. Hyde	Nehemih Waterman	Lucius H. Noyes
Johnson	Charles W. Taylor	Levi B. Vilas	"	Stoughton S. Pike
Mansfield	Ivory Luce	"	"	Annexed to Stowe.
Morristown	Luther Brigham	Joseph Sears	Luther P. Poland	Horace Powers
Sterling	Moses Vilas			Baruch Darling
Stowe	Daniel Moody	Orion W. Butler	Harry S. Camp	Orion W. Butler
Waterville		Moses Fisk	Alpheus Morse	Jesse C. Holmes
Wolcott	Jonathan Smith	Thomas Taylor	Nathaniel Jones	Samuel Pennock

Court, in March, 1778. The first Judge of Probate for Rutland County, in 1781, the Judge of the Court he held till Dec., 1783, and the Judge of Probate till his death in 1784. The year and place of his birth is unknown, and no stone marks the place where the stranger can learn where the re-

MEMBERS OF THE CONSTITUTIONAL CONVENTIONS.

ORANGE CO.	1791	1793	1814	1822
Bradford	John Barron	John Barron	Pelatiah Corliss	John Pickett
Braintree			Lyman Kidder	William Ford jr
Brookfield	Daniel Kingsbury	Elisha Allis	Frederick Griswold	Frederick Griswold
Chelsea			Josiah Dana	Thomas Jones
Corinth	Peter Sleeman	Samuel Hazeltine	Peter Eaton	"
Fairlee	Nathaniel Niles	Israel Morey	Nathaniel Niles	Solomon Mann
Newbury	Daniel Farrand	Jacob Bayley	James Spear	"
Orange			Thaddeus Clapp	Jonathan Emery
Randolph	Josiah Edson	Abner Weston	Dudley Chase	"
Strafford	Peter Pennock	William Denison	Jed. H. Harris	Martin Barrett
Thetford	Beriah Loomis	Israel Smith	Joseph Reed	Elijah Hammond
Topsham			Jonathan Jenness	Saml. Butterfield
Tunbridge	Elias Curtis	Reuben Hatch	Samuel Austin	
Vershire	Thomas Porter		Asa Smith jr	Nathaniel Jones jr
Washington			Daniel Peas'ee	Jacob Bliss
Williamstown	Cornelius Lynde		Jonathan Fisk	Joel Bass
ORLEANS CO.				
Albany	In consequence of a letter being seven days coming from Burlington to Middlebury, after it took the cars, I have to put the contents out of its proper place. Samuel C. Crafts was Register of Probate for Orleans district from Dec. 1796 to Dec. 1815. Ira H. Allen from 1815 to 1821. Salmon Nye from 1821 to 1825. Ira H. Allen from 1825 to 1826. John H. Kimball from 1826 to 1836. For remainder see the proper place.	The only surviving member of this convention, and the youngest one of the whole, is Samuel C. Crafts and he was the only member from Orleans Co. Daniel Chipman, the member from Rutland, died April 23, 1850, aged 83, and David Whitney, from Addison, May 10, 1850, aged 93.	William Rowell	Eli Chamberlin jr
Barton			Samuel Works	John Kimball
Brownington			George Nye	William Baxter
Charleston			Jonas Warren	"
Coventry			Peleg Redfield	John Ide
Craftsbury			Royal Corbin	Joseph Scott
Derby			William Howe	Luther Newcomb
Glover			Timothy Lyman	John Crane
Greensboro			Timothy Stanley	Sam. Woodman 2d
Holland				Eber Robinson
Irasburgh			Joshua Johnson	"
Lowell			Asahel Curtis	John Harding
Morgan				Ira Leavens
Newport				Josiah Rawson
Troy			Henry Corey	Charles Conant
Westfield			Walter Stone	Thos. Stoughton
RUTLAND CO.				
Benson		Asahel Smith	Oliver Parmelee	John Kellogg
Brandon	Nathan Daniels	David Buckland	John Conant	"
Castleton	Noah Lee	"	Enos Merrill	John Mason
Philadelphia			Howard Mitchell	
Chittenden	Samuel Harrison		Thomas Manley	Wolcott H. Keeler
Clarendon		Jonathan Parker	Seba French	Linsey Rounds
Danby	Daniel Sherman	Daniel Sherman	John H. Andrus	James M. Daniels
Fairhaven	Simeon Smith	Mathew Lyon	Ethan Whipple	John P. Colburn
Hubbardton	Janna Churchill	Ebenezer Wallis	James Whelpley	Seth Wallace
Ira		George Sherman	James Herrenton	Preserved Fish
Mendon			Zidon Edson	Elisha Estabrooks
Middletown	Jonathan Brewster	John Burnham	Jonas Clark	David McClure
Mount Holley		Abraham Jackson	Jed. Hammond	Abel Bishop
Mount Tabor		John Stafford	Gideon Tabor	"
Pawlet	Lemuel Chipman	Caleb Allen	James Leach	Benjamin Fitch
Pittsfield			Erastus Holt	Warner Durkee
Pittsford	Thos. Hammond	Augustine Hibbard	Wm Harrington	James Barlow
Poultney	William Ward	Isaac Hosford	John Stanley	Asahel Pond
Rutland	Nathaniel Chipman	Daniel Chipman	Wm. Denison	Robert Pierpoint
Shrewsbury		Emanuel Case	David Holden	Zidon Edson
Sherburne			Nath'l M. Fuller	"
Sudbury	Joseph Warner	Elijah Blake	John Jackson	Joseph Warner
Tinmouth	John Spafford	Orange Train	Estus Barker	"
Wallingford	Asahel Jackson	Joseph Randall	William Fox	Eliakim H. Johnson
Wells		Samuel Lathrop	Aaron Mosher	
Westhaven		Simeon Smith		

mains of the man are deposited, which the people of Rutland took so much pride to honor while living; and he left no descendants, nor is there any one living that is able to tell those less important items in his public life. I hope and trust for the honor of the town, that the State, County, or town will in some suitable manner raise something to his grave that will commemorate his memory.

MEMBERS OF THE CONSTITUTIONAL CONVENTIONS. 105

ORANGE CO.	1828	1836	1843	1850
Bradford	Jesse Merrill 2d	Geo. W. Prichard	Seth Austin	John B.Woodward
Braintree	Lyman Kidder	Elijah Flint	Jefferson P. Kidder	Levi Tracy
Brookfield	Frederick Griswold	"	Noah Paine	Fred'k G. Bigelow
Chelsea	David Wiggin	John W. Smith	H.E.G. M'Laughlin	Levi B. Vilas
Corinth	Peter Eaton	George Sleeper		William Spencer
Fairlee	Thomas Stratton	Phinehas Bailey	John M'Lane	"
Newbury	Moody Chamberlin	Tappan Stevens	John E. Chamberlin	Joseph Atkinson
Orange	Reuben White	Luther Carpenter	Preston Chamberlin	Luther Carpenter
Randolph	Lebbeus Edgerton	Calvin Blodgett	Jacob K. Parish	Philander Perrin
Strafford	Martin Barrett	Nathaniel Morrill	William Sanborn	Royal Hatch
Thetford	Simeon Short	*Lyman Fitch*	Abijah Howard jr	Lyman Hinckley
Topsham	Jonathan Jenness		"	John W.Batchelder
Tunbridge	Nathaniel King	Elijah Dickinson	Thomas S. Paine	Zebina Whitney
Vershire	Geo. W. Maltby		Simeon Bacon	William Boardman
Washington	Asa Burton	Wm. Huntington	John Colby	Lyman Perigo
West Fairlee	Isaac Lyon	William Niles	Stephen Thomas	"
Williamstown	Jedediah Smith	B. Newcomb	Darius Pride	William L. Beckett
ORLEANS CO.				
Albany	Eli Chamberlin jr	Enoch Rowell	Perley Hyde	Nathan Bedee
Barton	James May	"	Horace Pierce	Samuel A. Willard
Brownington	Amherst Stewart		Elisha White	John F. Skinner
Charleston	Abner Allyn	Ebenezer Cole	Kelton Brackett	Elijah Robinson
Coventry	Argalus Harmon	Philip Flanders	Charles Story	Isaac Parker
Craftsbury	*Samuel C. Crofts*	Joseph Scott	James A. Paddock	Nathan S. Hill
Derby	Luther Newcomb	Timothy Hinman	ElbridgeG.Johnson	John L. Edwards
Glover	John Crane	Warren Sartwell	Isaac B. Smith	H. S. Bickford
Greensboro	Stephen Sherman	"	Ezekiel Rand	HamiltonStimpson
Holland	Eber Robinson	Jason Hinman		Jason Hinman
Irasburgh	Roger Enos	John Kellam	George Nye	Thomas Jameson
Jay	Madison Keith	Walter Charlton		Willard Walker
Lowell	Abel Curtis	H W. W. Miller	John Harding	Andrew Dodge
Morgan	Rewell Cobb	Ira Leavens	Simeon Albee	Samuel Daggett
Newport	Nathan Daggett	Asa B. Moore	Orville Daggett	William Moon
Salem	Noyes Hopkinson	Samuel Blake	Noyes Hopkinson	"
Troy	Samuel H. Hovey	Frederick Fuller	Ralph Chamberlin	Frederick Fuller
Westfield	Luther Page	Luke Miller	Chester Coburn	Jairus Stebbens
Westmore		Peter Gilman	"	Thomas K. Bruce
RUTLAND CO.				
Benson	Chauncey Smith	Rowland P. Cooley	Philo Wilcox	Loyal C. Kellogg
Brandon	Daniel Farrington	Josiah W. Hale	Edward Jackson	Josiah W. Hale
Castleton	John Mason	Selah H. Merrill	Benj. F. Langdon	Almon Warner
Chittenden	Jonas Wheeler	Thos P. Leonard	Alvin Randall	Capen Leonard
Clarendon	Ozel H. Rounds	Linsey Rounds	Silas W. Hodges	Thomas Stewart
Danby	Andrus Eggleston	James M. Daniels	Galen J. Locke	"
Fairhaven	Moses Colton	Wm. C. Kittredge	Abram Graves	
Hubbardton	David Barber		Pliny Holmes	C. S. Rumsey
Ira	Leonard Mason	"	Russell Fish	Lester Fish
Mendon	Rufus Richardson	Timothy Gibson	Rufus Richardson	Jonas Wheeler
Middletown	Allen Vail	Jonathan Morgan	Jonas Clark	
Mount Holley	Nathan T. Sprague	David French	John Crowley	John Bryant
Mount Tabor	Caleb Buffum	Gideon S. Tabor	Azel Kelley	BenjaminB.Britton
Pawlet	Joel Simonds	Nathaniel Harmon	Geo. W Harmon	Robert H. Smith
Pittsfield	Wm. R. Blossom	Erastus Holt		John M'Collum
Pittsford	Caleb Hendee	"	German F. Hendee	"
Poultney	John Stanley	Joel Beaman	Henry G. Neal	John Lewis
Rutland	Robert Pierpont	Solomon Foote	Jonathan C.Dexter	
Shrewsbury	John Buckmaster	Noah Johnson	William Matherson	"
Sherburne	Josiah Wood		RichardEstabrooks	John Johnson
Sudbury	Barnard Ketchum	John C. Sawyer	ThomasJ.Goodrich	"
Tinmouth	Obadiah Noble jr	"	Payne Gilbert	Eliada Crampton
Wallingford	Amos Bucklin	Mosely Hall	Sam. M. Edgerton	Harvey Button
Wells	Seth Blossom	Westley Clement		Nathan Francis
Westhaven	Erastus Colman	Oliver Hitchcock	Curtis Kelsey	James Forbes
Debentures			$6,330 61	$8,967 81

MEMBERS OF THE CONSTITUTIONAL CONVENTIONS.

Town	1791	1793	1814	1822
WASHINGTON CO.				
Barre		Asaph Sherman	James Fisk	Denison Smith
Berlin			Bethuel Goff	Mathew Wallace
Calais			Samuel Fay	Benjamin Page
Duxbury		Walter Avery	Jesse Arms	Edward Crossett
Fayston				Daniel Wilder
Marshfield			Robert Cristy	Lovell Kelton
Middlesex		Seth Putnam	Rufus Chamberlin	"
Montpelier		Jacob Davis	Joseph Howes	Darius Boyden
Moretown			Ebenezer Hazeltine	Rufus Clapp
Northfield			Gilbert Hatch	Oliver Averill
Plainfield			Lovel Kelton	John Vincent
Roxbury			Darius Spaulding	Jonathan F. Ruggles
Waitsfield			Stephen Pierce	Mathias S. Jones
Warren			Joseph W. Eldridge	Amos Rising
Waterbury		Richard Holden	Dan Carpenter	Ezra Butler
Woodbury			John Bruce	Joel Cilley
Worcester			John Ridlon	Allen Vail
WINDHAM CO.				
Athens	James Shafter	Thad's Alexander	Samuel Bayley	Abraham Ball
Brattleboro	Gardner Chandler	Samuel Knight	Samuel Elliott	Jonas Mann
Dover			Reuben Deane	Amos Rice
Dummerston	Jason Duncan	Alexander Cathern	Jonathan Huntley	Marshall Miller
Grafton	David Palmer	Amos Fisher	Ebenezer Burgess jr	William Stickney jr
Guilford	Peter Briggs	"	John Phelps	Joseph Boyden
Halifax	Benjamin Henry		Joseph Henry	
Jamaica			Samuel Berry	Nathaniel Robbins
Londonderry		"	Benjamin Baldwin	Lawrence Pierce
Marlboro		Gershom C. Lyman	Joseph Olds	H. H. Winchester
Newfane	Jonas Whitney			
	Calvin Knowlton	Luke Knowlton	Sylvanus Sherman	
Putney	Daniel Jewett	John Campbell	Phinehas White	Theoph's Crawford
Rockingham	Elijah Lovwell	David Sanderson	Henry Lake	Eleazer Albee
Somersett			Sylvanus Parmeley	Saml. Worthington
Stratton			Sampson Bixby	Richard Scott
Townshend	Joshua Wood	Ephraim Wheelock	Ezekiel Ransom	Dana Bayley
Vernon	Jonathan Hunt	"	Cyrus Washburn	
Wardsboro		Daniel Reed		Asa Wheelock
Westminster	Stephen R. Bradley	Lott Hall	Gideon Warner	Samuel Mason
Whitingham	Isaac Lyman	Jabez Foster	James Roberts	John Roberts
Wilmington		Timothy Castle	Silas Axtel	Jesse Swift
Windham			Luther Stowell	Amos Emery
WINDSOR CO.				
Andover		Moses Warner	Samuel Manning	Oliver Farrar
Barnard	Silas Tupper	Aaron Barlow	John Foster	Thomas Freeman
Bethel	Michael Flynn	Joel Marsh	Jonathan Marsh	"
Bridgewater	Benjamin Perkins	"	James Southgate	Isaiah Raymond
Cavendish		Asaph Fletcher	Uriel C. Hatch	"
Chester		Daniel Heald	Aaron Leland	Joshua Leland
Hartford		John Clark	Frederick Marther	George E. Wales
Hartland	Oliver Gallup	George Denison	Elihu Luce	Simeon Willard
Ludlow			Asahel Smith	"
Norwich	Daniel Buck	Paul Brigham	"	"
Plymouth			Ephraim Moore	
Pomfret	William Perry	"	Ignatius Thomson	
Reading		Aron Kimball	Jonathan Shed	
Rochester	Enoch Emerson		Enoch Emerson	John Chaffee
Royalton	Heman Durkee	Elias Stevens	Daniel Rix jr	
Sharon		Zacheus Downer	James Parker	"
Springfield	Simeon Stevens	Lewis R. Morris Sec.	Asahel Powers	Leonard Walker
Stockbridge		John Whitcomb	Elias Keyes	Norman Webber
Weathersfield		Nath'l Stoughton	Paul Cook	Amos Hulett
Windsor	Benjamin Greene	Stephen Jacob	Jabez Delano	Rufus Root jr
Woodstock	Benjamin Emmons	Jabez Cottle	Titus Hutchinson	Jasper Hazen

MEMBERS OF THE CONSTITUTIONAL CONVENTIONS. 107

	1828	1836	1843	1850
WASHINGTON CO.				
Barre	Peter Nichols	Alvin Carter	Webber Tilden	John E. Palmer
Berlin	Ebenezer Bailey	Abel Knapp	Sheffield Hayward jr	Joseph Hill
Calais	Thomas Cole	Shubael Wheeler	Nelson A. Chase	"
Duxbury	Ira Arms	David Beldin	Luther Graves jr	Arad E. Graves
Fayston	Peter Drew	"	Benjamin Davis	Willard B. Porter
East Montpelier				Hazen Lyford
Marshfield	Josiah Hollister	Horace Hollister	James Pitkin	Jonathan Goodwin
Middlesex	Rufus Chamberlin	"	William X. Holden	O. A. Chamberlain
Montpelier	Stephen Foster	Nahum Kelton	Jer'h T. Marston	"
Moretown	David Belding	Ira Carpenter	Levi Spaulding	Roger G. Bulkley
Northfield	Amos Robinson	Elijah Smith jr	Jesse Averill	Moses Robinson
Plainfield	Nathaniel Bancroft	James Parmer	Nathaniel Bancroft	Nathaniel Sherman
Roxbury	Nathan Morse	"	Henry S. Royce	Thomas R. Shaw
Waitsfield	Jason Carpenter	Mathias S. Jones	Norman Durant	Benjamin Reid jr
Warren	Joseph A. Hyzer	Artemas Cushman	Gideon Goodspeed	Denslow Upham
Waterbury	Luther Cleaves	Paul Dillingham jr	Wm. Carpenter	Eliakim Allen
Woodbury	Ebenezer Bruce	"	Joel Cilley	Ira M'Lond
Worcester	Allen Vail	"	Daniel Adams	Allen L. Vail
WINDHAM CO.				
Acton		Nathan Fisher		
Athens	Ethalston Bayley	Abraham Ball jr	Nathaniel Balch	Mark Ball
Brattleboro	Lemuel Whitney	Samuel Clark	Henry Clark	Calvin Townsley
Brookline	William Perry	"	Edson Higgins	Hiram Whitney
Dover	Ebenezer Jones	Lewis Hall	Fayette Perry	Asaph Haskins
Dummerston	Jonathan Huntley	Samuel Knight	John Clark	Asa Dutton
Grafton	William Stickney jr	"	Benj. H. Bridgman	Abishia Stoddard
Guilford	Aaron Barney	Elisha Field	Barnard Lynde	John Lynde
Halifax	Sanford Plumb	James L. Stark	Robert Collins	Timothy Larabee
Jamaica	Timothy Goodale	"	Alpheus Kellogg	Joel Holton
Londonderry	Luther Stowell	Curtis Robinson	David Arnold	Sem Pierce
Marlboro	Simeon Adams	Phinehas Marther jr	"	"
Newfane	Martin Field	Walter Eager	Charles K. Field	"
Putney	John Campbell	Phinehas White	David Crawford	William Houghton
Rockingham	Manasseh Divoll	Eleazer Albee	Daniel Kellogg	Jeremiah Barton
Somersett	Charles Morse	Jonathan Pike	Ephraim Rice	Joseph Morse
Stratton	Richard Scott	Benjamin Thatcher	David Rice	Amos Parsons
Townshend	Waitstill R. Ranney	William R. Shafter	John Roberts	"
Vernon	Joseph Franklin	Elijah Stebbins	"	Nathan Wood
Wardsboro	Asa Wheelock	Emery Wheelock	"	Henry Rice
Westminster	Ellery Albee	Timothy Field	Nathan G. Pierce	David Gorham
Whitingham	Elisha Putnam	David Chase 2d	Hosea F. Ballou	"
Wilmington	Lancy Forbes	Charles K. Field	Perley Bartlett	Eleazer Gorham jr
Windham	Amos Emery	"	"	William Harris
WINDSOR CO.				
Andover	Edward Simons	Joel Balch	Joseph Dodge jr	John Adams
Baltimore	Joseph Atherton		John Piper	Levi Piper
Barnard	Thomas Freeman	Ebenezer Richmond	Joseph B. Danforth	Daniel Aikens
Bethel	Daniel Lillie	James Wallace	Averill Burnett	Calvin Morse
Bridgewater	James Topliff	David Thompson	Isaiah Raymond	Ovid Thompson
Cavendish	Levi Jackman	"	Salmon F. Dutton	John F. Deane
Chester	Rufus Bruce	"	Phine's O. Sargeant	H. E. Stoughton
Hartford	Willis Lyman	Andrew Tracy		John L. Lovering
Hartland	Aaron Willard	David H. Sumner	Eben M. Stocker	"
Ludlow	Asahel Smith	"	Sewall Fullum	Alexander Barton
Norwich	Aaron Loveland	John Wright	"	Alba Stimson
Plymouth	Asa Briggs	John S. Fullerton	Moses Pollard jr	Levi Slack
Pomfret	Henry Hewett	"	Martin D. Follett	A. L. Chamberlin
Reading	Henry Conant	John Watkins	Rufus Forbush	"
Rochester	Lyman Emerson	John Chaffee		Artemas Cushman
Royalton	Franklin Hunter	Jacob Collamer	John S. Marcy	"
Sharon	Rhodolphus Brown	Alex'r F. Bean	Wooster Downer	Warren C. French
Springfield	Leonard Walker	Nomlas Cobb	Bezaleel Wood	Wm. W. Whitney
Stockbridge	Norman Webber	Daniel Gay jr	"	Justin Morgan
Weathersfield	William Jarvis	Ebenezer Shedd	Daniel Bowen	William M. Pingrey
Weston	Amos N. Burton	Asa B. Foster	Perkins N. Willey	Stephen Smith
West Windsor				Samuel Parker
Windsor	Horace Everett	Asa Aikens	Darius Jones	Carlos Coolidge
Woodstock	Titus Hutchinson	Oliver P. Chandler	Lyndon A. Marsh	Norman Williams

CENSUS AT DIFFERENT TIMES.

ADDISON CO.	1791	1800	1810	1820	1830	1840	1850
Addison,	401	734	1100	1210	1306	1232	1279
Avery's Gore,				13	29		78
Bridport,	449	1124	1520	1511	1774	1480	1393
Bristol,	211	665	1179	1051	1274	1233	1344
Cornwall,	826	1163	1279	1120	1264	1164	1155
Ferrisburgh,	481	956	1647	1581	1822	1755	2075
Goshen,		4	86	290	555	621	486
Granville,	101	185	324	328	403	545	603
Hancock,	56	149	311	442	472	465	430
Leicester,	343	522	609	548	538	603	596
Lincoln,		97	255	278	639	770	1057
Middlebury,	395	1263	2138	2535	3468	3162	3517
Monkton,	450	889	1248	1152	1384	1310	1246
New Haven,	723	1135	1688	1566	1834	1503	1663
Orwell,	778	1386	1849	1730	1598	1504	1470
Panton,	220	363	520	546	605	670	559
Ripton,			15	42	278	357	567
Salisbury,	446	644	709	721	907	942	1027
Shoreham,	721	1447	2033	1881	2137	1674	1601
Starksboro',	40	359	726	914	1342	1263	1400
Vergennes, } Waltham, }	201	516 247	835 244	817 264	999 301	1017 283	1378 271
Weybridge,	175	502	750	714	850	797	804
Whiting,	250	404	565	609	653	659	629
	7267	14745	21613	21879	26503	25087	26550

BENNINGTON CO.							
Arlington,	991	1597	1468	1354	1207	1035	1084
Bennington,	2377	2243	2524	2485	3419	3429	3923
Dorset,	958	1286	1294	1359	1507	1432	1700
Glastenbury,	34	48	76	48	52	53	52
Landgrove,	31	147	299	341	355	345	337
Manchester,	1276	1397	1502	1508	1525	1590	1782
Peru,	71	130	239	314	455	578	567
Pownal,	1746	1692	1655	1812	1835	1613	1740
Readsboro',	64	234	410	530	662	767	857
Rupert,	1033	1648	1630	1332	1318	1091	1101
Sandgate,	773	1020	1187	1185	933	777	850
Searsburgh,				9	40	120	201
Shaftsbury,	1999	1895	1973	2022	2143	1835	1896
Stamford,	272	373	378	490	563	662	833
Sunderland,	414	557	575	496	463	437	479
Winhall,	155	202	429	428	571	576	762
Woodford,	60	138	254	212	395	487	423
	12254	14607	15893	15925	17443	16827	18587

CALEDONIA CO.							
Bradley Vale,					21	50	107
Barnet,	477	860	1301	1488	1764	2030	2522
Burke,		98	460	541	866	997	1103
Cabot,	122	349	886	1032	1304	1440	1356
Danville,	574	1514	2240	2300	2631	2633	2578
Deweysburgh,	48	152	200				
GoshenGore,North,				64	105		142	183
" " South,						44	32
Groton,	45	248	449	595	836	928	895
Harris Gore,						16	8
Hardwick,	3	260	735	867	1216	1354	1403
Kirby,		20	311	312	401	520	509
Lyndon,	59	542	1090	1296	1822	1753	1752
Newark,		8	88	154	257	360	434
Peacham,	365	873	1301	1294	1351	1443	1377
Ryegate,	187	415	812	994	1119	1223	1606
St. Johnsbury,	143	615	1334	1404	1592	1887	2758
Sheffield,			170	388	581	720	821	997
Sutton,			146	433	697	1005	1068	1001
Walden,	43	153	455	580	827	913	910
Waterford,	63	565	1289	1247	1358	1388	1412
Wheelock,	32	568	964	906	834	881	856
	2161	7556	14800	16393	19924	21891	23599

MEMBERS OF CONGRESS FROM VERMONT.

NAMES.	TERM.	
Nathaniel Niles,	1791 to	1795
Israel Smith,	1791	1797
Daniel Buck,	1795	1799
Mathew Lyon,	1797	1801
Lewis R. Morris,	1797	1803
Israel Smith,	1801	1803
Wm. Chamberlain,	1803	1805
"	1809	1810
Martin Chittenden,	1803	1813
James Elliott,	1803	1809
Gideon Olin,	1803	1807
James Fisk,	1805	1809
"	1810	1815
James Witherill,	1807	1808
Samuel Shaw,	1808	1813
Jona. H. Hubbard,	1809	1810
Wm. Strong,	1810	1815
"	1819	1821
Wm. C. Bradley,	1813	1815
"	1823	1827
Ezra Butler,	1813	1815
Richard Skinner,	1813	1815
Charles Rich,	1813	1815
"	1817	1824
Daniel Chipman,	1815	1817
Luther Jewett,	"	"
Chauncey Langdon,	"	"
Asa Lyon,	"	"
Charles Marsh,	"	"
John Noyes,	"	"
Heman Allen, of Col.,	1817	1819
Samuel C. Crafts,	1817	1825
Wm. Hunter,	1817	1819
Orsamus C. Merrill,	1817	1819
Mark Richards,	1817	1821
Ezra Meech,	1819	1821
"	1825	1827
Rollin C. Mallary,	1820	1831
Elias Keyes,	1821	1823
John Mattocks,	1821	1823
"	1825	1827
"	1841	1843
Phineas White,	1821	1823
D. A. A. Buck,	1823	1829
Henry Olin,	1824	1825
Geo. E. Wales,	1825	1829
Benjamin Swift,	1827	1831
Jona. Hunt,	1827	1832
Wm. Cahoon,	1827	1831
Horace Everett,	1829	1843
Heman Allen, of M.,	1832	1839
William Slade,	1831	1843
Hiland Hall,	1833	1843
Benj. F. Deming,	1833	1835
Henry F. Janes,	1835	1837
Isaac Fletcher,	1837	1841
John Smith,	1839	1841
Augustus Young,	1841	1843
Geo. P. Marsh,	1843	1849
Solomon Foot,	1843	1847
William Henry,	1847	1851
Paul Dillingham,	1843	1847
Jacob Collamer,	1843	1849
Lucius B. Peck,	1847	1851
Ahiman L. Miner,	1851	
Wm. Hebard,	1849	
James Meacham,	1849	
Thomas Bartlett, jr.,	1851	

CENSUS AT DIFFERENT TIMES.

	1791	1800	1810	1820	1830	1840	1850
CHITTENDEN CO.							
Buels Gore						13	18
Bolton	88	220	249	306	452	470	602
Burlington	332	815	1690	2111	3226	4271	7585
Charlotte	635	1231	1679	1526	1702	1620	1634
Colchester	137	347	657	960	1489	1739	2593
Essex	354	730	957	1089	1664	1824	2052
Hinesburgh	454	933	1238	1332	1669	1682	1834
Huntington	167	405	514	732	929	914	885
Jericho	381	728	1185	1219	1654	1685	1837
Milton	282	786	1546	1746	2100	2134	2451
Richmond		718	935	1014	1109	1054	1453
Shelburne	389	723	987	936	1123	1098	1257
St. George	57	65	68	120	135	121	127
Underhill	65	212	490	633	1052	1441	1599
Westford	63	647	1107	1025	1290	1352	1458
Williston	471	836	1195	1246	1608	1554	1669
	3875	9346	14497	15995	21202	22977	29054
ESSEX CO.							
Averill			9		1	11	7
Bloomfield		27	144	132	150	179	244
Brighton					105	157	193
Brunswick	66	86	143	124	160	130	119
Canaan	19	74	232	277	373	378	471
Concord	49	322	677	806	1031	1024	1153
Easthaven			30	34		79	94
Granby		69	120	49	97	105	127
Guildhall	158	296	544	529	481	470	501
Lemington	31	52	132	139	183	124	187
Lunenburgh	119	393	714	856	1054	1130	1123
Maidstone	125	152	177	166	236	271	237
Victory			6		53	140	168
Wenlock					24	28	26
	567	1471	2942	3112	3948	4226	4650
FRANKLIN CO.							
Avery's Gore				11	22	35	48
Bakersfield	13	222	812	945	1087	1258	1523
Berkshire		172	918	831	1308	1818	1957
Enosburgh		143	704	932	1560	2022	2009
Fairfax	254	786	1301	1359	1729	1918	2113
Fairfield	129	901	1618	1573	2270	2448	2592
Fletcher	47	200	382	497	793	1014	1184
Franklin	46	280	714	631	1129	1410	1647
Georgia	340	1068	1760	1703	1897	2106	2648
Highgate	103	437	1374	1250	2038	2292	2653
Montgomery		36	237	293	460	548	1007
Richford		113	440	440	704	914	1075
Sheldon	110	408	883	927	1427	1734	1814
St. Albans	256	901	1609	1636	2395	2702	3572
Swanton	74	858	1657	1607	2158	2312	2824
	1372	6525	14409	14635	20977	24331	28706
GRAND ISLE CO.							
Alburgh	446	750	1105	1172	1239	1344	1568
Grand Isle	337	680	826	898	648	724	666
Isle La Mott	47	135	338	312	459	435	470
North Hero	125	324	552	503	638	716	731
South Hero	200	600	623	842	714	664	705
	1155	2489	3445	3727	3701	3883	4140
LAMOILLE CO.							
Belvidere			217	198	185	207	256
Cambridge	359	733	990	1176	1613	1790	1849
Eden		29	224	201	461	703	668
Elmore	12	51	157	157	442	476	504
Hydepark	43	110	261	273	823	1080	1107
Johnson	93	255	494	778	1079	1410	1380
Mansfield		12	38	60	279	223	
Morristown	10	144	550	726	1315	1502	1441
Sterling		9	122	131	183	193	233
Stowe		316	650	957	1570	1371	1771
Waterville	15	51	193	273	488	610	837
Wolcott	32	47	124	123	492	910	909
	564	1751	4020	5153	8930	10475	10955

DAVID ROBINSON.

This man was born in Hardwick, Mass., Nov. 22, 1754, and was an early resident of Bennington and a soldier in the memorable battle in that town, August 16, 1777. He held the office of Sheriff of that county from 1787 to 1810, with the exception of two years, making 22 years, which is a longer time than that office has been held by any other person in the State. He was United States Marshall eight years, a Major General in 1812, and a member of the Constitutional Convention of 1828. He died at Bennington, Dec., 1843, aged 89,

GEN. SAMUEL FLETCHER

Was born in Grafton, Mass., in 1745. At the age of seventeen he enlisted as a soldier in the old French war, and served one year. On his return he learned the trade of a Blacksmith and followed it four years, when he married a young lady with a handsome property, and, resigning the sledge, removed to Townsend to wield the axe among the trees of the forest On the commencement of the war in 1775, he joined the American Standard at Bunker Hill, as orderly sergeant. He returned to Townshend in January, 1776, where he was chosen captain of Militia. Being a prominent man, he was ordered to raise as many minute men as possible in his vicinity, to be ready to march at the beat of the drum. His whole company volunteered, and in 1777 they marched to Old 'Ti, for the aid of the American army there besieged. On this expedition with 13 volunteers, he attacked a British force of 40 men, killed one and took seven prisoners, without loss to his own men. He soon after received a Major's commission, and continued in the service till after the capture of Burgoyne. After his return he rose to the office of Major General of Militia. He was the first representative from Townshend, in the first legislature holden after the adoption of the first Constitution in 1777, and was twice re-elected, and at the last election he was chosen Councillor also, and held that office till 1790, and two years afterwards, 13. In 1788 he was chosen Sheriff of the county, and held that office in succession 18 years, the longest held by one person in the State, in succession. He was two years or more Judge of the County Court. He died Sept. 15, 1814, aged 69 years.

CENSUS AT DIFFERENT TIMES.

	1790	1800	1810	1820	1830	1840	1850
ORANGE CO.							
Bradford,	651	1063	1592	1411	155	1655	1723
Braintree,	231	531	850	1033	1299	1232	1225
Brookfield,	421	983	1384	1507	1677	1789	1662
Chelsea,	239	908	1397	1462	1958	1959	1953
Corinth,	578	1490	1876	1907	1953	1970	1906
Fairlee,	213	386	490	570	656	644	575
Newbury,	873	1304	1363	1623	2225	2578	2984
Orange,		348	686	751	1016	934	1007
Randolph,	892	1841	2255	2487	2743	2578	2666
Strafford,	845	1642	1805	1921	1935	1762	1540
Thetford,	862	1478	1735	1915	2113	2065	2216
Topsham,	162	344	814	1020	1384	1745	1668
Tunbridge,	487	1324	1640	2003	1920	1811	1736
Vershire,	439	1031	1311	1290	1260	1198	1070
Washington,	72	500	1040	1160	1374	1359	1343
West Fairlee,	230	391	493	573	841	824	696
Williamstown,	146	839	1353	1481	1487	1620	1452
	7354	16318	21724	24114	27258	27873	27285
ORLEANS CO.							
Albany,			12	101	253	683	920	1052
Barton,			128	447	372	726	892	937
Brownington,			65	236	265	412	486	612
Charleston,				56	90	564	731	1008
Coventry,			7	178	282	735	796	867
Craftsbury,		18	229	566	605	982	2151	1223
Derby,			178	714	925	1469	1881	1751
Glover,			36	387	549	902	1119	1137
Greensboro,		19	280	566	625	781	883	1008
Holland,				126	100	422	605	669
Irasburgh,			15	392	432	860	971	1031
Jay,				28	52	196	308	371
Lowell,				40	139	314	431	637
Morgan,				135	116	331	422	486
Newport,			50	112	52	284	591	748
Salem,			16	58	80	236	299	455
Troy,			32	231	277	603	856	1008
Westfield,			16	149	225	353	370	509
Westmore,				71	18	32	122	152
		37	1064	4593	5457	10357	13534	15707
RUTLAND CO.							
Benson	658	1164	1561	1481	1493	1403	1305
Brandon	637	1180	1375	1495	1946	2194	2835
Castleton	800	1039	1420	1541	1783	1769	3016
Chittenden & Phil.	198	450	651	528	610	644	675
Clarendon	1478	1789	1797	1712	1585	1549	1477
Danby	1206	1487	1730	1607	1362	1379	1536
Fairhaven	280	411	645	714	675	633	902
Hubbardton	404	641	734	810	865	719	701
Ira	312	473	519	498	442	431	400
Mendon	34	87	111	174	432	545	504
Middletown	699	1066	1207	1039	919	1057	876
Mount Holly			658	922	1157	1318	1356	1534
Mount Tabor	165	153	209	222	210	226	309
Pawlet	1458	1938	2233	2155	1965	1748	1843
Pittsfield	49	164	338	453	505	615	512
Pittsford	850	1405	1936	1916	2005	1927	2027
Poultney	1121	1697	1905	1955	1909	1878	2330
Rutland	1407	2124	2379	2369	2753	2708	3717
Sherburne	32	90	116	154	452	498	578
Shrewsbury	383	748	990	1149	1289	1218	1268
Sudbury	258	521	754	809	812	796	794
Tinmouth	935	973	1001	1069	1049	780	717
Wallingford	536	912	1386	1570	1740	1608	1688
Wells	622	988	1040	986	880	740	804
Westhaven	265	340	679	684	724	774	718
	14787	22448	27638	28247	29723	29195	33066

HEMAN LOWRY, Of Jericho, was a member of the Legislature one year, and 10 years United States Marshall, and held the office of Sheriff of the county 18 years, the longest of any one in that county. He died at Burlington, where he resided a number of years, some 6 or 8 years since.

JONATHAN BELL, Of Rutland, is the next on the list and was Sheriff of the county 16 years, and has long occupied a small piece of land in the burying ground a little North of Rutland village.

JOSEPH SCOTT, Of Craftsbury, comes in for a short notice, by having held the office of Sheriff of Orleans Co., for a longer term than any other, 14 years. He was seven years a member of the Legislature, one year a member of the Council of Censors and two years a member of Constitutional Conventions, and Judge of Probate six years. He died about 1841. His son Joseph, was elected Town Clerk in 1829, in room of Governor Crafts, who had held that office since 1792, and is the present Town Clerk. The town have had but two clerks, both of which are now living, 1751. Joseph Jr., was two years a member of the Legislature and has held many important town offices of various kinds. Harvey Scott, which I presume is a son of the Sheriff, took the office of Sheriff one year after his father's time expired, and held it eleven years. So it seems that office is hereditary in the family.

CALVIN FLETCHER, Of Grand Isle County, was Sheriff 14 years, and a member of the Legislature once. Whether dead or living, is unknown to the compiler.

JOHN CHIPMAN, Was the first person that came into Middlebury with a view of settling in 1766, but soon abandoned it. In 1773 he came again, and was drove off with the

CENSUS AT DIFFERENT TIMES.

WASHINGTON CO.	1791	1800	1810	1820	1830	1840	1850
Barre	16	919	1669	1955	2012	2126	1845
Berlin	134	685	1067	1455	1664	1598	1507
Calais	45	443	841	1111	1539	1709	1410
Duxbury	39	153	326	440	652	820	845
East Montpelier							1448
Fayston		18	149	258	458	635	684
Marshfield		172	513	710	1271	1156	1102
Middlesex	60	262	401	726	1156	1270	1365
Montpelier	118	890	1877	2308	2985	3725	2310
Moretown	24	191	405	593	806	1128	1335
Northfield	40	204	426	690	1412	2013	2922
Plainfield		256	543	660	874	880	802
Roxbury	14	113	361	512	737	784	967
Waitsfield	61	473	647	935	958	1048	1021
Warren		58	229	320	766	943	962
Waterbury	93	644	966	1269	1650	1992	2352
Woodbury		23	258	432	824	1092	1070
Worcester		25	41	44	432	587	702
	644	5529	10719	14418	20196	23506	24649
WINDHAM CO.							
Acton,		49	131	245	204	170	
Athens,		450	459	478	507	415	378	359
Brattleboro,		1589	1867	1891	2017	2141	2624	3816
Brookline,			472	431	391	376	328	285
Dover,		270	616	804	829	831	729	710
Dummerston,		1501	1692	1704	1658	1592	1277	1645
Grafton,		561	1149	1365	1482	1439	1324	1246
Guilford,		2432	2256	1872	1862	1760	1525	1389
Halifax,		1309	1600	1758	1567	1562	1299	1139
Jamaica,		263	582	996	1313	1553	1586	1607
Londonderry,		362	330	637	958	1302	1210	1279
Marlboro,		629	1087	1245	1296	1218	1027	896
Newfane,		660	1000	1267	1500	1441	1403	1305
Putney,		1848	1574	1607	1547	1510	1383	1421
Rockingham,		1235	1684	1954	2155	2272	2336	2331
Somerset,		111	130	199	173	245	282	32
Stratton,		95	271	265	272	312	311	180
Townshend,		677	1083	1115	1406	1386	1515	1354
Vernon,		482	430	521	627	631	705	82
Wardsboro,		483	868	1159	1016	1148	1102	1127
Westminster,		1601	1942	1925	1974	1737	1556	1728
Whitingham,		442	868	1248	1307	1477	1391	1380
Wilmingham,		645	1011	1193	1309	1367	1296	1375
Windham,			429	782	931	847	757	763
		17693	23531	26751	28457	28788	27442	28972
WINDSOR CO.							
Andover,		275	1022	957	1000	975	877	725
Baltimore,			175	207	204	179	155	124
Barnard,		673	1244	1648	1691	1881	1774	1647
Bethel,		473	911	1041	1314	1667	1880	1730
Bridgewater,		292	779	1154	1125	1311	1363	1311
Cavendish,		491	921	1295	1551	1498	1427	1776
Chester,		981	1880	2370	2193	2320	2301	2001
Hartford,		988	1495	1831	2010	2044	2194	2159
Hartland,		1652	1959	2352	2553	2503	2341	2063
Ludlow,		179	409	877	1144	1227	1363	1619
Norwich,		1158	1487	1812	1935	2316	2218	1978
Plymouth,		106	495	834	1112	1237	1417	1296
Pomfret,		710	1109	1473	1632	1867	1774	1546
Reading,		747	1123	1565	1603	1409	1363	1171
Rochester,		215	523	911	1142	1392	1396	1493
Royalton,		748	1498	1758	1816	1893	1917	1850
Sharon,		569	1170	1363	1431	1459	1371	1240
Springfield,		1097	2038	2556	2702	2749	2625	2762
Stockbridge,		190	424	700	964	1333	1418	1327
Weathersfield,		1146	1946	2115	2301	2213	2031	1851
Weston,			17	629	890	972	1032	951
W. Windsor } Windsor, }		1542	2214	2757	2950	3134	2744	1002 / 1928
Woodstock,		1605	2130	2672	2601	3014	3315	3041
		15748	26969	34477	38233	40623	40356	38521

others in 1776. In 1784 returned the third time and remained till his death in Aug, 1829. He was a Captain in the Revolutionary war, and many curious things are among his records in the Town Clerk's office. He, Joshua Hyde and Stephen Goodrich, were the first selectmen chosen in town, in 1787, and all lived till 1829. He was 12 years Sheriff of the county, and held some other offices in town. In the other counties the Sheriff's term of office was shorter, Nathan Fuller, of Caledonia, held it 11 years. Asaph Fletcher, jr., of Windsor, and Joseph Edson, of Orange, 10 years each. Edson was Marshall 6 years. Prince B. Hall, of Franklin, Greenleaf Webb, of Essex, and John Peck, of Washington, 8 each, and all but one in Lamoille two each.

GOV. ISRAEL SMITH.

A few years since I was at Rutland on business, and spent the Sabbath there, and, as is my usual custom took a walk to the burying ground. I soon came to the grave stone of Ex-Gov. Israel Smith, who had filled a page of his country's history with honor to himself. He graduated at Yale College in 1781, studied law, and removed to Rupert in 1783, and commenced his profession. In 1785, 88, 89 and 90 he represented the town of Rupert in the Legislature, and in 1791 removed to Rutland, and in 1797 was chosen a representative in the General Assembly. He was in high repute as a lawyer, and such was the estimation of his talents that in 1789 he was chosen, together with such noted men as Isaac Tichenor, Stephen R. Bradley, Nathaniel Chipman, Elijah Paine, Ira Allen and Stephen Jacob, Commissioners, to adjust the controversy between Vermont and New York. In 1792 he was a member of the Convention that assented to, and adopted the United States Constitution, preparatory to its being admitted into the Union as a State, which was accomplished the same year. Vermont being entitled to two representatives in Congress, Gov. Smith was chosen for the western district

CENSUS. AGGREGATE BY COUNTIES.

COUNTIES.	1791	1800	1810	1820	1830	1840	1850
Addison,	7267	14745	21613	21879	26503	25087	26550
Bennington,	12254	14607	15893	15925	17443	16827	18587
Caledonia,	2161	7556	14800	16392	19924	21891	23599
Chittenden,	3875	9346	14497	15995	21202	22977	29055
Essex,	567	1471	2942	3112	3948	4226	4650
Franklin,	1372	6525	14409	14635	20977	24531	28706
Grand Isle,	1155	2489	3445	3727	3701	3883	4140
Lamoille,	564	1751	4020	5153	8930	10475	10955
Orange,	7354	16318	21724	24114	27258	27873	27285
Orleans,	37	1064	4593	5457	10887	13834	15707
Rutland,	14787	22448	27638	28247	29723	29195	33066
Washington,	644	5529	10719	14413	20196	23506	24649
Windham,	17693	23581	26751	23457	28788	27442	28972
Windsor,	15748	26969	34877	38233	40623	40356	38521
Total,	85478	154399	217921	235740	280103	292103	314441

The following is all I have been able to obtain in relation to the District Court and its Officers.

DISTRICT JUDGES.
Nathaniel Chipman from 1791 to 1793
Elijah Paine from 1801 to 1842
Samuel Prentiss from 1842 ——

DISTRICT CLERKS.
Frederick Hill from 1791 to 1799
Cephas Smith jr from 1801 to 1809
Jesse Gove from 1810 to 1842
Edward H. Prentiss from 1842 ——

DISTRICT ATTORNEYS.
David Fay from 1801 to 1809
C. P. Van Ness from 1810 to 1812
Titus Hutchinson from 1813 to 1820
William A. Griswold from 1821 to 1829
Daniel Kellogg from 1829 to 1840

Charles Davis from 1841 to 1845
Charles Linsley from 1845 to 1849
Abel Underwood from 1849 ——

MARSHALLS.
John Willard from 1801 to 1810
David Robinson from 1811 to 1818
Heman Allen of C., from 1819 to 1823
Joseph Edson from 1823 to 1829
Heman Lowry from 1829 to 1835
George W Barker from 1835 to 1837
Heman Lowry from 1837 to 1841
William Barron from 1841 to 1845
Jacob Kent jr from 1845 to 1849
John Pettis from 1849 ——

in 1791, and twice afterwards. During his third term in Congress, in 1796, he became identified with the rising republican party, by voting against the appropriation of funds to carry into effect Jay's Treaty. This being unsatisfactory to a majority of his constituents, Mathew Lyon was chosen a member in room of Gov. Smith. In 1797, the Legislature, of which he was a member, elected him Chief Judge of the Supreme Court. He was a noble looking man, and got the name of "the handsome Judge." At the Vergennes Slaughter in 1798, Gov. Smith was not re-elected. In 1800 he was again chosen a member of Congress which he held one term. and at the end of which he took his seat in the United States Senate in March, 1803, which office he resigned on being chosen Governor of the State in October, 1807. While Governor he called the attention of the Legislature to the mode of punishment then existing, and to his influence was the present penitentiary system adopted. He held the office but one year, during which his health was much impaired. His grave stone was worded so different from most others, that I took a copy of it, and is as follows:

"The Honorable Israel Smith, born at Suffield, Connecticut, April 4th, 1759,
and died at Rutland, Vermont, Dec. 2d, 1810.
No lengthened scroll, no praise encumbered stone,
My epitaph shall be my name alone ;
If that with honor fail to crown my clay,
Oh ! may no other fame my deeds repay.
That, only that, shall single out the spot,
By that remembered, or with that forgot."

DEMING'S STATISTICAL VIEW OF THE LEGISLATURE OF VERMONT, 1851:

WITH A LIST OF THE LIVING COUNCILLORS AND SENATORS OF THE STATE, AND THE FIRST REPRESENTATIVE OF EACH TOWN, WHO ARE NOW LIVING, AND SOME ADDITIONS AND CORRECTIONS IN THE FOREGOING PAGES, TO WHICH THIS IS A SUPPLEMENT, AND THE COUNTY OFFICERS FOR 1851-2, AS FAR AS ARE CHOSEN.

EXECUTIVE DEPARTMENT—1851.

STATE OFFICERS.	Politics.	Where and when born.	Occupation.	lodg.	term in leg.
His Excellency, CHS. K. WILLIAMS, *Rutland*, Governor,	w	Cambridge, Massachusetts, Jan 24, 1782,	attorney	Riker's	11 9
GEORGE HOWES, Treas., Montpelier,	w	Montpelier, November 14, 1814,	cashier	Howes'	5
FERRAND F. MERRILL, Secretary of State, Montpelier,	w	Montpelier, October, 24, 1814,	attorney	Merrill's	16
F. W. HOPKINS, Adj. & Inspec. General, Rutland,	w	Pittsford,	county clerk	Riker's	17
R. F. ANDREWS, Sec. of Civil & Military Affairs, Cavendish,	w	Westfield, Ohio, May 27, 1825,	attorney	Colby's	2
F. E. WOODBRIDGE, Auditor of Accounts, Vergennes,	w	Vergennes, August 29, 1819,	attorney	Pav.	23 3
LUTHER CROSS, Sergeant at Arms, Montpelier,	w	Swansey, New Hampshire, October 7, 1802,	merchant	Cross's	5
JOHN E. BADGER. Assistant & Stationer, Montpelier,	w	New Market, New Hampshire, May 4, 1795,	hatter	Badger's	7
GEO. NICHOLS, Lib., Northfield,	w	Northfield, Apr. 17, 1827,	physician	O. Smith's	3
F. F. HOVEY, Ass't, Montpelier,	w	Thetford, Jan. 16, 1827,	med. student	Ellis's	2
G. F. HOUGHTON, Ag't for International Exchanges, St. Albans,	w	Guilford, May 31, 1820,	attorney	Pav.	25 4

SENATE DEPARTMENT.

OFFICERS.	Politics.	Where and when born.	Occupation.	lodg.	term in leg
Hon. JULIUS CONVERSE, of Woodstock, *President*,	w	Strafford, Connecticut, December 27, 1798,	attorney	Pav.	21 10
SAMUEL M. CONANT, Brandon, *Secretary*,	w	Brandon, November 22, 1820,	editor	J W Howes'	3
WILLIAM M. DICKERMAN, Coventry, *Ass't Secretary*,	w	Burke, August 13, 1820,	attorney	Riker's	10 3

SENATE.

ADDISON COUNTY.
SENATORS.   s.   p.   Where and when born.   Occupation.   lodg.   term.

EDWARD SEYMOUR, Vergennes, 26 w Vergennes, Oct. 26, 1811,   farm Pav.   26   4
BELA HOWE, Shoreham,   30 w Shoreham, May 7, 1804,   farm Riker's 22   4

BENNINGTON COUNTY.
WM. BIGELOW, Bennington,   27 w Middletown, Nov. 9, 1791,   phys Pav.   20   1
IRA K. BATCHELDER, Peru,   28 w Mt. Vernon, N. H., Dec. 11, 1811, farm French 41   3

CALEDONIA COUNTY.
WM. MATTOCKS, Peacham,   5 fd Peacham, June 20, 1818,   atty & farm Silver's   3
EPHRAIM CHAMBERLIN, Lyndon,   6 fd Wheelock, May 4, 1808,   farm Union   9   2

CHITTENDEN COUNTY.
HEMAN BARSTOW, Shelburne,   24 w Shelburne,* April 11, 1790,   farm Burn.   20   3
A. G. WHITTEMORE, Milton,   25 w White Creek, N. Y., Jan. 16, 1797, atty Pav.   31   5

ESSEX COUNTY.
JOHN DEWEY, Guildhall,   7 w Hanover, N. H., Dec. 5, '94   far & phys Dewey's   10

FRANKLIN COUNTY.
HOMER E. ROYCE, E. Berkshire, 15 w Berkshire,* June 14, 1819,   atty Pav.   26   5
GEORGE GREEN, Swanton,   16 w Swanton, March 15, 1791,   farm French 43   7
HARMON NORTHROP, Fairfield, 17 w Fairfield, June 16, 1796,   farm French 43   1

GRAND ISLE COUNTY.
DAVID MARVIN, West Alburgh, 11 d Alburgh, Dec. 20, 1813,   clergy E. J. Scott's 2

LAMOILLE COUNTY.
GEORGE W. BAILEY, Elmore,   10 fd Berlin, July 27, 1798,   farm Burn.   2   3

ORANGE COUNTY.
GEO. P. BALDWIN, Bradford,   4 fd Bradford, Jan. 22, 1808,   farm Union   1   4
PHINEHAS MOULTON W R'nd'ph 12 fd Randolph, Feb. 22, 1790,   farm Union   1   1
BENJ. THURBER jr., Washingt'n, 23 fd Corinth, April 4, 1805,   merch Union   1   1

ORLEANS COUNTY.
HENRY M. BATES, Irasburgh,   29 w Hartland, July 3, 1809,   cashier Riker's 12   6

RUTLAND COUNTY.
JOHN CROWLEY, Mount Holly, 18 w Mount Holly, May 27, 1805,   phys French 35   7
JAS. K HYDE, Sudbury,   20 w Hydepark, Nov. 19, 1801, inn'k & farm Pav.   20   7
ELISHA LAPHAM, Danby,   19 w Danby, Dec. 14, 1792,   farm Eagle   11   2

WASHINGTON COUNTY.
CHAS. G. EASTMAN, Montpelier, 8 d Fryburg, Me., June 1, 1816,   editor Eastman's   1
LEONARD KEITH, Barre,   9 fd Uxbridge, Mass., July 15, 1795, farm Union   5   4

WINDHAM COUNTY.
ASA WENTWORTH jr., R'ki'gh'm, 1 w Alstead, N. H., April 4, 1797,   merch Pav.   32   6
JOHN R. BLAKE, Brattleboro',   2 w Brattleboro', Feb. 3, 1794,   merch Dr Sp'ldg"s 3
IRA GOODHUE, Westminster,   3 w Westminster, Dec. 20, 1803,   farm Riker's 24   4

WINDSOR COUNTY.
WARREN CURRIER, Windsor,   14 w Walpole, N. H., March 14, 1817, atty Riker's 25   2
DAN'L L. LYMAN, Royalton,   22 w Royalton, Feb. 2, '06,   surgeon dentist Pav.   21   2
ASA B. FOSTER, Weston,   21 w Nelson, N. H., March 28, 1795, merch Riker's 27   5
CROSBY MILLER, Pomfret,   13 w Pomfret, June 6, 1811,   farm J. A. Vail's 1

OFFICERS OF THE SENATE.

WILLIAM H. LORD, Montpelier,
   Chaplain,   Amherst, N. H.,   clergyman W.H.Lord's 1
MARCUS A. WEBB, Guildhall, Door-
   Keeper,   w Lunenburgh, Oct. 7, 1802,   farmer Burn.   42   2
JOHN A. CHANDLER, Randolph,
   Assistant Door-Keeper,   w Randolph, Jan. 18, 1830,   printer B.H. Snow's 1
GEORGE C. HICKS, Rutland, Mes-
   senger,   w Rutland, April 20, 1836,   student Riker's 10   2

HOUSE OF REPRESENTATIVES. 115

Addison County.

Towns, Members.	seats. pol.	Where and when born.	occupation.	lodgings.	term.	Who are now known to be alive in Oct. 1851, with the first year of their class.	
Addison, George Witmarth,	30 w	Addison,* January 19, 1792,	farm	Eagle	16	2 Robert Chambers,	1817
Bridport, Erwin E. Grosvenor,	126 w	Bridport, July 19, 1807,	jeweller	Riker's	23	1 Phinehas Kitchel,	1801
Bristol, Rollin Dunshee,	238 w	Bristol, July 29, 1820,	wheelwright	French	33	1 Amos Eastman,	1807
Cornwall, Marcus O. Porter,	234 w	Tinmouth, May 16. 1807,	phys	Riker's	21	1 Thos. P. Mathews,	1820
Ferrisburgh, Noah W. Porter,	51 w	Charlestown, N. H., Dec 4, 1781	farm	Eagle	16	2 Theoph. Middlebrooks	1799
Goshen, Silas D. Gale,	84 w	Irasburg, Sept. 9, 1809,	farm	Eagle	15	1 Abiather Knapp,	1829
Granville, Hiram Ford,	112 w	Granville, Nov. 7, 1802,	farm	Rust's		1 Joel Rice,	1807
Hancock, Augustus Taylor,	102 w	Windsor, Dec. 8, 1817,	farm	Rust's		1 Zerah Barnes,	1824
Leicester, Wm. F. Wright,	101 w	Leicester,* Jan. 3, 1817,	farm	Eagle	14	3 William Gile,	1820
Lincoln, Enos P. Hoag,	191 fd	Lincoln, Jan. 18, 1816,	farm	Riker's	15	1 Nathan Page,	1822
Middlebury, Joseph H. Barrett,	233 w	Ludlow, April 15, 1824,	editor	Riker's	14	3 Peter Starr,	1815
Monkton, John A. Beers,	175 fd	Monkton, May, 6, 1808,	farm	French	25	2 Johnson Finney,	1826
New Haven, Julius L. Eldredge,	180 w	New Haven, Feb. 19, 1807,	farm	French	33	2 Jonathan Hoyt jr.,	1809
Orwell, Champlin M. Fletcher,	176 w	Bridport, Feb. 14, 1822,	farm	Pav.	23	1 Samuel Young,	1830
Panton, Hiram Allen,	29 w	Bridport, Sept. 15, 1806,	farm	Eagle	16	1 Samuel Shepherd,	1804
Ripton, John R. New,	145 w	Cornwall, July 23, 1815,	farm	Riker's	16	2 Sam'l H. Hendrick,	1843
Salisbury, John Dyer,	185 w	Rutland, Oct. 28, 1802,	farm	French	35	1 Jonathan Gibson,	1815
Shoreham, Alonzo Birchard,	85 w	Shoreham, June 5, 1796,	farm	Riker's	22	3 Joseph Smith,	1814
Starksboro', Sam. D. Holcomb,	81 w	Starksboro', June 1, 1807,	farm	Burn.	21	1 Myron Bushnell,	1824
Vergennes, George W. Grandey,	247 w	Panton, Feb. 3, 1816,	atty	Pav.	28	4 E. D. Woodbridge,	1811
Waltham, Newton Rose,	222 w	New Haven, ct., M'ch. 10, 1789	farm	French	35	2 Solomon Hobbs,	1228
Weybridge, Edwin Hayward,	83 w	N Bridgewater Ms. M'ch 21 '03,	farm	Eagle	11	2 Asaph Hayward,	1810
Whiting, Wm, P. Wright,	44 w	Shoreham, Dec. 1, 1816,	phys	Riker's	21	1 James O. Walker,	1821

Bennington County.

Arlington, Willard Holden,	241 w	Arlington, Oct. 9, 1802,	farm	Pav.	19	2 Joshua Judson,	1812
Bennington, Silas Wilcox,	16 d	Stockbridge, Sept. 11, 1816,	phys	French	13	1 Noadiah Swift,	1814
Dorset, Daniel G. Williams.	60 w	Dorset, Feb. 16, 1808,	farm	French	31	2 Reuben H. Blackmer,	1823
Glastenbury, John Elwell,	215 fd	Shaftsbury, May 1, 1797,	farm	Union	22	4 Asa G. Hewes,	1835
Landgrove, James Martin,	111 fd	Landgrove,* Sept. 14, 1813,	farm	French	25	3 David Willey,	1814
Manchester, Amos F. Boorn,	242 w	Manchester,* Sept. 19, 1802,	farm	French	23	2 Joel Pratt,	1808
Peru, Edward Batchelder,	134 w	Peru, Feb. 14, 1817,	mechanic	French	29	2 Benj. Barnard jr.,	1834
Pownal, Eddy Perkins,	182 w	Pownal,* April 3, 1802,	farm	Riker's	15	1 Samuel Wright,	1811
Readsboro', Jason P. Lord,	236 d	East Windsor, Ct. Aug 25, '09	farm	Burn.	26	2 Richard Carpenter,	1817
Rupert, Thomas S. Beebe,	178 w	Sandgate, Nov. 29, 1810,	farm	French	33	2 Nathan Burton,	1818
Sandgate, none.						Reuben Thomas,	1800
Searsburgh,						Luther Park,	1833
Shaftsbury, Reuben R. Snow,	56 fd	Mansfield, Ms. Feb. 9, 1811,	tanner	Union	18	1 Gardner Barton,	1814
Stamford, Dalmon N. Stroud,	181 fd	Stamford, Jan. 28, 1796,	farm	Riker's	15	3 Levi Gillmore,	1818
Sunderland, Ira McLaughlin,	137 fd	Sunderland, July 9, 1807,	machinist	Union	10	2 William Landon,	1819
Winhall, Seth Taylor, jr.,	119 w	Winhall,* Oct. 17, 1809,	farm	French	41	2 Asa Beebe jr.,	1800
Woodford, John Bugbee,	155 d	Whitingham, Jan. 31, 1820,	farm	Eagle	10	1 Elhanah Danforth, 1st	1800

Caledonia County.

Barnet, Obed S. Hatch,	7 fd	Thornton, N. H., May 15, '90,	farm	French	31	2 John Duncan,	1808
Burke, Daniel Beckwith,	113 w	Acworth, N. H., July 21, 1799,	mer	Union	13	3 Thos. Bartlett, 1st,	1805
Cabot, Daniel Gould,	195 fd	Brookfield, Sept. 5, 1799,	farm	Union	16	2 Joseph Fisher,	1801
Danville, Charles Davis,	183 w	Mansfield, Ct., Jan. 1, 1789,	atty	Riker's	18	2 William A. Palmer,	1811
Dewensburgh,						Zenas Crossman,	1809
Groton, Robert F. Goodwin,	35 fd	Newbury, Oct. 8, 1809,	clergyman	French	31	1 Peter McLacklin,	1813
Hardwick, Wm. Sandborn,	4 fd	Hardwick,* Jan. 3, 1798,	farm	Badger's		1 Levi Goodrich,	1800
Kirby, Merit Newhall,	57 fd	Leominster, Ms., Dec. 25, '93,	farm	Cross's	11	2 Theophilus Grout,	1809
Lyndon, John D. Miller,	37 fd	D'mersv'n, Sep. 9, '19,	carriage ma.	Union	17	1 Job Randall,	1827
Newark, Jubez Smith,	157 w	Canaan, N. H., Oct. 16, 1812,	farm	Rust's		4 Eleazer Packer,	1811
Peacham, none.						John W. Chandler,	1797
Ryegate, Wm. T Whitelaw,	6 w	Ryegate,* July 4, 1809,	farm	French	19	1 John Nelson,	1814
Sheffield, Laban M. M. Gray,	38 fd	Sheffield,* Jan. 4, 1818,	farm	Union	17	1 Benj. Conner,	1820
St. Johnsbury, Hiram Knapp,	69 w	Alstead, N. H., May 16, 1804,	merch	Union	9	1 Pres. West,	1805
Sutton, Lorenzo D. Hall,	39 fd	Sheffield, April 1, 1806,	farm	Union	17	2 John Beckwith,	1827
Walden, Isaac Eastman,	3 fd	Walden,* June 29, 1815,	farm	Rust's		2 James Bell,	1815
Waterford, Alfred P. Bonney,	53 w	Littleton, N. H., Aug. 29, '21,	farm	Union	15	1 Jonah Carpenter,	1823
Wheelock, Edward M. Magoon,	1 d	Acton, Me., June 13, 1798,	farm	Rust's		3 Josiah Lane,	1826

Chittenden County.

Bolton, Daniel Colton.	92 d	Vershire, Nov. 5, 1805,	farm	Thomas's		2 John Pineo,	1805
Burlington, Henry B. Stacy,	235 w	Orange, Aug. 23, 1804,	farm	Pav.	31	3 Charles Adams,	1817
Charlotte, Midas Prindly,	46 w	Ferrisburgh, Aug. 22, 1799,	farm	Burn.	20	1 Ezra Meach,	1805
Colchester, none.						Heman Allen, of C.,	1812
Essex, Holman Bates,	163 d	Colchester, April 6, 1808,	farm	Burn.	22	2 Bille B. Butler,	1825
Hinesburgh, none.						Edmond Baldwin,	1814
Huntington, Geo. W. Bromley,	82 w	Pawlet, Sept. 17, 1818,	phys	Burn.	21	2 James Ambler jr.,	1812
Jericho, Lucius E. Barney,	80 fd	Underhill, Oct. 18, 1797,	farm	Burn.	5	2 Thomas D. Rood,	1798
Milton, Hector Adams,	174 w	Burlington, Sept. 27, 1800,	atty	Pav.	19	4 Phelps Smith,	1827
Richmond, Aaron B. Maynard,	43 w	Easton, N. Y., Oct. 22, 1816,	atty	Pav.	9	1 William Rhodes,	1814
Shelburne, Lyman Hall,	45 w	Shelburne, March 13, 1812,	farm	Burn.	27	1 Garrad Burrett,	1823
St. George, Nathan Lockwood,	117 w	St. George,* April 8, 1799,	farm	French	3	2 Lewis Higbee,	1813
Underhill, Wm. H. Martin,	36 d	Underhill,* May 6, 1813,	farm	Burn.	24	2 Cyrus Birge,	1827
Westford, Jacob K. Drury,	86 fd	Milton, March 30, 1808,	farm	Burn.	17	1 Ziba Woods,	1826
Williston, Roswell B. Fay.	213 fd	Richmond, July 5, 1808,	farm	Burn.	28	2 Truman Chittenden,	1807

Essex County.

Bloomfield, S. W. Holbrook,	32 fd	Bloomfield, Jan. 24, 1821,	farm	Union	20	1 Daniel Holbrook,	1816
Brighton, Wm. B. Rosebrook,	27 w	Guildhall, June 30, 1825,	farm	Union	22	1 Timothy Corey,	1832

HOUSE OF REPRESENTATIVES.

Essex County.

Towns. Members.	seats. pol.	When and where born.	occupation,	lodgings,	term.	Who are now known to be alive, with the first year of their election.	
Brunswick, John D. French,	33 fd	Orford, N. H., Mar 9, 1818.	farm	Union	20	2 Haines Schoff,	1816
Canaan, Wm. Trask,	170 fd	Beverly, Mass., June 14, 1801,	farm	Carter's	2	2 Oliver Ingham,	1808
Concord, Preston May,	52 w	Concord, Nov. 3, 1808,	farm	Union	15	1 Richardson Graves,	1809
East Haven, Horace B. Root,	54 w	Lyndon, July 29, 1817,	mechanic	Union	15	2 John Walter jr.,	1845
Granby,						Abraham Boynton,	1815
Guildhall, John P. Denison,	28 w	Weston, Mass., Sept. 20, 1808,	farm	Union	4	2 Elijah Foot,	1807
Lemington, Stephen Harris,	148 w	Woodstock, Ct., July 17, 1774,	farm	Eagle	8	1 Abraham Boynton,	1815
Lunenburgh, Jeremiah Glines,	66 ind	Loudon, N. H., Aug. 11, 1792,	cler	Rust's		1 Samuel Gates,	1790
Maidstone, Daniel C. Kimball,	34 fd	Bradford, Feb. 23, 1820,	farm	Union	20	2 Moody Rich,	1809
Victory, Wm. M. Stearns,	58 fd	Rockingham, Feb. 18, 1814,	farm	Cross's	11	1 Loomis Wells,	1841

Franklin County.

Bakersfield, Thomas Hooker,	124 w	Rutland, Mass., Nov. 16, '12,	merch	Burn.	28	1 Silas B. Hazeltine,	1821
Berkshire, Wm. S. Rublee,	168 w	Berkshire, Aug. 17, 1815,	merch	Eagle	5	1 Amherst Willoghby,	1803
Enosburgh, none.						John Adams,	1811
Fairfax, Homer E. Hubbell,	217 d	Cambridge, Aug 10. 1807,	atty	Pav.	4	8 Luther B. Hunt,	1822
Fairfield, Bradley Barlow,	224 d	Fairfield, April 12, 1814,	farm	Pav.	12	4 Jos. D. Farnsworth,	1801
Fletcher, Guy Kinsley,	162 d	Cambridge, May 8, 1800,	farm	Burn.	22	5 Joseph Robinson,	1810
Franklin, Lathrop Marsh,	121 w	Sheldon, Oct. 17, 1805.	farm	Eagle	5	2 William Felton,	1818
Georgia, Alvah Sabin,	198 w	Georgia,* Oct. 23, 1793,	clerg	French	43	13 Joel Barber,	1830
Highgate, Jacob Carman,	220 w	Highgate,* Jan. 1, 1800,	farm	French	21	1 John Averill,	1830
Montgomery, John L. Clapp,	14 w	Hubbardton, Ms., May 10, '95,	farm	Riker's	23	4 Seth Goodspeed,	1812
Richford, Calvin P. Dwyer,	164 d	Richford, Aug. 19, 1810,	farm	Burn.	18	1 Amherst Willoughby,	1808
Sheldon, Alfred Keith,	248 d	Rosseau, N. Y., Oct. 14, '17,	merch	Pav.	12	2 Stephen Royce jr.,	1815
St. Albans, Wm. Bridges,	193 d	Southboro', Ms., Feb. 18, '85,	scribe	Pav.	11	4 Nathan Green,	1806
Swanton, Isaac B. Bowdish,	223 d	Fairfield, Oct. 3, 1818,	atty	Pav.	12	2 James Brown,	1799

Grand Isle County.

Alburgh, Job Babcock, jr.,	123 w	Alburgh, Sept. 4, 1811,	far & mech	Burn.	16	2 Ephraim Mott,	1816
Grand Isle, Samuel B. Gordon,	59 w	Grand Isle, July 26, 1800,	farm	Burn.	18	2 Joel Allen,	1823
Isle La Mott, Peter Fleury,	221 d	Canada E., July 23, 1812,	far & mer	French	21	1 Samuel Fisk,	1802
North Hero, Jabez Hazen,	125 d	North Hero,* Nov. 20, 1808,	farm	Burn.	16	1 Irad Allen,	1822
South Hero, Lewis Mott,	173 w	South Hero,* Aug. 12, 1802,	farm	Pav.	31	3 Elisha Boardman,	1822

Lamoille County.

Belvidere, none.						Josiah W. Potter,	1832
Cambridge, Elisha Bentley,	105 fd	Jericho, Jan. 17, 1811,	merch	Burn.	2	1 John Wires,	1817
Eden, none.						Jeduthan Stone,	1806
Elmore, Hiram P. Doty,	89 fd	Montpelier, Aug. 30, 1822,	farm	Burn.	5	1 Martin Elmore,	1814
Hidepark, none.						Nathaniel P. Sawyer,	1812
Johnson, Stoughton S. Pike,	72 fd	Randolph, July 12, 1813,	atty	Burn.	2	1 David Boynton,	1812
Morristown, none.						Robert Kimball,	1815
Sterling, none.						Asaph Kentfield,	1834
Stowe, Jared D. Wheelock,	8 fd	Montpelier, Sept. 28, 1820,	phys	Wh'lock		2 Riverius Camp,	1818
Waterville, Eliphalet Brush,	106 fd	Cambridge, June 6, 1809,	blacks'th	Burn.	5	2 Luther Poland, 1st,	1828
Wolcott, John Hawes,	169 d	Goffstown, N. H., Aug. 1, '97,	join'r	Scott's		1 Ephraim Ladd,	1824
Mansfield,						Peter C. Lovejoy,	1815

Orange County.

Bradford, none.						Daniel Kimball,	1802
Braintree, Whitman Howard,	73 fd	Easton, Mass., Feb. 26, 1808,	farm	Burn.	17	1 Isaac Nichols, 1st.	1791
Brookfield, Ariel Burnham,	93 fd	Brookfield, Jan. 31, 1799,	farm	Union	5	1 Frederick Griswold	1817
Chelsea, Elihu Hyde,	144 w	Chelsea, March 20, 1805,	farm	Union	6	3 Elisha Hotchkiss,	1807
Corinth,						William Spencer,	1810
Fairlee, Stephen Chapman,	97 fd	Newbury, Oct. 22, 1793,	farm	Union	18	2 Moulton Morey,	1824
Newbury, Moody Chamberlin,	107 fd	Newbury, Sept. 12, 1787,	farm	Union	31	2 Simeon Stevens jr.,	1817
Orange, Orange Fifield,	187 w	Orange,* April 12, 1804,	merch	Pav.	9	2 Luther Carpenter,	1812
Randolph, Ammi Burnham,	94 fd	Randolph,* Feb. 22, 1806,	farm	Burn.	2	2 William Nutting,	1816
Strafford, Benjamin Gilman,	143 w	Strafford, May 24, 1801,	farm	Union	6	1 Jedediah H Harris,	1810
Thetford, Josiah Coburn,	232 fd	Fairlee, May 10, 1804,	saddler	Union	5	2 Joseph Reed,	1818
Topsham, James Chamberlin,	77 fd	Topsham,* Sept. 27, 1800,	farm	Burn.	23	1 Gilman White.	1815
Tunbridge, Wm. Putnam,	65 w	Tunbridge, Oct. 5, 1799,	tanner	Union	21	2 Nathaniel King,	1805
Vershire, none.						Asa Smith,	1801
Washington, none.						Jacob Bliss,	1823
West Fairlee, J. P. Southworth,	98 fd	West Fairlee, Nov. 11, 1804,	farm	Union	18	2 Isaac Lyon,	1827
Williamstown, Milton Martin,	194 fd	Williamstown, Feb. 19, '09,	black'h	Union	8	2 Thomas Howe,	1813

Orleans County.

Albany, Hiram Moore,	79 d	Plainfield, N. H., Nov. 3, '98,	farm	Burn.	23	1 William Rowell,	1817
Barton, Lyndon Robinson,	202 fd	Barton, Jan. 18, 1800,	farm	Burn.	12	2 Joseph Owen,	1805
Brownington, T. C. Stewart,	199 w	Coventry, Oct. 26, 1804,	farm	Burn.	10	2 George C. West,	1829
Charleston, Loren W. Clarke,	12 w	Weathersfield, Oct. 24, 1807,	merch	Union	19	1 Ebenezer Cole,	1812
Coventry, Sam'l. S. Kendall,	40 w	Windsor, Jan. 14, 1799,	phys	Burn.	22	2 John Ide jr.,	1805
Craftsbury, none.						Samuel C. Crafts,	1796
Derby, Elmera Stewart,	136 d	Derby, Feb. 24, 1810,	farm	Burn.	20	1 Benj. Hinman,	1820
Glover, Joseph H. Dwinell,	203 fd	Keene, N. H., June 21, '02,	cabinet	Union	32	3 Charles Hardy,	1816
Greenboro', none.						Levi Stevens,	1817
Holland, Levi Pinney,	11 w	Canada, April 12, 1818,	farm	Union	19	1 Jason Hinman,	1814
Irasburgh, G. Worthington, jr.,	227 w	Montpelier, Oct. 8, 1808,	merch	Worth'ton.		2 Samuel Conant,	1816
Jay, none.						Madison Keith,	1828
Lowell, Charles Leland,	158 fd	Baltimore, Jan. 19, 1806,	farm	Union	22	1 John Harding,	1815
Morgan, Samuel Daggett,	135 w	Newport, June 12, 1810,	farm	Burn.	20	1 William Colby,	1828

HOUSE OF REPRESENTATIVES. 117

Orleans County.

Towns, Members	seats, pol.	Where and when born,	occupation-	lodgings,	term.	Who are now known to be alive, with the first year of their election,	
Newport, Freeman Miller,	192 d	Canada, April 20, 1808,	farm	French	19	2 Nathaniel Daggett,	1825
Salem, Isaac C. Smith,	201 fd	Brownington, Sept 30, 1812,	farm	Burn.	10	1 Noyes Hopkinson,	1828
Troy, A. Judson Rowell,	139 fd	Waterville, Nov. 4, 1818,	merch	Poland's		1 Samuel H. Hovey,	1819
Westfield, Arad Hitchcock,	160 d	Westfield, Oct. 21, 1811,	farm	Union	22	3 Walter Stone,	1813
Westmore, Wm. Gilfillan,	200 w	Barnet, Jan. 13, 1802,	farm	Burn.	10	1 Peter Gilman,	1838

Rutland County.

Benson, Loyal C. Kellogg,	246 d	Benson,* Feb. 13, 1816,	atty	Pav.	30	3 Simeon Goodrich,	1798
Brandon, Ebenezer J. Bliss,	184 fd	Shoreham, Jan. 3, 1817,	merch	Pav.	27	1 John Conant,	1809
Castleton, Isaac T. Wright,	245 w	Pownal, July 18, 1810,	atty	Pav.	30	1 Nehemiah Hoyt,	1833
Chittenden, Joseph Parker,	243 fd	Clarendon, March 2, 1806,	farm	Eagle	13	1 Jonas Wheeler,	1813
Clarendon, Joseph Congdon.	244 fd	Clarendon,* June 17, 1797,	farm	Eagle	13	2 Eleazer Flagg,	1808
Danby, Hiram H. Kelly,	55 d	Danby, Sept. 17, 1810,	farm	Eagle	6	1 William Hitt,	1817
Fairhaven, Abram Graves,	13 w	Rupert, July 15, 1797,	farm	Riker's	19	2 Artemas Wyman,	1822
Hubbardton, Perry Dikeman,	186 w	Ballston, N. Y.. Mar. 18, '88,	farm	Union	22	1 David Barber,	1813
Ira, Erwin Collins,	179 w	Ira,* Aug. 15, 1796,	farm	French	29	2 Leonard Mason,	1826
Mendon, Eben C. French,	230 w	Wallingford, March 17, 1819,	farm	Eagle	3	1 Zidon Edson,	1813
Middletown, Eliakim Paul,	128 w	Wells, Jan. 19, 1798,	phys	French	17	7 Jonas Clark jr.,	1808
Mount Holly, Daniel Packer,	91 w	Guilford, Sept. 23, 1783,	clerg	French	50	1 Nathan T. Sprague,	1816
Mount Tabor, David Stimson,	141 fd	Mendon, Mass., Nov. 14, 1800,	farm	Eagle	8	2 Caleb Buffum,	1820
Pawlet, Robert H. Smith,	129 w	Pawlet, Sept. 25, 1796,	farm	Riker's	20	2 Oliver Hanks,	1823
Philadelphia,						Wolcott H. Keelet,	1812
Pittsfield, none.						Erastus Holt,	1816
Pittsford, Simeon Gilbert,	62 fd	Pittsford,* Dec. 19, 1801,	farm	Riker's	27	2 Caleb Hendee jr.,	1803
Poultney, John Lewis,	88 w	Poultney, Jan. 30, 1792,	farm	French	23	1 Harvey D. Smith,	1821
Rutland, Martin G. Everts,	249 w	Salisbury, July 2, 1818,	atty	Pav.	20	2 Charles K. Williams,	1809
Sherburne, Rufus Richardson,	231 d	Mendon, Sept. 10, 1818, inn	keeper	Union	11	2 Josiah Wood jr.,	1813
Shrewsbury, John P. Bowman,	229 d	Clarendon, Jan. 26, 1816,	tanner	Eagle	3	1 Zidon Edson,	1822
Sudbury, Tho's. J. Goodrich,	132 d	Benson, April 4 1801,	farm	Eagle	2	3 Barnard Ketchum,	1818
Tinmouth, Judah H. Round,	127 w	Clarendon, Dec. 12, 1809,	farm	French	17	1 Obadiah Noble jr.,	1811
Wallingford, Robinson Hall,	172 w	Wallingford,* Nov. 5, 1797,	farm	Pav.	20	2 John Fox,	1822
Wells, John C. Hopson, jr.,	130 w	Wells,* March 22, 1801,	farm	Riker's	20	1 Aaron Mosher,	1812
West Haven, John H. Wyman,	48 w	West Haven,* Oct. 11, 1804,	farm	Riker's	15	2 Josiah Bascomb,	1823

Washington County.

Barre, Jesse Scott,	190 d	Barre, Dec. 8, 1797,	farm	Union	14	1 Peter Nichols,	1823
Berlin, Elijah H. Covell,	2 fd	Berlin,* July 9, 1802,	farm	Rust's		2 Jabez Ellis,	1815
Calais, Rufus P. Moses,	103 fd	Gilmanton, n. h., Sept 13, '06,	f.&m	Union	16	1 Lemuel Perry,	1804
Duxbury, Lorenzo Davis,	152 fd	Duxbury, Nov. 2, 1819,	farm	Burn.	25	2 Ebenezer Corse,	1807
E. Montpelier, J. P. W. Vincent,	210 fd	Middlesex, Dec. 16, 1818,	farm	Union	12	1 Nathaniel C. King,	1849
Fayston, Willard B. Porter,	150 fd	Fayston, March 1, 1817,	farm	Burn.	24	1 Theophilas Bixby,	1823
Marshfield, Asa Spencer,	196 w	Woodbury, Sept. 14, 1811,	farm	Union	4	1 Wm. Martin,	1820
Middlesex, O. A. Chamberlin,	211 fd	Middlesex, Sept. 30, 1804,	farm	Union	12	1 David Harrington,	1809
Montpelier, Hezekiah H. Reed,	188 w	Hamstead, N. H., May 25, '95	atty	at home		1 Joseph Howes,	1813
Moretown, Uriah Howe,	153 fd	Jericho, May 3, 1810,	mechanic	Burn.	24	2 Cephas Carpenter,	1805
Northfield, John Gregory,	212 fd	Norwalk, Ct., Nov. 18, 1810,	cler.	Burn.	28	2 Cephas Carpenter,	1807
Plainfield, Lewis Chamberlin,	189 fd	Barre, Jan. 4, 1816,	atty. & farm	Union	14	1 Israel Goodwin,	1829
Roxbury, Henry S. Boyce,	76 fd	Sangersfield, N. Y. Ap. 22, '04	farm	Burn.	17	1 Samuel Robinson,	1806
Waitsfield, Roderi'k Richardson,	218 fd	Stafford, Ct., Aug. 7, 1807,	farm	Union	5	7 Ralph Turner,	1821
Warren, Gideon Goodspeed,	151 w	Sharon, Aug. 5, 1808,	farm	Burn.	25	2 Amos Rising,	1816
Waterbury, Calvin Blodgett,	216 d	Randolph, Jan. 5, 1798,	merch	Pav.	4	3 Dan Carpenter,	1807
Woodbury, Stephen C. Burnham,	68 d	Woodbury, March 5, 1801,	farm	Burn.	16	1 Elisha Benjamin, jr.,	1812
Worcester, Nath'l. A. Kelly,	90 fd	Pembroke, N. H., Jan. 5, 1818,	farm	Burn.	5	1 Allen Vail,	1822

Windham County.

Athens, Chester D. Ingraham,	26 fd	Sharon, July 22, 1818,	clerg	Scott's		1 Timo. H. Whitney,	1810
Brattleboro', Samuel Earl, jr.,	99 w	Brattleboro', April 19, 1796,	farm	Eagle	17	2 Samuel Clarke,	1820
Brookline, Wm. Adams,	226 w	Dummerston. July 15, 1810,	farm	Eagle	12	4 Benjamin Ormsbee,	1823
Dover, Asaph Huskins, .	133 fd	Dover, Dec. 9, 1790,	farm	Eagle	10	1 Amos Rice,	1811
Dummerston, Asa Dutton,	146 w	Dummerston, May 10, 1791.	farm	Eagle	9	1 Marshall Miller,	1824
Grafton, Ambrose Burgess,	131 w	Grafton,* Oct. 7, 1798,	farm	Eagle	12	4 Thaddeus Taylor,	1798
Guilford, Ben. W. Stevens,	237 fd	Guilford, Jan. 1, 1789,	phys	Pav.	32	1 Gilbert Denison,	1805
Halifax, Jonas Scott,	251 w	Halifax, May 27, 1812,	tanner	Eagle	7	3 Stephen Otis,	1808
Jamaica, John E. Butler,	120 fd	Jamaica, Dec. 14, 1809,	atty	French	41	5 Peter R. Taft,	1827
Londonderry, none.						Luther Stowell,	1819
Marlboro', Emory Dunklee,	139 fd	Brattleboro', Nov. 10, 1804,	farm	Eagle	10	1 H. H. Winchester,	1828
Newfane. Fred O. Burditt,	138 d	Brookline, March 7, 1821,	cab. m	Union	10	1 Sylvanus Sherwin,	1805
Putney, Mark Crawford,	250 w	Putney,* Oct. 20, 1800,	farm	Carter's		2 Theophilus Crewford,	1822
Rockingham, Russell Hyde,	225 w	Guilford, Feb. 16, 1798,	farm	Pav.	32	4 Ellery Albee,	1821
Somerset, Joseph Morse,	156 fd	Paxton, Ms., Aug. 16, 1794,	farm	French	31	2 Hazleton Rice,	1821
Stratton, Rufus Lyman,	95 fd	Northfield, Ms., Sept. 3, 1815,	farm	Union	10	2 Richard Scott,	1824
Townshend, Francis D. Sawyer,	239 fd	Westminster, Ms. Apr. 7, 1813,	mer	Riker's	24	1 Peter R. Taft,	1818
Vernon, Ebenezer Howe, jr.,	197 w	Vernon, Dec. 21, 1799,	farm	Eagle	17	8 Cyrus Washburn,	1812
Wardsboro', Wales A. Bridges,	96 d	Medway, Ms., April 9, 1800,	farm	Union	5	1 Loland Fairbanks,	1826
Westminster, David C. Gorham,	238 w	Westminster, March 9, 1818,	farm	Riker's	24	1 Wm. C. Bradley,	1806
Whitingham, Eli Green,	252 w	Whitingham, Oct. 9, 1812,	farm	Eagle	7	4 Amos Brown,	1818
Wilmington, none.						Ephraim Tyler,	1827
Windham, Wm. A. Chapin,	240 w	Salem, N. Y., June 28, 1816,	phys	Riker's	24	2 Luther Stowell,	1814

HOUSE OF REPRESENTATIVES.

Windsor County.

Town, Members.	seats, pol.	Where and when born,	occupation, lodgings,	tacro,	Who are now known to be alive, with the first year of their election.
Andover, none.					Samuel Burton, 1804
Baltimore, none.					Lyman Litch, 1839
Barnard, none.					Apollos Warner, 1823
Bethel, Almon Burkee,	19 w	Stockbridge, Aug. 12, 1808,	tanner Scott's	2	Peleg S. Marsh, 1819
Bridgewater, none.					Isaiah Raymond, 1823
Cavendish, Wm. Smith,	177 w	Cavendish, July 31, 1800,	manu Riker's	27	4 Salmon Dutton, jr., 1818
Chester, none.					Abiel Richardson, 1822
Hartford, Albert G. Dewey,	20 w	Hartford, Dec. 16, 1805.	manu. Riker's	27	2 James Udall, 1819
Hartland, Daniel Denison,	5 w	Hartland, May, 15, 1794,	farm Eagle	11	3 Luban Webster, 1810
Ludlow, none.					Asahel Smith, 1806
Norwich, Samuel Goddard,	87 w	Royalston, Ms., June 11, 1808,	farm Union	8	1 Israel Newton, 1814
Plymouth, John W. Stickney,	42 w	Grafton Sept. 16, 1818.	farm Eagle	15	1 Moses Priest, 1795
Pomfret, Joshua Vail,	116 w	Pomfret,* Feb. 10, 1804,	farm Vail's		2 Eben Snow, 1822
Reading, Luther Carlton,	22 w	Reading, Jan. 21, 1792,	farm Eagle	15	2 Wm. L Hawkins, 1813
Rochester, David Eaton,	100 w	Rochester, Sept. 29, 1805,	farm Rust's		3 Daniel Huntington, 1817
Royalton, Daniel Woodward,	122 w	Royalton, April 15, 1804,	mech Riker's	12	2 Moses Cutter, 1819
Sharon, Colcord Quimby,	115 fd	Springfield. N. H., Aug 24 1799, farm Eagle		15	1 Wm. Steele, 1822
Springfield, Russell Burke,	61 w	Westminster, Mar. 26, 1797, iron fo Eagle		2	3 Joseph Selden, 1810
Stockbridge, Zeb Twitchell,	25 fd	Stockbridge, April 10, 1802, clergy Scott's			2 Dwight Gay, 1826
Weathersfield, John C. Haskell,	21 w	Weathersfield,* Apr. 18, 1793, farm Eagle		2	2 Oliver Whipple, 1814
Weston, Amos N. Burton,	49 w	Wilton, N. H , Jan. 2. 1785,	farm French	3	3 Henry Gray, 1824
West Windsor, M. Worcester,	50 w	West Windsor, June 22, 1815, farm Eagle		15	1 Daniel Read, 1849
Windsor, Hiram Harlow,	64 w	Rockingham, Oct. 16, 1810,	farm Riker's	25	6 Jabez Delano, 1806
Woodstock, Tho's. E. Powers,	176 w	Woodstock, Nov. 16, 1808,	farm Riker's	11	6 Titus Hutchinson, 1804

OFFICERS OF THE HOUSE OF REPRESENTATIVES.

THOMAS E. POWERS, Woodstock,
Speaker, w Woodstock, November 16, 1808, physician Riker's 11 6
CHALON F. DAVEY, Burlington, Clerk, w Fairhaven, August 28th... 1817, attorney Riker's 13 6
ELISHA F. MEAD, Hinesburgh, Ass't. Clerk, w Hinesburgh, June 25th , 1824, attorney Pavilion 5 2
CHARLES K. WRIGHT, Shoreham, 2d. Assistant Clerk, w Shoreham, June 3d, 1825, attorney Riker's 19 1
PLINY H. WHITE, Brattleboro', 3d. Assistant Clerk, w Springfield, Oct. 6th, 1822, attorney & editor Riker's 19 1
David C. Davenport, Lowell, Door Keeker, w Dummerston, April 27th., 1821, farmer Cross's 2 1
George C. Fry, Concord, w Concord, June 29th., 1831. farmer Union 15 1
Charles H. Joyce, Northfield, w England, January 3ᵈ, 1829. law student Cadwell's 1
Albert Barrows, Stowe. w Stowe, December 11th., 1829, medical student Snow's 1
Charles Camp, Montpelier, w Montpelier, April 29th., 1832, Camp's 1

In the Senate are 6 new members, 21 whigs, 7 free Democrats, and 2 old line democrats, farmers, 16, atty., 4, merchants, 4, phys., 4. clergy., 1, cashier, 1, Inn keeper, 1, editor 1. The oldest is Phinehas Moulton of Orange, the youngest, Homer E. Royce of Franklin, 22 were natives of Vermont. In the House are 94 new members, 80 of 2 yrs..; farmers, 145; attorneys, 13; merchants, 14; physicians, 10; mechanics, 8; tanners, 3; machinist, 1; manufacturers, 2 carriage makers, 2: scribe, 1; blacksmiths, 2; inn-keeper, 1; iron-founder, 1. Whigs, 112; Free Democrats,67 ; Old Line Democrats. 32; Free Soil 1; Independent, 1 The oldest member is Mr. Harris of Lemington, 77; the youngest is Mr. Rosebrook of Brighton 26 ; and 166 natives of Vermont.

Councillors that are living, and Senators which are dead.

On pages 12 and 13 are to be found the old Councillors. In the first column, Joel Pratt, O. C. Merrill, Myron Clark, John S. Pettibone are the only now living. Column 2d., Gilbert Denison, William C. Bradley, Theophilas Crawford, Charles Phelps, John Roberts, Austin Birchard and David Crawford. Column 3d., Henry F. Janes and Milton Brown. Column 4th., S. C. Crafts, Ira H. Allen and E. H. Starkweather. Col. 5, S. H. Holley, S. S. Phelps. Column 6th., T. Chittenden, S. C. Loveland, Job Lyman Wm. G. Hunter, and Allen Wardner. Page 13, column 1, George C. Cahoon and Walter Harvey., Column 2d., Joseph Berry, R. Pierpoint and Zimri Howe. Column 3d., Horatio Seymour, James Davis, Joseph H. Brainard and George Green. Column 4th., John W. Chandler, Jedediah H. Harris, Daniel Cobb and Martin Flint. Column 5th., Samuel Clark, and Geo. P. Marsh. Last column, George Worthington, Richardson Graves and H. R. Beardsley. The remainder are among the dead,

Senators not alive.

Windham County, Phineas White, Samuel F. Thompson and John Phelps. Rutland County, Tho's. D. Hammond and Orson Clark. Addison county, Jesse Grandy, Joseph Simonds and Harvey Bell. Franklin county, Geo. W. Foster, Lucius R. Beamen and Jacob Wead. Caledonia county, Elias Bemis, jr. Essex county, William Gates. Orange county, Lebbeus Edgerton, Jonathan Jenness, Elijah Farr.

COUNTY COURTS, &c. 119

ERRATA.

On page 5th 6th line from bottom, for Feb, 15, read Feb. 12.
    4th, 14th line from the bottom, for Missisco Leg, read Missisco Tongue.
    10, before Oct. 12 1786, for Windsor, read Rutland.
    11, 17th line from bottom, on 1st column, for three, read two.
    11, 15th line from bottom, after the word office. insert a town representative.
    14, 1st column, near the bottom, for Edmond Weston, read William Weston.
    20, Under 1786, against Danby, insert John Burt.
    31, on the last column, for Horace Wilcox, read Roswell Bottom, jr.
    34, between S. C. Croft and H. Seymour, insert Gilbert Denison.
    34, for Mills De Forest, 1801; read Noah Sabin, 1807.
    34, for Myron Clark, 1824, read Nathan Burton and John H. Olin 1817.
    34, after Joshua Y. Vail. add, and William Nutting.
    52. 3d line from bottom, for 24, read 25.   Cavendish, population in 1850, is 1576.
    53. first column, against Benson, insert Chauncey Smith. Stratton, 286.
    64, at the bottom, add Betsey Munson died in June 1850: Montgomery, 973.
    55, 2nd column, change the places of Wm. Colby, and John Harding. Fletcher, 1086.
    72, The first town clerk of Chester was John Goulding, 1761.
    88, first column, against 19, for Erastus, read Erasmus.
    78, The judges for Orange county, 1796, should read the same as 1797.
    88, Ira Kidder, Judge of Orange county for '50 died, and Carlos Carpenter appointed to his place.
    66, between the last 7 and 9, insert "8, Wm. Strong.
    59, bottom line but one, for C. Hopson, jr., read John C. Hopson, jr.
    59, The first town clerk of Lowell was Abel Curtis, not Asahel.
    104, 2nd column, between Benson and Asahel Smith, add " Asahel Smith."
When the foegoing pages were issued, through the difficulty of obtaining correct and perfect returns from the hasty perusal of old documents and records, I omitted to procure complete returns from Orange and Windham counties. I now add so those counties some very ancient proceedings, and correct some errors that have been found in the work

Kingsland, Glouster County, Province of New York May 29th 1770 }   The Court meet for the first time, and the ordinance and Comitions Being Read

          John Taplin   } Judges being appointted
          Samuel Sleeper } by the Government of
          Thomas Sumner } Newyork were present,
          and the Courts opened as is usual in other Courts, also present
N. B. these Courts were the Courts   James Pennock   }
of Quarterly sessions, and the Court   Abner Fowler   } Justices of the Quorum
of Common Pleas of Said County   John Peters   }
                               John Taplin jr Sheriff

The Court adjourned to the Last Tuesday in August next to be Held in said Kingsland, opened accordingly and appointed four Constables Simeon Stevens for Newbury, Jesse McFarland for Moretown, Abner Howard for Thetford, and Samuel Pennock for Strafford, and adjourned to the last Tuesday in Nov. Nov 27. Court opened at Kingsland, called over the docket of 8 causes only, put over, and dismissed them and appointed Ebenezer Green Constable for Thetford, and Samuel Pennock, Ebenezer Martin & Ebenezer Green and James Allen Surveyors for the County ; and adjourned to Feb next Last Tuesday

Feb 25 } Sett out frome Moretown for Kings Land, travelled untill Knight there Being No Road, and the Snow very
1771 } Depa, we traveled on Snow Shoes or Racats, on the 26th we travelled Some ways and Held a Council when it was Concluded it was Best to open the Court as we Saw No Line it was not whether in Kingsland or Not But we Concluded we were farr in the woods we Did not Expect to See any House unless we marched three miles within Kingsland and No one lived there when the Court was Ordered to be opened on the Spot, Present   John Taplin Judge
      all Causes Continued or adjourned   John Peters of the Quorum
      over to Next term   John Taplin jr. Sheriff
      the Court if one adjourned over untill the Last Tuesday in may Next at which it was opened.
      and after disposing of one case of bastardy, adjourned to August next.
                                                         John Peters Clerk

No further records of the New York Court.
There was a Court of General Sessions held at Newbury in August. 1772. &c.

August, 1772	Nov. 1772	Feb., 1773	1774
Judges,	1 John Taplin	"	"
* 1 Jacob Bailey,	2 "	"	"
2 Thomas Sumner,	2 "	"	James Pennock,
2 Jacob Kent,	2 "	James Pennock,	Jacob Kent,
2 Joel Marsh		Jacob Kent,	John Hatch,
2 Thomas Chamberlin,		Thomas Chamberlain,	
2 Samuel Hale,		Samuel Hale,	
2	3 John Peters,		"
4 John Taplin, jun.,			

WINDHAM COUNTY COURT.

In February, 1781, the county of Cumberland was divided into three counties, Windham, Windsor and Orange.

June Term, 1781.	1782.	May Term, 1783.	Dec. Term, 1783.	1784.	1785
1 John Sessions,	"	"	"	"	Luke Knowlton
2 Luke Knowlton,	"	"	"	"	John Bridgman,
2 John Bridgman,	"	Benjamin Burt:	Samuel Fletcher,	"	"
2 Benjamin Burt,	"	Stephen R Bradley,	Benjamin Burt,	"	"
3 Micah Townsend,	"	"	"	"	"
4	Jonathan Hunt,				
5 Stephen R. Bradley,	"	Samuel Knight,	S. R. Bradley,	"	"
†					

* No. 1, Chief Judge—2, assistant Judges—3, Clerks—4, Sheriffs—5, States Attorney—6, Judges of Probate—7, Registers of Probate.
† For Judges and Registers of Probate in Westminster district, see the bottom of page 6, and the 75th to the 88th.

COUNTY OFFICERS FOR 1851-2.

ORANGE COUNTY COURT,

After its organization in 1781, the first session was holden at Thetford on the second Tuesday in June, 1781.

1781, present,	1782.	1783.	1784.	1785.
1 Jacob Bailey,	"	1 Israel Smith,	"	1 Jacob Bailey,
2 Israel Smith,	"	2 Noah White,	"	2 Israel Smith,
2 Noah White,	"	2 Alexander Harvey,	"	2 Noah White,
2 Thomas Russell	Alexander Harvey	2 Joshua Tucker	"	2 Alexander Harvey
3 Davenport Phelps	"	2 Benjamin Baldwin	"	2 Israel Morey
4		3 & Daniel Burt	"	3 Nathan Goddard
5		4 Abner Chamberlain	"	"

Isaac Bailey was clerk of Orange county court from 1787 to 1811, and in 1814. Harris E. G. McLaughlin was clerk from 1815 to 1833. Harry Hale was clerk in 1832 and 1834. J. W. Parker was clerk in 1835 and 6. Pearly C. Jones was clerk in 1837, 39, 41 and 42, John Smith in 1838. Robbins Dinsmore in 1840. Calvin Blodgett was clerk from 1843 to 1848, both years. Joseph Berry in 1849. Samuel M. Flint 1850.

Judges and Registers of Probate in Randolph District, in addition to those in the proper place for them. The first Judge was Elijah Paine, of Williamstown, appointed in 1789; he held the office 2 years, but no record is left of his having done any Probate business, being enquired of some years afterwards for his records, he replied, that, as he did no business in that line, he had kept no record of it, and he found that nobody died in those days. The first case on the records is that of Ezra Dudley, of Roxbury, June 15, 1792, while Israel Converse was Judge, who was of course appointed in 1791, and held the office till Aaron Storrs was appointed in 1796, and James Converse was Register from 1792 to 1796. David Storrs was Register from 1797 to 1799. Aaron Storrs and Moses Hubbard the remainder of the year Dec. 1800, when Jonathan Fisk was appointed Judge, and with James Converse and Joseph Roberts for Registers for two years. The Judge did his own recording till Dec. 1818. Under Frederick Griswold, Jacob K. Parish was Register to Dec. 1832. Wm. Hebard Register to 1833. Wyman Spooner Register to Dec. 1834. Wm. Hebard Register to Dec. 1836. Jacob K. Parish Register to Dec. 1837. William Hobard Register to Dec. 1838. Calvin Blodgett to 1839. Edward C. Redington to 1840. John Colby to 1842. Daniel F. Weymouth to 1843. Philander Perrin to 1844. Gustavus Rolfe to 1845. Philander Perrin to 1846. Jonathan Smith jr. to July, 1848. Cornelius W. Clark to Dec. 1848. Philander Perrin 1849. John B. Hutchinson to Dec. 1850. Cornelius W. Clark to the present time.

P. S. Judges of the Supreme Court, (just elected,) Stephen Royce, Isaac F. Redfield, and Pierpoint Isham. Peter T. Washburn, Woodstock, Reporter.

Addison County.
2 Joseph Hayward
2 Roswell Bottum jr.
3 George S. Swift
4 David S. Church
5 John W. Stewart
6 Horatio Seymour
6 Harvey Munsill
7 Jed. S. Bushnell
7 John Pierpont

Bennington County.
2 Simeon Rising
2 C. E. Houghton
3 Sam'l H. Blackmer
4 Jas. S. Merrill
5 Harmon Canfield
6 Leonard Sergeant
6 Joseph Eames
7 Harvey K. Fowler
7 A. B. Gardner

Caledonia County.
2 Alden E. Judevine
2 Andrew McMillan
3 Gustavus A. Burbank
4 George Ide
5 Joseph Potts
6 Theron Howard
7 Gustavus A. Burbank

Chittenden County.
2 Ransom Jones
2 Aaron L. Beach,
3 D. B. Bulkley

4 Isaac Sherwood
5 Edward J. Phelps
6 Charles Adams
7 Bradford Rixford

Essex County.
2 David Hubbard jr.
2 Oramel Crawford
3 Wm. H. Hartshorn
4 Joseph W. Cooper
5 Wm. Hayward jr.
6 Reuben W. Freeman
7 Wm. Chandler

Franklin County.
2 Alvah Sabin
2 Augustus Young
3 Joseph H. Brainerd
4 Orson Carpenter
5 George F. Houghton
6 William Bridges
7 Jeptha Bradley

Grand Isle County.
2 William L. Sowles
2 Daniel Wait
3 Elijah Haynes
4 Charles H. Clark
5 John M. Sowles
6 Sealand Whitney
7 Augustus Knight

Lamoille County.
2 James M. Hotchkiss
2 Giles A. Barber
3 E. B. Sawyer

4 Samuel Pennock
5 George Wilkins
6 Stoughton S. Pike
7 Wm. G. Ferrin

Orange County.
2 Gouldsburn Taplin jr.
2 Alvah Smith
3 Samuel M. Flint
4 John E. Chamberlin
5 Asa M. Dickey
6 Royal Hatch
6 Philander Perrin
7 Charles B. Leslie
7 Cornelius W. Clark

Orleans County.
2 William Moon
2
3 Hubbard Hastings
4 Elisha White
5 Wm. M. Dickerman
6 Isaac N. Cushman
7 Henry M. Bates

Rutland County.
2 Samuel H. Kellogg
2 Baines Frisbie
3 F. W. Hopkins
4 Jacob Edgerton
5 Caleb B. Harrington
6 Harvey Button
6 Almon Warner
7 Henry Hall

Washington County.
2 David W. Hadley
2 Joseph Hancock
3 Shubael Wheeler
4 Isaac W. Brown
5 Stoddard B. Colby
6 Jacob Scott
7 Lyman Briggs

Windham County.
2 Ellery Allbee
2 Horace Alvord
3 Royal Tyler
4 Cyrus Carpenter
5 George B. Kellogg
6 Royal Tyler
6 Abishai Stoddard
7 Frederick Holbrook
7 Benjamin W. Dean

Windsor County.
2 Hampden Cutts
2 Calvin French
3 Norman Williams
4 Lorenzo Richmond
5 Warren C. French
6 Salmon F. Dutton
6 John Porter
7 Henry Closson
7 Lyndon A. Marsh

For Clerks of Courts, and Probate Registers, I have inserted those now in.

INDEX.

Executive and Senate Department, page, 113
House of Representatives, alphabetically by Counties, 115
Councillors and Senators, denoting which are not living, 118
Errata, and ancient County Officers, 119
County Officers for 1851-2   120

If any person wishes to purchase the whole work, they can have it by forwarding to Leonard Deming, at Middlebury, Vt., one dollar, post paid, and two copies will be sent to them post paid, or of his son E. C. Deming, 56 Brattle street, Boston, or requesting their Representatives to purchase one for them during the session.

www.ingramcontent.com/pod-product-compliance
Lightning Source LLC
Chambersburg PA
CBHW071220160426
43196CB00012B/2360